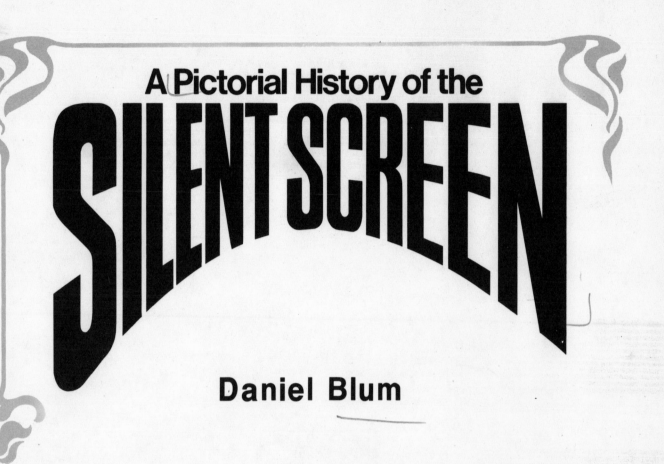

A Pictorial History of the
SILENT SCREEN

Daniel Blum

Spring Books

London · New York · Sydney · Toronto

ACKNOWLEDGMENTS
I WISH TO THANK the following for the loan of pictures and assistance in compiling this book: *Photoplay Magazine*, The Museum of Modern Art, The New York Public Library, The Museum of the City of New York, *The New York Post* and *The Motion Picture Magazine*. Also John Willis, Louis Melancon, Vernon Rice, May Davenport Seymour, Raymond Frederick, Dorothy Ansen, Jean Gillette, William H. Matthews, George Freedley, Joanne Godbout, Richard Griffith, Lillian Gish, Clara Kimball Young, Kathlyn Williams, Harriet Parsons, Irving Cummings, Edwin August, Nance O'Neil, Ben Grauer, Hildegarde Halliday, Tony Gray, Suzanne Nicholl, Earle Forbes, Walter Latwaite and William Thomas.

© Copyright 1953 by Daniel Blum
First published in the United Kingdom in 1962 by
The Hamlyn Publishing Group Limited
London · New York · Sydney · Toronto
Hamlyn House, Feltham, Middlesex, England
by arrangement with G. P. Putnam's Sons, New York
3rd Impression 1973
Printed in Czechoslovakia by Naše vojsko, Prague
ISBN 0 600 03104 7
51657/3

TO
MY SISTER ADELE
—whom I love dearly

GRETA GARBO

FOREWORD

THE NICKELODEONS, as the first movie theatres were called, in no way resembled the luxurious picture palaces of today, but what an aura of magic and mystery, of laughter and tears clung to them! There, to the sounds of a tinkling and appropriately emotional piano, Pearl White faced her perils, Francis X. Bushman caused fluttering hearts, Theda Bara wrecked homes, Chaplin and Arbuckle and Mack Sennett set zany standards, never to be excelled, and a host of beautiful ladies smiled and wept and were alluring. It was a realm of fantastic and childish make-believe situated in a never-never land called Hollywood, but gradually the whole world came to treasure its heroes and heroines and clowns, and to ape them.

Whatever role the silent screen has played in our social history—and I believe it was an important one—no one can underestimate the enormous pleasure the films of this era gave to audiences everywhere. It has been my thought in compiling this book to recall the varied and fascinating personalities and photoplays of the years from the earliest films to the advent of the sound screen, when stars were *really* stars, when the fashions and activities of the Hollywood greats echoed around the world and 100,000 people could gather in London and even in Moscow to greet Mary Pickford and Douglas Fairbanks on their triumphal tour of Europe.

Here was an art peculiarly American and yet universal. Its essence was entertainment; its success, financial and otherwise, was stupendous. Perhaps today, in a more troubled age, we can look back on these people and their films not only with nostalgia but also with a sincere desire to learn what made glamor so glamorous and laughter so hearty, and the world a happier place to live in. It was a memorable age, and I hope I have captured some of its quality to preserve in this book.

Daniel Blum

THOMAS ALVA EDISON

EDISON'S FIRST
KINETOSCOPE (1889)

KINETOSCOPE PARLOR (1895)

PROGRAM OF FIRST PUBLIC
VITASCOPE PRESENTATION (1896)

THE EARLY YEARS

To Thomas Alva Edison goes the credit for motion pictures, though at the time he did not regard his invention too seriously. He considered movies, as did many others, a novelty that would soon wear off. In 1889 the original motion picture machine came into being. It was called the Kinetoscope. It consisted of a cabinet inside which a length of film revolved on spools. When a coin was dropped into a slot an electric light shone on the film which was projected on the end of the cabinet. You saw the "moving picture" through a peephole just big enough for the human eye. These films were about fifty feet in length and ran for less than a minute. The subjects of Edison's films were simple—a baby being bathed, a dog with a bone, portions of boxing matches, dances and vaudeville turns—all suitable to show movement, jerky of course, but movement. To supply these films for the peepshow Kinetoscopes the first motion picture studio in the world was built by Edison in East Orange, New Jersey, at the cost of $637. Completed on February 1, 1893, it was dubbed "The Black Maria" and was swung from a pivot post to permit the stage to follow the light of the sun. In 1894 the Edison Kinetoscope machines were sold in the open market and presented commercially to the New York public in what were called Kinetoscope Parlors. Before the end of the year natives of Chicago, San Francisco, Atlantic City, Washington and Baltimore were introduced to the new wonder and soon Kinetoscope Parlors were flourishing all over the United States. This same year Alexander Black, who later became a well-known writer, discovered the photoplay. A series of photographic slides taken from life were projected on a screen by a magic lantern machine. They illustrated a story Black would read from the stage. He showed four slides a minute for his presentation and each picture was a step forward in action. For his first picture play he wrote 14,000 words and took as his subject the adventures of a girl reporter, "Miss Jerry." Blanche Bayliss, a well-known artist's model, played the title role and William Courtenay, who later became a celebrated stage star, was the hero. The first recorded film, in 1893, was made of a sneeze performed by Fred Ott, an assistant in the Edison West Orange Laboratory. The list of films made during those early years included Mme. Bertholdi, a contortionist; Annie Oakley; Colonel William Cody, the original Buffalo Bill; Eugene

FRED OTT'S
SNEEZE (1893)

ANNABELLE'S BUTTERFLY
DANCE (1897)

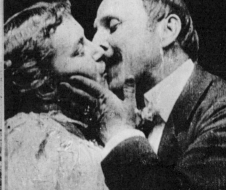

"WASHDAY TROUBLE"
(EDISON—1895)

FIRST MOTION PICTURE STUDIO (1893)

MAY IRWIN, JOHN C. RICE IN "THE
KISS" (EDISON—1896)

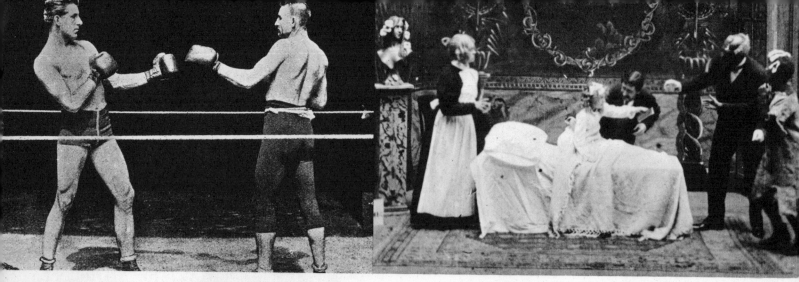

JAMES J. CORBETT, PETER COURTENAY IN FIRST FIGHT
FILM (1894)

"UNCLE TOM'S CABIN" (EDISON—1903)

"CRIPPLE CREEK BARROOM" (EDISON—1898)

SCENE FROM A LUBIN FILM (1900)

Sandow, the strong man; the Butterfly Dance by Annabelle, who later as A
belle Whitford became one of Ziegfeld's first glorified beauties; and a film lab
simply "Dance" made with Miss Ruth Dennis, a young lady from Brooklyn
became a famous dancer as Ruth St. Dennis. In 1894 James J. Corbett
Peter Courtenay made the first fight film before the Edison camera at West Or
for the peepshow machines. That same year Woodville Latham devised a
jector which he called the Pantoptikon. It was far from perfect, the pict
flickered, jumped and glimmered but it projected moving pictures on the new
screen. On May 20, 1895, the first public showing took place on the roof of
Madison Square Garden. About the same time that Latham launched his
perfect projector, Louis and Auguste Lumiére of France patented their first
jection machine. Others engaged in nearly parallel efforts which were to a
the course of the screen were Thomas Armat of Washington, D. C., and Ro
W. Paul of London. On April 20, 1896, Koster and Bial's Music Hall be
presenting Edison's Vitascope pictures as one of the "acts" of their variety
The same year one of the most famous of the early films was made showing
kissing scene between May Irwin and John C. Rice from their stage success "
Widow Jones." On March 17, 1897, the Corbett-Fitzsimmons fight at Ca
City was filmed for Edison by a camera made especially for the event by Er
J. Rector. Eleven thousand feet of film were used, at that time the world's re
for photographing a single event. Edison was now due for competition. Will
Kennedy and Laurie Dickson, who had formerly been associates of Edison, for
the American Mutoscope and Biograph Company on October 12, 1896, for
purpose of making motion pictures. The next year, Sigmund Lubin in Ph
delphia made his first film "Horse Eating Hay" and J. Stuart Blackton, Albert
Smith and William T. Rock joined forces to form the Vitagraph Company
America. France was entering the competition too with such pioneers as Gec
Méliés, Charles Pathé and Leon Gaumont. On April 16, 1902, the first mo
picture theatre, the Electric, opened its doors in Los Angeles. That same y
Méliés, who had formerly been a magician, made the first narrative film,
now famous "Trip To The Moon." In 1903 Edison followed with his equ
famous first American narrative film, "The Great Train Robbery." It was
feet long and directed by Edwin S. Porter. Joseph Jefferson filmed scenes f
his famous stage success "Rip Van Winkle" for Biograph and in 1904 Vitagr

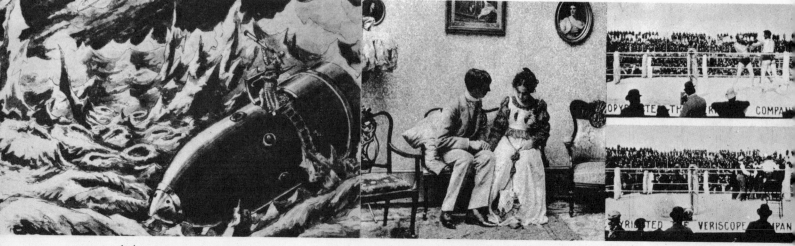

GEORGE MÉLIÉS' "TRIP TO THE MOON" (1902)

WILLIAM COURTENAY, BLANCHE BAYLISS
IN "MISS JERRY" (1894)
(ALEXANDER BLACK PHOTOPLAY)

THE CORBETT-FITZSIMMONS FIGHT AT
CARSON CITY (1897)

THE EDISON STOCK COMPANY (1907)—IN THE GROUP ARE CHARLES OGLE, PAT O'MALLEY, HERBERT PRIOR, FRANK McGLYNN

"THE NIGHT BEFORE CHRISTMAS" (EDISON—1906)

uaded Kyrle Bellew, noted actor, to film a tabloid version of "A Gentleman 'rance" which he had performed on the stage. In 1905 Vitagraph made lles, The Amateur Cracksman" as a thousand-foot feature with J. Barney ry in the title role. It was directed by G. M. Anderson who began his career actor in "The Great Train Robbery" and who later became famous as Broncho , the first motion picture cowboy. Companies were hiring actors by the week, it was to be several years before their names were known or they were given publicity. William Sorrelle, an obscure stage actor, was the first member of Edison Stock Company. He was paid $30 a week. Maurice Costello, a juvenile the Cecil Spooner Stock Company in Brooklyn, joined Edison. In 1906 ence Turner, the daughter of an actor who lived near the Vitagraph Company latbush, was hired for $18 a week. She doubled as actress and wardrobe ress and later became known as "The Vitagraph Girl." The next year Mary er began her film career at Vitagraph. Motion pictures were prospering and were theatres showing them. In Chicago, William N. Selig, George Kleine and rge K. Spoor entered the field. G. M. Anderson had left Vitagraph and joined g. In 1907 he met Spoor and together they formed the Essanay Film Manu-uring Company. The name was derived from their initials. The Kalem pany, which got its name from its founders George Kleine, Samuel Long and nk Marion, also started in 1907 with $400 cash capital. They engaged Sidney ott as actor and director. He had had some picture experience at Biograph was then playing on the road with Joseph Santley and Marion Leonard in ly The Kid." Robert Vignola of the company was also hired as an actor. He r became a famous director. In December of 1907, Kalem produced "Ben ." It was advertised as "positively the most superb moving picture spectacle made in America in sixteen magnificent scenes with illustrated titles." Kalem not acquire the rights to the famous Lew Wallace drama and they were sued he publishers, producers and the author's estate. In 1911 Kalem finally settled $25,000. Until this suit was instigated motion picture rights were unknown. s year a young actor named Lawrence Griffith made a film for Edison called scued From An Eagle's Nest." His real name was David Wark Griffith. Pathé not yet opened a studio in this country but were importing their French lucts. One was "Cinderella" in 967 feet and "partly colored."

"THE GREAT TRAIN ROBBERY" (EDISON—1903)

"THE GREAT TRAIN ROBBERY" (EDISON—1903)

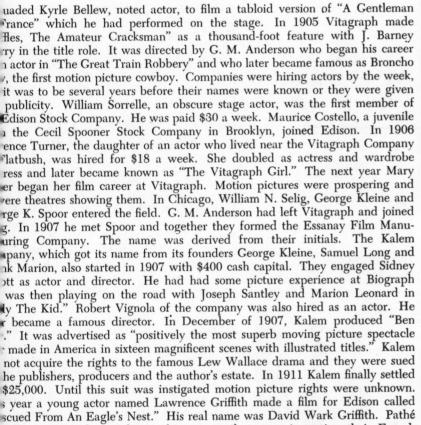

D. W. GRIFFITH IN "RESCUED FROM AN EAGLE'S NEST" (EDISON—1907)

ADVERTISEMENT FROM "FILM INDEX" (MARCH 2, 1907)

D. W.
GRIFFITH

LINDA
ARVIDSON

LINDA ARVIDSON, D. W. GRIFFITH, UNKNOWN PLAYER, HARRY
SALTER IN "WHEN KNIGHTS WERE BOLD" (BIOGRAPH)

HOBART
BOSWORTH

FLORENCE LAWRENCE IN
"INGOMAR, THE BARBARIAN" (BIOGRAPH)

KATHLYN WILLIAMS

PAUL W.
PANZER

BETTY HARTE, HOBART BOSWORTH
IN "THE ROMAN" (SELIG)

KATHLYN WILLIAMS, HAROLD
LOCKWOOD IN "HARBOR
ISLAND" (SELIG)

G. M.
ANDERSON

MARION LEONARD, D. W. GRIFFITH IN
"AT THE CROSSROADS OF LIFE" (BIOGRAPH)

1908 Nickelodeons, as motion picture t[...] tres were then called, were sprin[...] up all over the country, and to sa[...] the demand film companies were humm[...] Edison built a new studio in the Bronx, V[...] graph was now operating in Flatbush, Lubin [...] a new studio in Philadelphia, while Selig [...] Essanay in Chicago were working at top sp[...] In the fall of the year, G. M. Anderson to[...] company to Niles, California, where he ope[...] a western branch of the Essanay Studio and [...] the next seven years turned out one-reel [...] later two-reel Broncho Billy cowboy films e[...] week. Biograph, which played such an [...] portant part in the history of the early s[...] films, was turning out two films a week, [...] average footage of these being between [...] hundred and a thousand feet. These were fil[...] at 11 East 14th Street, New York, an old bro[...] stone house which had been turned into a stu[...] In the spring, actor Lawrence Griffith and [...] wife Linda Arvidson were acting before [...] Biograph cameras. In June, Wallace [...] Cutcheon, who had been directing most of t[...] pictures, became ill and Lawrence Griffith, a[...] became D. W. Griffith, director. The first [...] he directed was "The Adventures of Dolly" [...] it had its world premiere at Keith and Proc[...] Union Square Theatre, July 14, 1908. His [...] and a young stage actor named Arthur Joh[...] had the leads. Johnson became one of the [...] popular leading men of the period. Among [...] other Biograph players were Eddie Di[...] Harry Salter, Charles Inslee, Mack Sen[...] Herbert Yost, Wilfred Lucas, Owen M[...] David Miles, Frank Gebhardt, John Comp[...] Tony O'Sullivan, Mabel Sloughton, Flor[...] Auer, Ruth Hart, Flora Finch, Anita [...] dry, Dorothy West, Eleanor Kershaw [...] later married Thomas H. Ince, Violet [...] sereau and Jeanie Macpherson who becan[...] famous scenario writer. The child actors of [...] company were Johnny Tansy, Gladys Egan [...] Adele De Gardes. No one received bil[...] Among the unknown players who joined [...] Selig Company were Kathlyn Williams, Ha[...] Lockwood and Hobart Bosworth. Vitag[...] was making one-reel features of Shakespe[...] "Romeo and Juliet," "The Merchant of Ven[...] "Antony and Cleopatra," "Julius Caesar" [...] "Richard III." Thomas H. Ince played bit [...] in some of these. The role of Romeo was pla[...] by Paul Panzer who became a well-known vi[...] in Pearl White serials, while Juliet was pla[...] by Florence Lawrence who as "Baby Flo, [...] Child Wonder Whistler" had been touring [...] country since she was four. Near the end of [...] year Florence Lawrence, who had been get[...] $15 a week at Vitagraph, was lured over to [...] graph with a salary of $25 weekly. Miss L[...] rence's pictures became very popular and s[...] since the company did not allow the name[...] actors to be given out, she became known [...] "The Biograph Girl." It was an anonymous [...] dom and eventually led to companies revea[...] the names of their players and the star sys[...] in films.

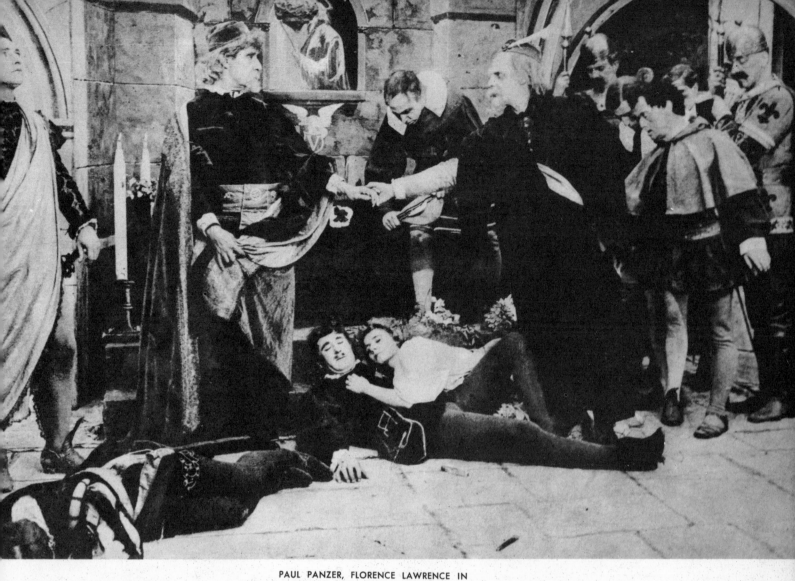

PAUL PANZER, FLORENCE LAWRENCE IN
"ROMEO AND JULIET" (VITAGRAPH)

VITAGRAPH FILMS
12 CENTS PER FOOT — 12 CENTS PER FOOT
THE FILMS OF "QUALITY"

TUESDAY, SEPTEMBER 22nd

HER NEWSBOY FRIEND

COPYRIGHT, 1908, BY THE VITAGRAPH CO. OF AMERICA.

A splendid drama in which a newsboy who is be-
friended by a factory girl repays the kindness by thwarting
the plans of a designing villain, and effecting a reconcilia-
tion with her lover.   LENGTH, 985 FEET.

SATURDAY, SEPTEMBER 26th

Another Positive Winner

RICHARD III.
A SHAKESPEARIAN TRAGEDY

COPYRIGHT, 1908, BY THE VITAGRAPH CO. OF AMERICA.   LENGTH, 990 FEET.

A grand reproduction of Shakespeare's sublime tragedy. A magnificent subject surpassing in every detail all previous efforts. The most powerful effusion of
Shakespeare's genius, elaborately staged, gorgeously costumed and superbly acted.

SPECIAL

Elaborate Views of CONEY ISLAND "MARDI GRAS" CARNIVAL
Including CHILDREN'S PARADE, ready for release, Tuesday, September 29th

A magnificent view of the Democratic nominee WILLIAM JENNINGS BRYAN receiving congratulations
after his nomination.   LENGTH, 160 FEET.

THE VITAGRAPH COMPANY OF AMERICA, { NEW YORK, 116 Nassau Street
CHICAGO, 109 Randolph Street
LONDON, 25 Cecil Court
PARIS, 15, Rue Sainte-Cécile.

"ANTONY AND CLEOPATRA"
(VITAGRAPH)

FLORENCE LAWRENCE, PAUL PANZER
IN "ROMEO AND JULIET"

ADVERTISEMENT FOR "RICHARD III"

HARRY
SALTER

FLORENCE
LAWRENCE

11

JEANIE MACPHERSON, FLORENCE LAWRENCE, JOHN COMPSON, TONY O'SULLIVAN IN "MRS. JONES ENTERTAINS"

TONY O'SULLIVAN, DOROTHY BERNARD, FLORENCE LAWRENCE, MARY PICKFORD, JOHN COMPSON, HARRY MYERS IN A "JONESY" PICTURE

OWEN MOORE, MARY PICKFORD IN "IN A LONELY VILLA"

MARY PICKFORD, OWEN MOORE, HENRY B. WALTHALL, KATE BRUCE IN "IN OLD KENTUCKY"

JAMES KIRKWOOD, BILLY QUIRK, FLORENCE LAWRENCE IN "THE MENDED LUTE" ABOVE: MACK SENNETT (on floor), ARTHUR JOHNSON, FLORENCE LAWRENCE IN "THE SONG OF THE SHIRT"

FLORENCE LAWRENCE, ARTHUR JOHNSON, CLARA T. BRACEY
IN "RESURRECTION"

ARTHUR JOHNSON
(BIOGRAPH)

ARTHUR JOHNSON, FLORENCE LAWRENCE IN
"RESURRECTION"

MARY PICKFORD, BILLY QUIRK IN
"THEY WOULD ELOPE"

1909 With the public showing an increased interest in this new kind of entertainment, more motion picture companies were being formed. Carl Laemmle, a German immigrant who had given up a clothing business in Oshkosh to run a theatre in Chicago and who was at this time head of a film exchange, decided to go into production. He rented space in the independent Actophone Studio at Eleventh Avenue and Fifty-third Street, New York, formed the Imp Company and started to make pictures. His first production was "Hiawatha," a one-reel feature with Gladys Hulette, and it was released October 25, 1909. Adam Kessel, who also ran a film exchange, formed a corporation to make pictures with Charles Bauman, Fred Balshofer, friends, and Louis Burston, an attorney. They called it Bison Films and their first effort was "A True Indian's Heart." It was made in Coytesville, New Jersey, with Charles French playing the title role. P. A. Powers, a jobber in talking machines, opened a studio—the Powers Picture Plays—at Mount Vernon, New York, with Irving Cummings, an actor who had played in Lillian Russell's company, as the leading man. Other independent companies formed included the Yankee and Rex. Lois Weber and Phillips Smalley appeared in the early Rex pictures. Meanwhile, the already established companies were forging ahead.

FLORENCE LAWRENCE, HARRY SALTER,
MACK SENNETT (extreme right) IN
"THE SLAVE"

FLORENCE LAWRENCE FILMS
BOTTOM: WITH OWEN MOORE

JAMES KIRKWOOD
ABOVE: MARION LEONARD

DAVID MILES, MARY PICKFORD IN "THE VIOLIN
MAKER OF CREMONA"
TOP: BILLY QUIRK, MARY PICKFORD IN
"THE HESSIAN RENEGADES"

MABEL NORMAND

ANNETTE KELLERMANN

MAURICE COSTELLO

ARTHUR JOHNSON, MARION LEONARD, BILLY QUIRK, MACK SENNETT, FRANK EVANS, JAMES KIRKWOOD IN "THE GIBSON GODDESS"

1909 At Biograph, Florence Lawrence, "The Biograph Girl," was their most valuable property and for a time was making two films each week. Her early releases included a one-reel version of Tolstoi's "Redemption" directed by D. W. Griffith, and a series of domestic comedies called the "Jonesy Pictures" with John Compson playing Mr. Jones. Mary Pickford, who had been playing child roles in stock companies since she was five, joined the Biograph Company in May and made her motion picture debut June 7, 1909, in "The Violin Maker of Cremona." Her second picture was "The Lonely Villa" which was written by Mack Sennett. She then was teamed with Billy Quirk for a series of comedies. Others who joined Biograph were Henry B. Walthall, James Kirkwood, Marion Leonard (from the stage) and Florence La Badie, an artist's model. Alice Joyce, also a model, joined Kalem. Maurice Costello left Edison for Vitagraph. They also contracted Mabel Normand, a fashion model. In the early days actors were often pressed into service as carpenters and scene painters, but when Costello joined Vitagraph and became known as "The Dimpled Darling," he set a precedent with his declaration: "I am an actor and will not build sets or paint scenery." Among the outstanding one-reel features Vitagraph produced were "King Lear," "Launcelot and Elaine," "Oliver Twist" with Elita Proctor Otis as Nancy Sykes, and a film of Annette Kellermann "in her physical culture exercises, diabolo playing, fancy swimming and diving displays." Edison's most notable film was "The Prince and The Pauper" with Miss Cecil Spooner in the dual role.

HERBERT YOST, LINDA ARVIDSON IN "EDGAR ALLAN POE"

CHARLES INSLEE, DOROTHY BERNARD, OWEN MOORE, VIOLET MERSEREAU, HERBERT PRIOR, LINDA ARVIDSON IN "THE CRICKET ON THE HEARTH"

GLADYS EGAN, HENRY B. WALTHALL, JAMES KIRKWOOD IN "A CONVICT'S SACRIFICE"

"GERTIE THE DINOSAUR," FIRST IMPORTANT ANIMATED CARTOON

CECIL SPOONER IN "THE PRINCE AND THE PAUPER"

MARION LEONARD, JAMES KIRKWOOD "COMATO THE SIOUX"

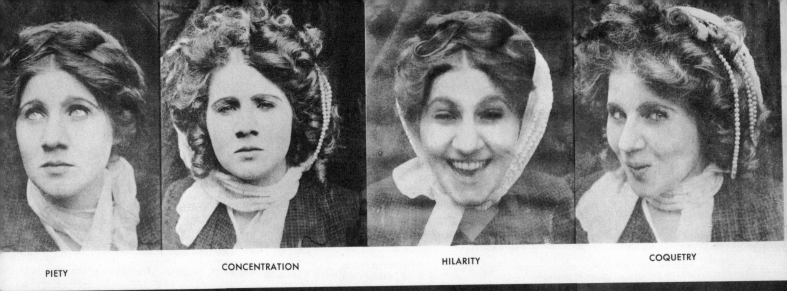

PIETY   CONCENTRATION   HILARITY   COQUETRY

HORROR   MIRTH   DETERMINATION   SADNESS

15

FLORENCE LAWRENCE, "THE BIOGRAPH GIRL"

J. WARREN KERRIGAN IN
"THE HAND OF UNCLE SAM" (ESSANAY)

GENE GAUNTIER
"THE KALEM GIRL"

MARY FULLER IN "ELEKTRA" (VITAGRAPH)

ALICE JOYCE
(KALEM)

J. WARREN KERRIGAN
(ESSANAY)

ETHEL CLAYTON
(ESSANAY)

MACK SENNETT
(BIOGRAPH)

ANNA Q. NILSSON
(KALEM)

WILLIAM GARW
(THANHOUSE

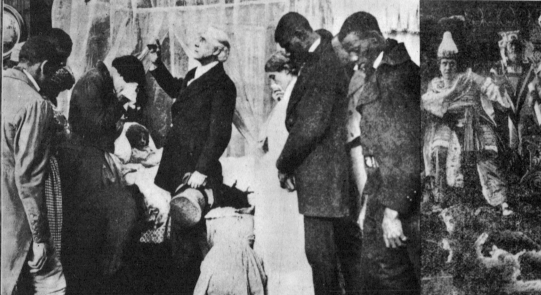

CHARLES KENT (center) IN "UNCLE TOM'S CABIN" (VITAGRAPH)

"LIFE OF MOSES" (VITAGRAPH)

BLANCHE SWEET, EDWIN AUGUST IN
"SMILE OF A CHILD" (BIOGRAPH)

EDWIN AUGUST IN
"SMILE OF A CHILD"

MLLE. VICTORIA LEPANTO
IN "CARMEN" (PATHÉ)

ALPHONSE ETHIER, MISS ROSAMONDE
IN "THELMA" (THANHOUSER)

FINCH, JOHN TROJANO, FLORENCE TURNER, JOHN BUNNY,
RICE COSTELLO, E. R. PHILLIPS IN "THE NEW STENOGRAPHER"
(VITAGRAPH)

ALICE JOYCE IN
"ENGINEER'S SWEETHEART"
(KALEM)

FLORENCE TURNER, CARLYLE BLACKWELL, NORMA TALMADGE,
CHARLES KENT IN "A DIXIE MOTHER" (VITAGRAPH)

CHARLES KENT
(VITAGRAPH)

EDNA PAYNE
(LUBIN)

VAN DYKE BROOKE
(VITAGRAPH)

BLANCHE SWEET
(BIOGRAPH)

ROBERT VIGNOLA
(KALEM)

CLARA WILLIAMS
(SELIG)

PEARL WHITE
(POWERS)

1910

"While the pictures have attained a distinct prominence and are now recognized as a standard attraction, the people playing in them are very sensitive about having their identity become known. They have an impression that the step from regular stage productions to the scenes before the camera is a backward one." This is a quote from a trade journal. The original "Biograph Girl," Florence Lawrence, changed all that. Shortly after the formation of Laemmle's independent Imp Company, Miss Lawrence vanished and a story was published in St. Louis newspapers that she had been killed by a streetcar. This false report produced advertisements to the effect that "The Biograph Girl" was very much alive and now an Imp star. It was the beginning of the star system. It was also the beginning of "publicity stunts" for picture stars. To squelch the death rumors, Miss Lawrence made a personal appearance in St. Louis and more people met her train to welcome her than appeared the week before to welcome visiting President Taft. Companies were advertising their products "artistically enacted by REAL actors," and when Vitagraph released "Uncle Tom's Cabin" they stated: "It will be the real thing in every respect—real ice, real bloodhounds, real negroes, real actors, real scenes from real life as it really was in the antebellum days!" Exhibitors were seeking other attractions and soon singers with illustrated song slides were included as part of the show. Color too was again bidding for attention.

MARY PICKFORD
(BIOGRAPH)

KATHLYN WILLIAMS IN "THE FIRE CHIEF'S
DAUGHTER" (SELIG)

MARY PICKFORD, MACK SENNETT IN
"AN ARCADIAN MAID" (BIOGRAPH)

"THE WIZARD OF OZ" (SELIG)

MARTIN FAUST, FRANK CRANE, MISS ROSAMONDE, AMELIA BARLEON IN "A WINTER'S TALE" (THANHOUSER)

EXAMPLE OF SLIDES USED IN THIS PERIOD

LINDA ARVIDSON, ARTHUR JOHNSO "THE UNCHANGING SEA" (BIOGRA

SONG SLIDES FOR "THE DUBLIN RAG" and "I'LL BE WITH YOU WHEN THE SOUTHERN ROSES BLOOM"

TYPICAL NICKELODEON OF THE PERIOD

TYPICAL SLIDES

DOROTHY WEST, HENRY B. WALTHALL IN
"THE HOUSE WITH CLOSED SHUTTERS" (BIOGRAPH)

MARION LEONARD, HENRY B. WALTHALL, ARTHUR
JOHNSON IN "IN OLD CALIFORNIA" (BIOGRAPH)

CHARLES KENT, JULIA SWAYNE GORDON, MARIN
SAIS IN "TWELFTH NIGHT" (VITAGRAPH)

FLORENCE LAWRENCE IN
"THE ANGEL OF THE STUDIO"

1910 Pathé announced their film "In Ancient Greece" in all color with "the flesh tints so natural that it is hard to believe that the people are only pictures on a screen." More independent companies were formed. Thanhouser, American, Majestic, Reliance, Nestor, Eclair and Champion were new competitors. Pathé opened an American studio. This year saw the beginning of many important screen careers. John Bunny, from the stage, joined Vitagraph and became the first famous film comedian. His popularity lasted until his death in 1915. Flora Finch played opposite him. King Baggot, a St. Louis stock actor, joined Imp and became a popular star and later a director. Norma Talmadge, a Brooklyn schoolgirl with no theatrical background, took two of her photographs to Vitagraph, filled out an application, and was accepted as a member of their stock company. She played bits before being given a role in "A Dixie Mother." Carlyle Blackwell, also in this film, had been in college plays at Cornell and a chorus boy before signing with Vitagraph. By 1913 he was a prominent film star. Tom Mix was a United States marshall of a small Oklahoma town when a Selig company arrived there to film a western. Mix thought he would participate. In July Selig released "Ranch Life in The Great Southwest" and Tom Mix was on his way. Other events this year worth noting: Vitagraph filmed "The Life of Moses" in five reels and released a reel a week. D. W. Griffith took a company of Biograph players to California. Mack Sennett directed his first film, "Comrades," for Biograph. Victoria Lepanto appeared in probably the first film version of "Carmen" for Pathé.

FLORENCE TURNER IN
"ST. ELMO" (VITAGRAPH)

TWO SCENES FROM "RIP VAN WINKLE"
(THANHOUSER)

JOHN BUNNY
(VITAGRAPH)

MARY PICKFORD, FRANCIS GRANDIN IN "RAMONA"
Above: HENRY B. WALTHALL, MARY PICKFORD
IN "RAMONA" (BIOGRAPH)

FLORENCE TURNER
AS LUCY

NORMA TALMADGE, MAURICE COSTELLO IN
"A TALE OF TWO CITIES" (VITAGRAPH)

MAURICE COST
AS SYDNEY CA

JEANIE MACPHERSON, LINDA ARVIDSON, WILFRED
LUCAS, EDDIE DILLON, KATE TONERAY IN
"FISHER FOLKS" (BIOGRAPH)

BLANCHE SWEET, LIONEL BARRYMORE IN
"FIGHTING BLOOD" (BIOGRAPH)

BLANCHE SWEET, FRANK GRANDON, WILF
LUCAS IN "THE LONEDALE OPERATOR" (BIOG

NORMA TALMADGE
Above: LARRY TRIMBLE

THE ORIGINAL IMP COMPANY
Top Row (L. to R.): GEORGE L. TUCKER, DAVID MILES, MRS. SMITH (Mother of the Pickfords), BOB DALY, TONY GAUDIO
2nd Row: WILLIAM E. SHAY, ANITA HERNDON, J. FARRELL MacDONALD, HAYWARD MACK, MRS. MacDONALD, JACK
HARVEY   3rd Row: TOM INCE, OWEN MOORE, MARY PICKFORD, KING BAGGOT, COL. JOE SMILEY   Bottom Row:
ISABEL REA, JACK PICKFORD, LOTTIE PICKFORD

EDITH HALLA
Above: WILLIAM

EDITH STOREY
(MÉLIÉS)

JEAN, THE VITAGRAPH DOG

G. M. ANDERSON
(BRONCHO BILLY)
(ESSANAY)

RAY MYERS, ETHEL GRANDIN IN
"ACROSS THE PLAINS" (INCE)

1911 Producers were realizing players had selling value even though the public at this time did not know many of them by name. There was a mad scramble to sign prospective favorites and they were now given billing and publicity. Florence Lawrence was still the most valuable actress at the box office when she left Imp and joined Lubin. She teamed up with Arthur Johnson and their comedies were very popular. Mary Pickford, who was becoming a great favorite, left Biograph for Imp. Owen Moore, whom she had married, went with her. She remained with Imp only eight months, made a few pictures for Majestic and then returned to Biograph. Vitagraph, where Maurice Costello and Florence Turner were top-ranking players, had acquired Larry Trimble as an actor and writer.

MIRIAM NESBITT, MARC MacDERMOTT, MARY FULLER
IN "AIDA" (EDISON)

WALLACE REID IN
"THE DEERSLAYER" (VITAGRAPH)

EVELYN DOMINICUS, HARRY MOREY, WALLACE REID, FLORENCE TURNER, HAL REID
IN "THE DEERSLAYER" (VITAGRAPH)

MASTER KENNETH CASEY

WILLIAM HUMPHREY

KATE PRICE

HARRY MOREY

VITAGRAPH PLAYERS

FLORA FINCH

LEO DELANEY

JULIA SWAYNE GORDON
IN "LADY GODIVA" (VITAGRAPH)

EARLY VITAGRAPH STUDIO IN BROOKLYN

DANTE'S "INFERNO"

THE STORY THAT NEVER GROWS OLD

THE TWO ORPHANS

SELIG'S IMMORTAL MASTERPIECE
IN THREE REELS

"YOU MUST SING, I'LL DO THE BEGGING"

JAMES O'BURRELL, LEIGHTON STARK, KATHLYN WILLIAMS,
WINNIFRED GREENWOOD, LILLIAN LEIGHTON IN
"THE TWO ORPHANS" (SELIG)

POSTER

WINNIFRED GREENWOOD, KATHLYN WILLIAMS
IN "THE TWO ORPHANS"

FREDERIC SANTLEY
(KALEM)

ELSIE McLEOD
(EDISON)

HARRY C. MYERS
(LUBIN)

LAURA SAWYER
(EDISON)

SIDNEY DREW
(KALEM)

DOT FARLEY
(AMERICAN)

1911 PICTURE PLAYS AND PLAYERS

ROBERT BROWER
(EDISON)

GERTRUDE ROBINSON
(RELIANCE)

JACK CLARK
(KALEM)

DOROTHY DAVENPORT
(NESTOR)

J. P. McGOWAN
(KALEM)

JANE FEARNLEY
(RELIANCE)

FLORENCE LAWRENCE, OWEN MOORE
IN "FLO'S DISCIPLINE"

DOROTHY DAVENPORT, RUSSELL BASSETT, ALICE DAVENPORT,
GORDON SACKVILLE IN "THE BEST MAN WINS" (NESTOR)

"IL TROVATORE"
(PATHÉ)

RRY C. MYERS, ARTHUR JOHNSON, FLORENCE
LAWRENCE IN "HER TWO SONS" (LUBIN)

JOHN BUNNY, LEO DELANEY, HELEN
GARDNER, ROSE TAPLEY IN "VANITY FAIR" (VITAGRAPH)

TOM MIX, KATHLYN WILLIAMS, CHARLES CLARY IN
"BACK TO THE PRIMITIVE" (SELIG)

RALPH INCE
(VITAGRAPH)

ETHEL JEWETT
(EDISON)

SPOTTISWOODE AITKIN
(LUBIN)

CLAIRE MERSEREAU
(NESTOR)

GEORGE MELFORD
(KALEM)

VIOLET MERSEREAU
(NESTOR)

1911 PICTURE PLAYS AND PLAYERS

23

FLORA FINCH, JOHN BUNNY, MABEL NORMAND IN
"THE SUBDUING OF MRS. NAG"

JOHN BUNNY AND JEAN IN
"BACHELOR BUTTONS"
JOHN BUNNY VITAGRAPH COMEDIES

JOHN BUNNY, WALLACE REID, VAN DYKE BROOKE
IN "THE LEADING LADY"

EDISON FILMS

"MOTHER" MARY MAURICE
(VITAGRAPH)

Tuesday, September 5th
The Three Musketeers

By Alexandre Dumas
Part One
Cast.

D'Artagnan, a young Gascon....Sydney Booth
Athos ⎫   Herbert Delmar
Porthos ⎬ The Three   Jack Chagnon
Aramis ⎭ Musketeers   Harold Shaw
King Louis XIII............William Bechtel
The Queen................Miriam Nesbitt
Constance, her attendant.......Mary Fuller
De Treville, Captain of the King's
Musketeers ....Robert Brower
Duke of Buckingham.....Herbert Barrington
Dumas' famous story of the time of Louis
XIII of France, showing the celebrated
Three Musketeers and their dashing young
comrade, D'Artagnan. A complete story full
of adventure.

FRANCIS X. BUSHMAN
(ESSANAY)

Wednesday, September 6th
The Three Musketeers

By Alexandre Dumas
Part Two.
Cast.

D'Artagan a young Gascon......Sydney Booth
Athos ⎫   Herbert Delmar
Porthos ⎬ The Three   Jack Chagnon
Aramis ⎭ Musketeers   Harold Shaw
Cardinal Richelieu ....Marc McDermott
King Louis XIII............William Bechtel
The Queen................Miriam Nesbitt
Constance, her attendant.......Mary Fuller
Milady, the Cardinal's spy........Carey Lee
Duke of Buckingham ....Herbert Barrington
D'Artagnan, the famous young musketeer,
is entrusted by the Queen's attendant, with
whom he is in love, on a confidential mission.
Through many perils he is successful. This
story is complete in itself and is splendidly
presented.

HAL REID
(VITAGRAPH)

WINNIFRED GREENWOOD
(SELIG)

MASTER PAUL KELLY
(VITAGRAPH)

THE AMERICAN FILM MANUFACTURING COMPANY
(L. to R.) W. W. KERRIGAN, PETER MORRISON, GEORGE PERIOLAT, ROBERT COFFEE, ALLAN DWAN, J. WARREN
KERRIGAN, LOUISE LESTER, MRS. MORRISON, PAULINE BUSH, A. G. HEIMERAL, JACK RICHARDSON, S. BEAL.

EVA PROUT AS LITTLE RI
RIDING HOOD (ESSANA

THOMAS J. CARRIGAN, MABEL TALIAFERRO
IN "CINDERELLA" (SELIG)

FRANK WEED, MABEL TALIAFERRO, JOSEPHINE MILLER,
LILLIAN LEIGHTON, OLIVE COX IN "CINDERELLA"
(SELIG)

FRANK GRANDON, LINDA ARVIDSON
IN "ENOCH ARDEN" (BIOGRAPH)

"CINDERELLA"
(THANHOUSER)

1911 One day the director of Miss Turner's picture was having trouble with a Pomeranian. Trimble appeared with Jean, his pet collie, who performed like a trouper and was put on the payroll for $25 a week. Jean became the first dog star of films. Hal Reid, who had signed to write and act too, brought along his nineteen-year-old son with ambitions to be a cameraman. The casting man took one look at the son and put Wallace Reid in front of the camera. Helen Gardner, a teacher of pantomime, was playing minor parts before she received attention in the role of Becky Sharp in "Vanity Fair." Essanay acquired Francis X. Bushman, an actor and sculptor's model. At Biograph, Lionel Barrymore, just returned from studying painting in Paris, began his career as a screen actor. Companies continued filming the classics. Thanhouser did "David Copperfield" and "Romeo and Juliet." Edison made "The Three Musketeers" and a film version of the opera "Aida," while Pathé released "Faust" and "Il Trovatore." D. W. Griffith directed "Enoch Arden" for Biograph, and Selig made a three-reel film of "The Two Orphans." Vitagraph's contribution to the screening of well-known novels included "A Tale of Two Cities," "Vanity Fair" and "The Deerslayer." Monopol distributed Dante's "Inferno." Both Selig and Thanhouser made a film of "Cinderella." Thomas H. Ince, an erstwhile actor, directed his first picture in California, entitled "Across The Plains."

MARY MAURICE, JAMES MORRISON, EARLE WILLIAMS,
TOM POWERS, FRANK NEWBERG IN
"SAVING AN AUDIENCE" (VITAGRAPH)

RUTH STONEHOUSE, PAT O'MALLEY IN
"THE PAPERED DOOR" (ESSANAY)

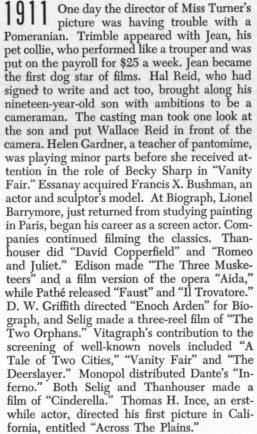

JACK STANDING, FLORENCE LAWRENCE IN
"A GOOD TURN" (LUBIN)

PEGGOTY, DAVID AND HIS MOTHER

DAVID AND EMILY AS CHILDREN
SCENES FROM "DAVID COPPERFIELD" (THANHOUSER)

DAVID AND AGNES

SARAH BERNHARDT IN SCENES FROM "QUEEN ELIZABETH" (FAMOUS PLAYERS)
WITH LOU TELLEGEN

BESSIE LEARN   BEN WILSON   GERTRUDE McCOY   AUGUSTUS PHILLIPS   BLISS MILFORD   EDWARD O'CONNOR

EDISON COMPANY PLAYERS

HAROLD SHAW, MARION BROOKS
IN "MARTIN CHUZZLEWIT" (EDISON)

RÉJANE IN "MADAME SANS-GENE"
(FILM d'ART)

MARC MacDERMOTT, MARY FULLER
IN "WHAT HAPPENED TO MARY" (EDISON)

JAMES YOUNG
(VITAGRAPH)

LENORE ULRICH
(ESSANAY)

IRVING CUMMINGS
(CHAMPION)

1912

Motion Pictures, well established now as entertainment, were taking the place of the resident stock companies and the road show. The old nickelodeon was a thing of the past. Better theatres were being built and most of them were charging ten-cent admissions. The screen was gradually getting away from the one- and two-reelers. The feature craze of four- and five-reelers was opposed by the old-guard film makers because they cost more money and also entailed creative thought. Three- and four-reel pictures were no longer a rarity. Animated cartoons, which were born in 1909 with "Gertie The Dinosaur," were becoming part of the "motion picture show" and so was the newsreel. Famous stage stars looked upon motion pictures as beneath them, but Adolph Zukor changed this. An Hungarian emigrant, he progressed from sweeping in a fur store to his own fur business, to penny arcades, to nickelodeons, and finally to the treasurer of the Marcus Loew Enterprises which controlled screen and vaudeville theatres. His next step was the purchase of the American rights of a four-reel French film, "Queen Elizabeth," starring Sarah Bernhardt. Its success gave him the idea of filming famous plays with famous stars. With Daniel Frohman and the Loew Enterprises he formed the Famous Players Film Company. The French-American Film Company imported a two-reel version of "Camille" with Mme. Bernhardt, and also "Mme. Sans-Gene," a three-reel feature with Mme. Réjane. American stars began to look on motion pictures with more favor. Nat C. Goodwin made a film of his stage success "Oliver Twist." Blanche Walsh was the next important stage star to appear in pictures. She filmed Tolstoy's "Resurrection" in three reels. It was the beginning of a trend. Important stage stars of the period who never appeared in films were Maude Adams, David Warfield, Julia Marlowe, John Drew, Mary Mannering, Henry Miller, Eleanor Robson, and Rose Stahl. Many of them, including Douglas Fairbanks, Marie Dressler, John and Lionel Barrymore, Marguerite Clark, George Arliss, Nazimova, Elsie Ferguson, Pauline Frederick and Victor Moore, achieved as great, and in some instances, greater fame from films than the stage.

J. WARREN KERRIGAN
Top: FLORENCE TURNER

CLARA KIMBALL YOUNG
Top: WALLACE REID

HARRY BENHAM   FLORENCE LA BADIE   JAMES CRUZE   MARGUERITE SNOW   WILLIAM RUSSELL   MIGNON ANDERSON

THANHOUSER PLAYERS

WILLIAM RUSSELL IN
"THE STAR OF BETHLEHEM"

HARRY BENHAM, FLORENCE LA BADIE
IN "THE MERCHANT OF VENICE"
THANHOUSER RELEASES

JAMES CRUZE, MARGUERITE SNOW, WILLIAM RUSSELL
IN "LUCILE"

JAMES YOUNG, MAURICE COSTELLO, ROBERT GAILLARD, LEO DELANEY IN "AS YOU LIKE IT"

ROSE COGHLAN, ROSE TAPLEY, JAMES MORRISON. IN "AS YOU LIKE IT"

EARLE WILLIAMS, WILLIAM R. DUNN, MARY MAU WALLACE REID, JAMES MORRISON, ROBERT GAIL IN A VITAGRAPH DRAMA

EDITH HALLERAN, EDITH STOREY, NORMA TALMADGE, DOROTHY KELLY, LILLIAN WALKER, JULIA SWAYNE GORDON, JOHN BUNNY IN "THE TROUBLESOME STEPDAUGHTERS"

FLORA FINCH, JOHN BUNNY IN "LEAP YEAR PROPOSALS"

WILLIAM SHEA, JOHN BUNNY, WALLACE REID, MARSHALL P. WILDER, LEAH BAIRD IN "CHUMPS"

TEFFT JOHNSON, CLARA KIMBALL YOUNG, JULIA SWAYNE GORDON, HAL REID IN "CARDINAL WOLSEY"

EARLE WILLIAMS, CLARA KIMBALL YOUNG IN "HAPPY-GO-LUCKY"

HELEN GARDNER IN "A PRINCESS OF BAGDAD"

HELEN GARDNER IN "CLEOPATRA"

CLARA KIMBALL YOUNG, ETIENNE GIRARDOT, JAMES YOUNG, SHEP IN "THE VIOLIN OF MONSIEUR"

CLARA KIMBALL YOUNG, HELENE COSTELLO, MAURICE COSTELLO
1912 VITAGRAPH RELEASES

WILLIAM RAYMOND, HECTOR DEAN, FLORENCE TURNER IN "FRANCESCA DA RIMINI"

"BABY" PARSONS (HARRIET PARSONS), FRANCIS X. BUSHMAN and BEVERLY BAYNE
IN SCENES FROM "THE MAGIC WAND" (ESSANAY) SCENARIO WRITTEN BY LOUELLA O. PARSONS

THE ESSANAY EASTERN COMPANY

Seated on Floor: ELEANOR KAHN and JACK, THE BULLDOG MASCOT; 1st Row: CHARLES HITCHCOCK, WHITNEY RAYMOND, EVA PROUT, BABY PARSONS, RUTH STONEHOUSE, WILLIAM MASON; 2nd Row: LILY BRANSCOMBE, FRANK DAYTON, DOLORES CASSINELLI, FRANCIS X. BUSHMAN, BEVERLY BAYNE, WILLIAM WALTERS, MILDRED WESTON; 3rd Row: JOSEPH ALLEN, ELEANOR BLANCHARD, JOHN STEPPING, MARTHA RUSSELL, HARRY CASHMAN, HELEN DUNBAR, HARRY MAINHALL; Top Row: E. H. CALVERT, WILLIAM BAILEY, HOWARD MISSIMER, FRED WULF

"LAST ROUND-UP" "WHEN LOVE AND HONOR CALLED" "THE COWBOY COWARD"
"BRONCHO BILLY" PICTURES WITH G. M. ANDERSON
MARGUERITE CLAYTON WAS HIS LEADING LADY

GEORGE LARKIN
(ECLAIR)

MAE HOTELY
(LUBIN)

J. W. JOHNSTON
(RELIANCE)

ROSEMARY THEBY
(VITAGRAPH)

THOMAS J. CORRIGAN
(SELIG)

ADRIENNE KROELL
(SELIG)

PAUL SCARDON
(MAJESTIC)

EDWIN AUGUST IN "THE HAND
THAT ROCKED THE CRADLE" (UNIVERSAL)

MONA DARKFEATHER
(KALEM)

TOM MIX
(SELIG)

MARGARET JOSLIN, AUGUSTUS CARNEY IN
"ALKALI IKE'S MOTORCYCLE" (ESSANAY)

NAT C. GOODWIN IN
"OLIVER TWIST"

CARLYLE BLACKWELL, ALICE
JOYCE IN "A BELL OF PENANCE"
(KALEM)

KING BAGGOT IN
"LADY AUDLEY'S SECRET"
(IMP)

OWEN MOORE, FLORENCE LAWRENCE
IN "IN SWIFT WATERS" (VICTOR)

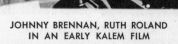

GERTRUDE SHIPMAN, IRVING CUMMINGS, ARTHUR
EVERS IN "CAMILLE" (CHAMPION)

GUY OLIVER, ROBERT FRAZER, BARBARA
TENNANT IN "ROBIN HOOD" (ECLAIR)

JOHNNY BRENNAN, RUTH ROLAND
IN AN EARLY KALEM FILM

KEYSTONE FILMS

A QUARTET OF POPULAR FUN MAKERS

MACK SENNETT
MABEL NORMAND
FRED MACE
FORD STERLING

SUPPORTED BY AN
ALL STAR COMPANY
IN SPLIT REEL COMEDIES

A KEYSTONE EVERY MONDAY

MABEL NORMAND

FIRST RELEASE SEPTEMBER 23

"Cohen Collects a Debt" and "The Water Nymph"

Featuring MABEL NORMAND, the beautiful Diving Venus

MONDAY, SEPTEMBER 30

"Riley and Schultze" and "The New Neighbor"

Amusing subjects, cleverly acted by world-famous actors

KEYSTONE FILM COMPANY

Mutual Film Corporation, 60 Wall St., New York City, Sole Agents for U. S. and Canada

1912 In March, Harry E. Aitken and John R. Freuler, who had controlled the Western Film Exchange of Milwaukee in 1906, formed the Mutual Film Corporation to combine several independent exchanges into a pattern like General Film Company, which had been formed in 1910 to engage in the distribution of films. The companies joining Mutual included Thanhouser, American, Reliance and Majestic. Carl Laemmle, whose Imp Company was prospering, countered with the formation on June 8, 1912, of the Universal Film Manufacturing Company. Companies releasing through Universal, besides Imp, included Victor, Rex, Eclair, Powers and Nestor. The independents were now in two camps bucking General Film. Adam Kessel and Charles Bauman, the founders of the Bison Film Company, were impressed with Mack Sennett's work at Biograph and put up $1,500 as a trial for Sennett to make three pictures of one reel each. He was to have a share of the profits and a salary of one hundred dollars a week. It was the beginning of the famous Keystone Comedies. The name and the trade-mark were adopted from the Pennsylvania Railroad. Mack Sennett signed Mabel Normand, Ford Sterling and Fred Mace, and the first Keystone Comedy, called "Cohen At Coney Island," was released September 23, 1912. Helen Gardner left Vitagraph and formed the Helen Gardner Picture Corporation, with a studio at Tappan-on-the-Hudson. She was the first star to form her own company.

FRANCIS X. BUSHMAN
PIN-UP BOY, 1912 VINTAGE

MABEL NORMAND
PIN-UP GIRL, 1912 VINTAGE

MACK SENNETT, MABEL NORMAND IN
"BARNEY OLDFIELD'S RACE FOR A LIFE"

MACK SENNETT, MABEL NORMAND, FRED
MACE IN A "KEYSTONE COMEDY"

OLORES CASSINELLI, FRANCIS X. BUSHMAN
IN "WHEN SOUL MEETS SOUL" (ESSANAY)

HOBART BOSWORTH IN
"THE COUNT OF MONTE CRISTO" (SELIG)

EUGENIE BESSERER, HERBERT RAWLINSON,
HOBART BOSWORTH IN "THE COUNT OF
MONTE CRISTO" (SELIG)

LILLIAN WALKER
(VITAGRAPH)

MAURICE COSTELLO
(VITAGRAPH)

MAE MARSH, ROBERT HARRON
IN "MAN'S GENESIS"

LIONEL BARRYMORE, MARY PICKFORD
IN "THE NEW YORK HAT"

DOROTHY BERNARD, WILFRED LUCAS
IN "THE GIRL AND HER TRUST"

MABEL NORMAND, EDWIN AUGUST, BLANCHE SWEET
IN "THE ETERNAL MOTHER"

MARY PICKFORD
IN "FRIENDS"

LILLIAN AND DOROTHY GISH
IN "AN UNSEEN ENEMY"

D. W. GRIFFITH DIRECTED BIOGRAPH FILMS 1912

MARY FULLER
(EDISON)

KING BAGGOT
(IMP)

1912 Meanwhile companies were exploiting and contracting stars. Vitagraph, where Lillian Walker and Earle Williams were favorites, signed Clara Kimball Young, a stock company actress, and her husband, James Young. Her first film was "Anne Boleyn." Mary Pickford, a big box office draw, had returned to Biograph bringing with her two young actress friends, Lillian and Dorothy Gish, who had appeared with her in road companies. Their first important film appearance was in "The Unseen Enemy." Alice Joyce and Carlyle Blackwell were Kalem's top stars. Kathlyn Williams and Tom Mix headed Selig's stars, while J. Warren Kerrigan was America's best bet. King Baggot was Imp's attraction. Florence Lawrence, still popular, had left Lubin for the newly formed Victor Company. Edison released "What Happened to Mary?" starring favorite Mary Fuller. It was a series of pictures and a forerunner of the serial. Each of the series was independent and complete, and one was released each month. G. M. Anderson and his Broncho Billy pictures were gaining in popularity and so was Francis X. Bushman at Essanay. Beverly Bayne, a Minneapolis society girl, became Bushman's leading lady and soon they were the most popular team in films. Essanay also starred "Baby Parsons," little daughter of Louella O. Parsons, who later as Harriet Parsons became the top woman producer in the industry.

OTHY BERNARD, CHARLES WEST
HE GODDESS OF SAGEBRUSH
GULCH" (BIOGRAPH)

LILLIAN GISH, WALTER MILLER
IN "THE MUSKETEERS OF PIG
ALLEY" (BIOGRAPH)

GENE GAUNTIER, JACK CLARK IN
"FROM THE MANGER TO THE CROSS"
(KALEM)

MARSHALL NEILAN, J. WARREN KERRIGAN, PAULINE
BUSH IN "THE STRANGER AT COYOTE" (AMERICAN)

PEARL WHITE, HAL FORDE IN
"MAYBLOSSOM" (PATHÉ)

ROBERT FRAZER
(ECLAIR)

ETHEL GRANDIN
(GEM)

NORMA PHILLIPS
"OUR MUTUAL GIRL"

VICTORIA FORDE
(NESTOR)

LOUISE FAZENDA
(JOKER)

WILLIAM STOWE
(SELIG)

J. WARREN KERRIGAN
IN "FOR THE FLAG"
(AMERICAN)

ARTHUR MAUDE IN
"PELLEAS AND MELISANDE"
(UNIVERSAL)

FLORENCE ROBERTS
IN "SAPPHO"

ROBERT LEONARD
IN "ROBINSON CRUSOE"
(REX)

MIRIAM NESBITT IN "THE
FOREMAN'S TREACHERY"
(EDISON)

HENRI KRAUSS
IN "LES MISERABLE

MAE MARSH, ROBERT HARRON
IN "JUDITH OF BETHULIA" (BIOGRAPH)

HENRY B. WALTHALL, BLANCHE SWEET
IN "JUDITH OF BETHULIA" (BIOGRAPH)

KATE BRUCE

W. CHRISTIE MILLER

LILLIAN GISH

ROBERT HARRON

DOROTHY GISH

WALTER MILLER

34   BIOGRAPH PLAYERS

WIN CAREWE   OCTAVIA HANDWORTH   ROMAINE FIELDING   LOTTIE BRISCOE   FLORENCE HACKETT   EDGAR JONES

LUBIN PLAYERS

SCENES FROM "QUO VADIS" (KLEINE CINES)

1913 Feature pictures received new impetus with the great success of "Quo Vadis." In eight reels, it was the longest film shown in America until this time. Produced by Cines Film Company in Italy, it was imported by George Kleine, a leader of the Motion Picture Patents Company group. It was presented in "legitimate" theatres and ran 22 weeks at the Astor Theatre, New York, at a one-dollar top. Kleine also imported "The Last Days of Pompeii." "Les Miserables" and "Shylock" were other foreign films that had American success. D. W. Griffith made his first "spectacle"—"Judith of Bethulia," in four parts. It was his last film produced under the Biograph banner. He signed with Mutual and was put in charge of the amalgamated Reliance-Majestic Companies. Famous Players' first American-made release was James K. Hackett in "The Prisoner of Zenda." Actually, "The Count of Monte Cristo," starring James O'Neill, was filmed first, but they held up release because of the three-reel Selig version shown in 1912. Other Famous Players features starred Mrs. Fiske, Mrs. Lily Langtry and Carlotta Nillson. They also signed Mary Pickford, who had left Biograph again and was appearing on the stage for David Belasco in "The Good Little Devil." Her first Famous Players feature was "In The Bishop's Carriage" and her second, "Caprice."

SCENES FROM "THE LAST DAYS OF POMPEII"
(GEORGE KLEINE)

SCENES FROM "LES MISERABLES"
(ELECTRIC)

BEL VAN BUREN   HAROLD VOSBURGH   MYRTLE STEDMAN   KATHLYN WILLIAMS   CHARLES CLARY   BESSIE EYTON

SELIG PLAYERS

MARY PICKFORD, OWEN MOORE
IN "CAPRICE"

MARY PICKFORD IN
"IN THE BISHOP'S CARRIAGE"
(FAMOUS PLAYERS)

M. JOUBE, HARRY BAUER AS SHYLOCK, M. HARVE, MLLE. P
BONAFE IN "SHYLOCK" (KLEINE-ECLIPSE)

RAYMOND BUNDEL, MRS. FISKE

SCENES FROM "TESS OF THE D'URBERVILLES" (FAMOUS PLAYERS)

LEAH BAIRD, HERBERT BRENON, KING BAGGOT
IN "IVANHOE" (IMP)

KING BAGGOT
IN "IVANHOE" (IMP)

MAX ASHER, HARRY McCOY, LOUISE FAZENDA, BOBBY
VERNON IN "MIKE AND JAKE AT THE BEACH" (JOKER)

ALEXANDER GADEN, CARLOTTA NILLSON, HOUSE PETERS,
ELINE TRAVERS IN "LEAH KLESCHNA" (FAMOUS PLAYERS)

EDDIE LYONS
IN "SOME RUNNER" (NESTOR)

JAMES O'NEILL IN
"THE COUNT OF MONTE CRISTO" (FAMOUS PLAYERS)

HARRY CAREY
(UNIVERSAL)

BEATRICE BECKLEY, JAMES K. HACKETT
IN "THE PRISONER OF ZENDA" (FAMOUS PLAYERS)

RUTH ROLAND
(KALEM)

HOUSE PETERS, CECILIA LOFTUS
IN "LADY OF QUALITY" (FAMOUS PLAYERS)

SIDNEY MASON, LILY LANGTRY
IN "HIS NEIGHBOR'S WIFE" (FAMOUS PLAYERS)

TOM MOORE, ALICE JOYCE
IN "NINA OF THE THEATRE" (KALEM)

JOHN BUNNY, LILLIAN WALKER, WALLY VAN
IN "LOVE, LUCK AND GASOLINE" (VITAGRAPH)

JOHN BUNNY
(VITAGRAPH)

MATT MOORE
(VICTOR)

WALLACE REID, CLEO MADISON
IN "THE HEART OF A CRACKSMAN"
(POWERS)

ROSE TAPLE
(VITAGRAPH)

BILLIE RHODES, CARLYLE BLACKWELL
IN "PERILS OF THE SEA" (KALEM)

RUTH ROLAND, GEORGE LARKIN
IN "WHILE FATHER TELEPHONED" (KA

NORMA TALMADGE
(VITAGRAPH)

EARLE WILLIAMS, REX INGRAM, LILLIAN WALKER
IN "THE ARTIST'S MADONNA" (VITAGRAPH)

JAMES YOUNG, CLARA KIMBALL YOUNG
IN "THE LITTLE MINISTER" (VITAGRAPH)

FRANK BORZAGE
(KAY-BEE)

TOM MIX
IN "THE ESCAPE OF JIM DOLAN"
(SELIG)

MABEL TRUNNELLE
(EDISON)

ARTHUR V. JOHNSON
(LUBIN)

13 Companies were still filming the classics. Universal made "Uncle Tom's Cabin," "Robinson Crusoe," "Ivanhoe" and "Dr. Jekyll and Mr. [Hyd]e." Vitagraph features included "Pickwick Papers" and "The Little Minis[ter.]" and Famous Players made "Tess of The D'Urbervilles" and "The Count of [Mon]te Cristo." Frederick Warde, Shakespearean actor, filmed "Richard III." [Mar]guerite Snow and Marion Leonard both starred in versions of "Carmen," [whil]e Constance Crawley and Arthur Maude appeared in "Pelléas and Méli[san]de." Among the actors who were playing supporting roles in films but later [beca]me more famous as directors were Herbert Brenon, who appeared in ["Iva]nhoe," and Rex Ingram, who was supporting Clara Kimball Young and [Ly]an Walker at Vitagraph. Theatres were showing the first adventure subject, ["Rain]ey's African Hunt" in nine reels. The films were shot by Paul J. Rainey, a [weal]thy Philadelphia sportsman, during one of his hunting expeditions. It was [a] [fo]rerunner and paved the way for Martin Johnson's adventure films, Robert J. [Flah]erty's "Nanook of The North," and Merian C. Cooper's "Grass" and "Chang."

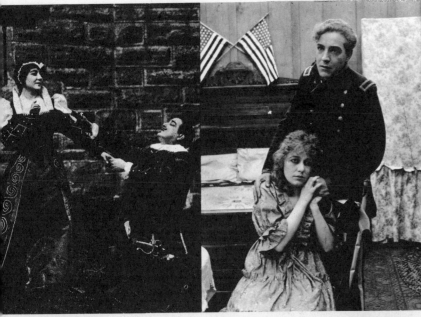

MARY FULLER, BIGELOW COOPER
IN "MARY STUART" (EDISON)

MARGARET THOMPSON, GEORGE FISHER
IN "THE MAN WHO WENT OUT" (DOMINO)

CLARA KIMBALL YOUNG
(VITAGRAPH)

MARION LEONARD IN "CARMEN"
(MONOPOL)

HARRY, LELAND, DOROTHY and ETHYLE BENHAM
(THANHOUSER)

WILLIAM GARWOOD, MARGUERITE SNOW
IN "CARMEN" (THANHOUSER)

SCENE FROM "THE SEA WOLF" (BOSWORTH)
Above: HERBERT RAWLINSON, HOBART BOSWORTH
IN "THE SEA WOLF" (BOSWORTH)

TOM MOORE
(KALEM)

FREDERICK WARDE IN SCENES FROM
"KING RICHARD III" (STERLING)

CHARLES OGLE
(EDISON)

ADELE LANE
(SELIG)

ALEC B. FRANCIS
(VITAGRAPH)

FRITZI BRUNETTE
(SELIG)

BILLY QUIRK
(PATHÉ)

JULIA STEWART
(ECLAIR)

SYDNEY AYRES
(AMERICAN)

HELEN MARTEN
(LUBIN)

JAMES CO
(RELIAN

CLARA KIMBALL YOUNG, JULIA SWAYNE GORDON,
JAMES YOUNG IN "BEAU BRUMMEL"
(VITAGRAPH)

BOBBY CONNELLY, CLARA
KIMBALL YOUNG IN
"LOVE'S SUNSET"
(VITAGRAPH)

KATHLYN WILLIAMS, HAROLD
LOCKWOOD IN "A MANSION
OF MISERY" (SELIG)

GERDA HOLMES, WILLIAM RUSSELL IN
"ROBIN HOOD" (THANHOUSER)

JANE GAIL, KING BAGGOT IN
"DR. JEKYLL AND MR. HYDE" (IMP)

WILLIAM CAVANAUGH, ETHEL GRANDIN, HOWARD
CRAMPTON IN "TRAFFIC IN SOULS" (IMP)

JOHN BUNNY
IN "PICKWICK PAPERS" (VITAGRAPH)

DOLORES AND HELENE COSTELLO
(VITAGRAPH)

JOHN BUNNY
IN "PICKWICK PAPERS" (VITAGRAPH)

1913 Keystone Comedies were becoming very popular. Among the new comics who joined forces with Mack Sennett, Mabel Normand and Ford Sterling were Roscoe Arbuckle, a rotund comedian sometimes known as "Fatty" Arbuckle, Mack Swain, Hank Mann, Al St. John, and a young Englishman named Charles Chaplin who had been playing the big-time vaudeville from coast to coast in Alf Reeves' act "Karno's Pantomime Company." Adam Kessel had caught the act and hired Chaplin for $150 a week. In November he appeared in his first film, a one-reeler, "Kid's Auto Races," made on the Keystone lot in Los Angeles. Chaplin's character of the little man with the baggy pants, oversized shoes and cane became famous before he was known by name. After Zukor first showed "Queen Elizabeth" at New York's Lyceum Theatre, and with the "Quo Vadis" success at the Astor, the legitimate theatres were coming more into use for exploitation purposes. "Traffic In Souls," a Universal release directed by a former actor, George Loane Tucker, was shown at Joe Weber's Theatre where it gave four showings daily for a twenty-five-cent admission. It was advertised as "a $200,000 spectacle in 700 scenes with 800 players and showing the traps cunningly laid for young girls by vice agents." Actually it had cost $5,700 and was made in four weeks. It grossed over half a million dollars.

'D PAGET
)GRAPH)

ALICE HOLLISTER
(KALEM)

RICHARD BUHLER
(LUBIN)

ALICE WASHBURN
(EDISON)

ALLAN DWAN
(AMERICAN)

BESSIE BARRISCALE
(KAY-BEE)

GEORGE A. LESSEY
(EDISON)

EDNA FLUGRATH
(EDISON)

GEORGE LOANE
TUCKER
(MAJESTIC)

  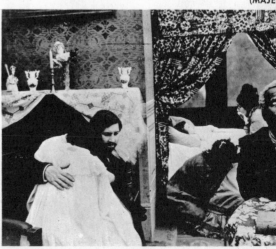

ELIZA CROSSING THE ICE

MARGARITA FISCHER

DEATH OF LITTLE EVA

SCENES FROM "UNCLE TOM'S CABIN" (UNIVERSAL) WITH EDWARD ALEXANDER as SINCLAIRE, MARGARITA FISCHER
as TOPSY, GERTRUDE SHORT as LITTLE EVA, IVY SHEPHERD as TESSIE, HARRY POLLARD as UNCLE TOM.

JEANIE McPHEARSON
(UNIVERSAL)

EARLE METCALFE
(LUBIN)

PEARL SINDELAR
(PATHÉ)

GUY COOMBS
(KALEM)

PAULINE BUSH
(UNIVERSAL)

OWEN MOORE
(VICTOR)

CHARLOTTE BURTON
(AMERICAN)

HERBERT RAW
(UNIVERS

BEVERLY BAYNE, WILLIAM BAILEY, LILY
BRANSCOMBE IN "THE SNARE"
(ESSANAY)

SYDNEY AYRES, CHARLOTTE BURTON
IN "TRAPPED IN A FOREST FIRE"
(AMERICAN)

RUTH STONEHOUSE, FRANCIS X. BUSHMAN
IN "THE SPY'S DEFEAT"
(ESSANAY)

WHEELER OAKMAN, BESSIE EYT
IN "THE LONG AGO"
(SELIG)

LILLIAN DREW
(ESSANAY)

SLIM SUMMERVILLE
(ESSANAY)

JULIA SWAYNE GORDON
(VITAGRAPH)

FRED MACE
(KEYSTONE)

ANNA LUTHER
(KEYSTONE)

TOM POWERS
(VITAGRAPH)

MARY ANDERSON
(VITAGRAPH)

SIDNEY AINSW
(ESSANA

MACK SWAIN
KEYSTONE COMEDIES

ROSCOE ARBUCKLE
KEYSTONE COMEDIES

MACK SWAIN

ROSCOE ARBUCKLE

FORD STERLING

MACK SENNETT'S KEYSTONE COMEDIANS

FORD STERLING, AL ST. JOHN, HANK MANN, ROSCOE ARBUCKLE AND KEYSTONE COPS
IN "IN THE CLUTCHES OF A GANG"

MABEL NORMAND, ROSCOE ARBUCKLE IN
"FATTY'S FLIRTATION"
Above: FORD STERLING AND KEYSTONE COPS

FORD STERLING, MABEL NORMAND
IN "THE GUSHER"
KEYSTONE COMEDIES

CHARLES CHAPLIN IN "MAKING A LIVING"
Above: FORD STERLING, MACK SENNETT, MABEL
NORMAND IN "A STRONG REVENGE"

BARBARA TENNANT, O. A. C. LUND
IN "FIRELIGHT" (ECLAIR)

J. WARREN KERRIGAN, PAULINE BUSH
IN "THE WISHING SEAT" (AMERICAN)

ANITA STEWART
(VITAGRAPH)

"SLEEPING BEAUTY"
(MONARCH)

ANITA STEWART
IN "THE WOOD VIOLET"
(VITAGRAPH)

HELEN GARDNER IN
"A SISTER TO CARMEN"

WILLIAM DUNCAN
(SELIG)

MATT MOORE, FLORENCE LAWRENCE, OWEN
MOORE IN A VICTOR COMEDY

WILLIAM CARPENTER, KATHLYN WILLIAMS,
THOMAS SANTSCHI

KATHLYN WILLIAMS

KATHLYN WILLIAMS

KATHLYN WILLIAMS

1913 On December 29, Selig released the first of fifteen episodes of "The Adventures of Kathlyn," a serial named for and starring Kathlyn Williams, a young Butte, Montana, girl who had appeared on the stage before becoming Selig's most popular star. Thomas Santschi played the hero while Charles Clary was the villain. This first serial ever shown was the beginning of a vogue. The public waited eagerly for a new adventure every second week, and for the next few years serial films flooded the country.

LAFAYETTE McKEE, KATHLYN WILLIAMS
THOMAS SANTSCHI

KATHLYN WILLIAMS, WILLIAM CARPENTER

KATHLYN WILLIAMS, GOLDIE
COLWELL

SCENES FROM "THE ADVENTURES OF KATHLYN" (SELIG)

PEARL WHITE

"The Perils of Pauline"

1914 The most famous of all serials was probably "The Perils of Pauline," released by Pathé. The first episode appeared April 4, 1914, and advertised announcements stated: "The action of the story includes flying machine accidents, thrilling rescues, fires at sea, train wrecks, automobile accidents, in fact, everything that can be introduced as a thrill." Paul Panzer was hissed as the villain, Crane Wilbur applauded as the hero, and Pearl White, as Pauline, became the outstanding serial queen. Born in Glen Ridge, Missouri, she ran away and joined a circus while in her teens. She trouped with various stock companies, and in 1910 she joined Powers Film Company at thirty dollars a week. When she died in 1938 she left an estate of over a million dollars. Her experience as a trapeze artist during her circus days was valuable. Scorning a double, she did all those hazardous serial stunts herself.

SCENES FROM "THE PERILS OF PAULINE" (PATHÉ)
WITH PEARL WHITE, CRANE WILBUR AND PAUL PANZER

CRANE WILBUR
(PATHÉ)

FLORENCE LA BADIE
(THANHOUSER)

FRANCIS FORD
(UNIVERSAL)

GRACE CUNARD
(UNIVERSAL)

SCENES FROM "THE MILLION DOLLAR MYSTERY"
(THANHOUSER) WITH FLORENCE LA BADIE
JAMES CRUZE, MARGUERITE SNOW

SCENES FROM "LUCILLE LOVE"
(UNIVERSAL) WITH
GRACE CUNARD AND FRANCIS FORD

SCENES FROM "THE TREY O' HEARTS"
(UNIVERSAL) WITH
CLEO MADISON AND GEORGE LARKIN

FLORENCE LA BADIE, JAMES CRUZE
IN "THE MILLION DOLLAR MYSTERY"
(THANHOUSER)

CLEO MADISON
(UNIVERSAL)

GEORGE LARKIN
(UNIVERSAL)

GEORGE LARKIN, CLEO MADISON
IN "THE TREY O' HEARTS"
(UNIVERSAL)

LEAH BAIRD
(VITAGRAPH)

IRVING CUMMINGS
(UNIVERSAL)

GERTRUDE McCOY
(EDISON)

CHARLES RAY
(KAY-BEE)

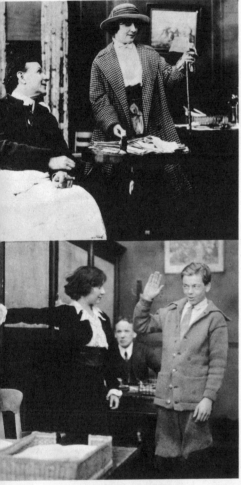

1914 In April also, Universal announced its first serial, "Lucille Love," which co-starred Grace Cunard and Francis Ford, and followed it with "The Trey O' Hearts" featuring Cleo Madison and George Larkin. Thanhouser joined the serial cycle with "The Million Dollar Mystery" starring Florence La Badie, James Cruze, who later became a famous director, and Marguerite Snow. Edison continued to release "series" pictures. Mary Fuller appeared in "Dolly of The Dailies." Andy Clark, a child actor, made an "Andy" series, while Ben Wilson, William Wadsworth, Marc MacDermott and Barry O'Moore (known on the stage as Herbert Yost) all appeared in their own series. The Universal popular players included Florence Lawrence, King Baggot, Edwin August, Pauline Bush, Frank Lloyd, Herbert Rawlinson, Margarita Fischer, Robert Leonard, Ethel Grandin, Irving Cummings, Wallace Reid, and their most popular star, J. Warren Kerrigan. Of this group, Cummings, Leonard and Lloyd all became famous as directors. Universal's outstanding films included "Samson" with Kerrigan and "Neptune's Daughter" with Annette Kellermann. "The Spoilers," filmed in nine reels by Selig from Rex Beach's novel, was a landmark, and a fight scene between William Farnum and Thomas Santschi became film history. The cast also included Kathlyn Williams and Bessie Eyton. Famous Players was signing more stage stars including May Irwin, Henrietta Crosman and H. B. Warner. Also, John Barrymore whose first film was "An American Citizen," Marguerite Clark who made her debut in "Wildflower," and Hazel Dawn whose initial film was "One of Our Girls."

MARY FULLER, YALE BOSS
Above: CHARLES OGLE, MARY FULLER
SCENES FROM "DOLLY OF THE DAILIES" (EDISON)

JAMES CRUZE, MARGUERITE SNOW (Also Above) IN
"JOSEPH IN THE LAND OF EGYPT" (THANHOUSER)

GARITA FISCHER, ROBERT LEONARD
IN "THE PRIMEVAL TEST"

MATT MOORE, FLORENCE LAWRENCE
IN "A SINGULAR CYNIC"

HERBERT RAWLINSON IN
"KID REGAN'S HANDS"

PAULINE BUSH, LON CHANEY IN
"WHERE THE FOREST ENDS"

J. WARREN KERRIGAN

J. WARREN KERRIGAN
SCENES FROM "SAMSON" (UNIVERSAL)

MAYME KELSO, J. WARREN KERRIGAN

JACK RICHARDSON
(AMERICAN)

DOROTHY PHILLIPS
(IMP)

WILLIAM CLIFFORD
(UNIVERSAL)

JANE GAIL
(UNIVERSAL)

EDWIN AUGUST
(UNIVERSAL)

CLARA HORTON
(ECLAIR)

MISS HAZELTONE, IRVING CUMMINGS, ETHEL GRANDIN
IN "JANE EYRE" (IMP)

ETHEL GRANDIN IN
"THE DAWN OF A ROMANCE"
(UNIVERSAL)

FORD STERLING IN
"A DRAMATIC MISTAKE"
(STERLING)

THOMAS SANTSCHI, WILLIAM FARNUM
WILLIAM FARNUM, THOMAS SANTSCHI, KATHLYN WILLIAMS
FAMOUS FIGHT SCENE BETWEEN THOMAS
SANTSCHI AND WILLIAM FARNUM
SCENES FROM REX BEACH'S "THE SPOILERS" (SELIG)
WILLIAM FARNUM, BESSIE EYTON, FRANK CLARK
Top: WILLIAM FARNUM, WHEELER OAKMAN, KATHLYN WILLIAMS

WHEELER OAKMAN
(SELIG)

ELEANOR WOODRUFF
(PATHÉ)

LEW CODY
(BALBOA)

MURIEL OSTRICHE
(THANHOUSER)

SIDNEY BRACY
(THANHOUSER)

MILDRED HARRIS
(OZ)

WALLACE REID, FRANK LLOYD
IN "THE TEST" (NESTOR)

HERBERT RAWLINSON IN
"FLIRTING WITH DEATH"
(UNIVERSAL)

IVA SHEPARD, EDWIN AUGUST, HAL AUGUST
IN "THE ROMANCE OF AN ACTOR"
(POWERS)

51

HAROLD LOCKWOOD, MARY PICKFORD, OLIVE GOLDEN
IN "TESS OF THE STORM COUNTRY"
Top: MARY PICKFORD, HAROLD LOCKWOOD IN "HEARTS ADRIFT"

ERNEST TRUEX, WILDA BENNETT, MARY PICKFORD IN
"A GOOD LITTLE DEVIL"
Top: OWEN MOORE, MARY PICKFORD IN "CINDERELLA"

MARY PICKFORD, JAMES KIRKWOOD IN
"THE EAGLE'S MATE" Top: MARY PICKFORD, CARL
BLACKWELL IN "SUCH A LITTLE QUEEN"

HAROLD
LOCKWOOD
(FAMOUS PLAYERS)

BILLIE RHODES
(MUTUAL)

WILLIAM SHAY
(UNIVERSAL)

HELENE ROSSON
(AMERICAN)

MAX FIGMAN
(LASKY)

LOLITA ROBERTSON
(LASKY)

WHITNEY RAYMOND
(ESSANAY)

HELEN DUNBAR
(ESSANAY)

THOMAS
COMMER
(ESSANAY)

JOHN BARRYMORE IN
"THE MAN FROM MEXICO"

WALTER CRAVEN, HAROLD LOCKWOOD, LORRAINE HULING,
GERTRUDE NORMAN, HENRIETTA CROSMAN IN
"THE UNWELCOME MRS. HATCH"

HAZEL DAWN IN
"ONE OF OUR GIRLS"

DOBSON MITCHELL, LOIS MEREDITH, JOHN EMERSON,
HAROLD LOCKWOOD IN "THE CONSPIRACY"

ELMER BOOTH, MAY IRWIN, CHARLES LANE
IN "MRS. BLACK IS BACK"
FAMOUS PLAYERS PRODUCTIONS

CARLYLE BLACKWELL
IN "THE SPITFIRE"

SCENES FROM "CABIRIA" (KLEINE) WITH UMBERTO MOSZATO, ERNESTO PAGANI, EDOUARD DAVESNES, ITALIA MANZINE, ANTONIO BRANIONI

JOHNSTONE
(AIR)

DOLORES CASSINELLI
(ESSANAY)

GEORGE FISHER
(MUTUAL)

GLADYS HULETTE
(THANHOUSER)

DARWIN KARR
(VITAGRAPH)

JOE MOORE
(UNIVERSAL)

TSURU AOKI
(KAY-BEE)

HAL AUGUST
(UNIVERSAL)

HOWARD ESTABROOK
(PATHÉ)

GLADYS HANSON, WILLIAM RUSSELL
IN "THE STRAIGHT ROAD"

1914 Films without established names were also popular if they were elaborate enough. "Cabiria," another Italian large-scale spectacle, was an example of this. Jesse Lasky, a vaudeville producer, now entered the picture business. With a capital of $26,500, the Jesse Lasky Feature Play Company was born. Samuel Goldfish, his brother-in-law who became famous as Samuel Goldwyn and Cecil B. de Mille, a former actor, joined the organization. De Mille directed the first film, "The Squaw Man," which was made in an old barn on the corner of Vine and Selma Streets in Hollywood. It starred Dustin Farnum who had been offered a substantial interest in the concern for his services. Farnum said he would rather have $5,000 in cash—a decision that cost him a fortune.

WILLIAM FARNUM, ROSINA HENLEY
IN "THE SIGN OF THE CROSS"

DARWELL, MONROE SALISBURY, BESSIE BARRISCALE
IN "THE ROSE OF THE RANCHO"

BETTY HARTE, HOUSE PETERS
IN "THE PRIDE OF JENNICO"
JESSE LASKY PRODUCTIONS

EDWARD ABELES
IN "BREWSTER'S MILLIONS"

THE LASKY COMPANY

Standing (L. to R.): OSCAR APFEL, MAX FIGMAN, CHARLES RICHMAN, WILFRED BUCKLAND, THEODORE ROBERTS, ROBERT EDESON, EDWARD ABELES, CECIL B. DE MILLE
Seated: LOLITA ROBERTSON, JESSE L. LASKY, BESSIE BARRISCALE

1914 Later in the year Paramount Pictures Corporation was formed with Adolph Zukor at the head and Jesse Lasky as vice-president to release the feature films of Famous Players, Lasky and Bosworth—a company that had been formed by Hobart Bosworth, an actor in early Selig films. William Fox, who had been a cloth sponger and had risen from his penny arcade business to a prominent exhibitor, decided to make films. The first Fox feature was "Life's Shop Window," made on Staten Island. It cost $4,500 and starred Claire Whitney and Stuart Holmes. Winfield Sheehan, a former reporter, joined the Fox organization. Another new organization was the Alco Film Corporation formed by Al Lichtman, formerly connected with Famous Players. During its short and

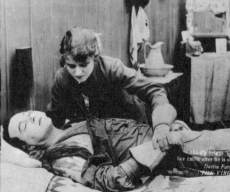

WINIFRED KINGSTON, ART ACORD, MONROE SALISBURY, BILLY ELMER, DUSTIN FARNUM IN "THE SQUAW MAN"
Center: WINIFRED KINGSTON, DUSTIN FARNUM, RED WING IN "THE SQUAW MAN" (LASKY)

LASKY BARN, HOLLYWOOD

DUSTIN FARNUM, WINIFRED KINGSTON IN "THE VIRGINIAN"
Center: J. W. JOHNSTON, H. B. CARPENTER, DUSTIN FAR... BILLY ELMER IN "THE VIRGINIAN" (LASKY)

S WEBER AS PORTIA, DOUGLAS GERRARD, RUPERT JULIAN AS ANTONIO, PHILLIPS SMALLEY AS SHYLOCK IN "THE MERCHANT OF VENICE" (UNIVERSAL)

PHILLIPS SMALLEY AS SHYLOCK

PHILLIPS SMALLEY, LOIS WEBER, RUPERT JULIAN IN "THE MERCHANT OF VENICE" (UNIVERSAL)

LEAH BAIRD, WILLIAM SHAY, ANNETTE KELLERMANN IN "NEPTUNE'S DAUGHTER" (UNIVERSAL)

JACK PICKFORD, MARGUERITE CLARK, HAROLD LOCKWOOD IN "WILDFLOWER" (FAMOUS PLAYERS)

stormy existence, it released Lubin's "Michael Strogoff," starring Jacob Adler; Ethel Barrymore in her first film, "The Nightingale"; Andrew Mack in "The Ragged Earl"; Olga Petrova's first film, "The Vampire"; and Beatriz Michelena in "Salomy Jane." They also handled Mack Sennett's Keystone Comedy "Tillie's Punctured Romance." In six reels, it was the first film Sennett ever made over two reels. It starred Charles Chaplin, Mabel Normand and Marie Dressler, then a stage star, and it became one of the early comedy classics. Among the independent films made were "Manon Lescaut" with opera stars Lina Cavalieri and Lucien Muratore, Effie Shannon and Herbert Kelcey in their stage success "After The Ball," and "Three Weeks," from Elinor Glyn's popular novel.

CE HOLLISTER, ALICE JOYCE, TOM MOORE, MARY ROSS IN "THE BRAND"
ALICE HOLLISTER, ALICE JOYCE IN "THE VAMPIRE'S TRAIL"

JAMES B. ROSS, JERE AUSTIN, GUY COOMBS, ALICE JOYCE IN "THE SCHOOL FOR SCANDAL" SCENES FROM ALICE JOYCE FEATURES (KALEM)

ALICE JOYCE, HENRY HALLAM, TOM MOORE, and Center: TOM MOORE, ALICE JOYCE IN "THE MYSTERY OF THE SLEEPING DEATH"

RICHARD TRAVERS, GLORIA SWANSON, RUTH STONEHOUSE IN "THE ROMANCE OF AN AMERICAN DUCHESS"

FRANCIS X. BUSHMAN, BEVERLY BAYNE IN "ONE WONDERFUL NIGHT"

FRANCIS X. BUSHMAN, LILLIAN DREW, BEVERLY BAYNE IN "ONE WONDERFUL NIGHT"

BEVERLY BAYNE

1914 Francis X. Bushman won *The Ladies' World* Hero Contest over such favorites as J. Warren Kerrigan, Crane Wilbur, Carlyle Blackwell, Maurice Costello, Arthur Johnson and King Baggot. Other Essanay players in the limelight were Beverly Bayne, Bushman's leading lady, Ruth Stonehouse, Richard Travers, and Wallace Beery who was comical in a "Sweedie" comedy series. His wife at that time was a young extra named Gloria Swanson. Constance Talmadge joined Vitagraph as a bit player. Clara Kimball Young and Earle Williams, both Vitagraph stars, won a popularity contest conducted by the *Motion Picture Magazine*. Miss Young, whose fame and box office appeal were mounting, made a big hit in "My Official Wife."

WALLACE, NOAH AND WILLIAM BEERY

WALLACE BEERY

BRYANT WASHBURN, MARGUERITE CLAYTON IN "THE PROMISE LAND"

ROD LA ROCQUE, NELL CRAIG IN AN EARLY FILM ESSANAY FILMS

RUTH STONEHOUSE, FRANCIS X. BUSHMAN IN "BLOOD WILL TELL"

FRANCIS X. BUSHMAN

CHESTER CONKLIN

MABEL NORMAND, CHARLES CHAPLIN, FORD STERLING,
CHESTER CONKLIN IN "BETWEEN SHOWERS"

ROSCOE ARBUCKLE, CHARLES CHAPLIN
IN "THE ROUNDERS"

MARIE DRESSLER

CHARLES CHAPLIN, MABEL NORMAND, MARIE DRESSLER
IN "TILLIE'S PUNCTURED ROMANCE"

CHARLES CHAPLIN

CHARLES CHAPLIN, MARIE DRESSLER, MABEL NORMAND
IN "TILLIE'S PUNCTURED ROMANCE"
KEYSTONE COMEDIES

CHARLES CHAPLIN, MARIE DRESSLER
IN "TILLIE'S PUNCTURED ROMANCE"

BEATRIZ MICHELENA
(ALCO)

BEATRIZ MICHELENA, WILLIAM NIGH, HOUSE PETERS
IN "SALOMY JANE" (ALCO)

ANTONY NOVELLI IN
"JULIUS CAESAR" (KLEINE)

DIGBY BELL IN
"THE EDUCATION OF MR. PIPP" (ALCO)

GEORGE PIERCE, MADALINE TRAVERSE
IN "THREE WEEKS" (RELIABLE)

PHILLIPS SMALLEY
(UNIVERSAL)

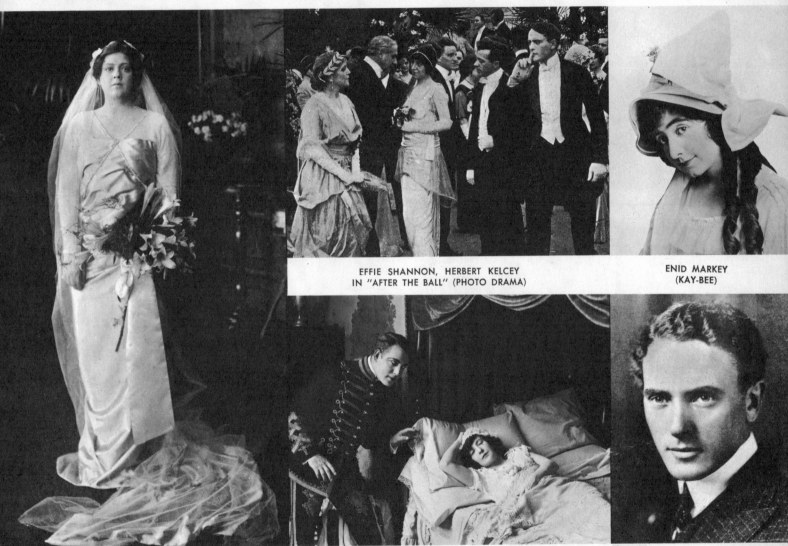

ETHEL BARRYMORE
IN "THE NIGHTINGALE" (ALCO)

EFFIE SHANNON, HERBERT KELCEY
IN "AFTER THE BALL" (PHOTO DRAMA)

ENID MARKEY
(KAY-BEE)

VICTOR SUTHERLAND, CECIL SPOONER
IN "THE DANCER AND THE KING" (WORLD)

HERBERT RAWLINSON
(UNIVERSAL)

CONWAY TEARLE, ETHEL BARRYMORE, IDA DARLING
IN "THE NIGHTINGALE" (ALCO)

ANDREW MACK IN
"THE RAGGED EARL" (ALCO)

MAUDE FEALY
(THANHOUSER)

CLARA KIMBALL YOUNG   CLARA KIMBALL YOUNG, HARRY T. MOREY   CLARA KIMBALL YOUNG, LEON TROTSKY   EARLE WILLIAMS

SCENES FROM "MY OFFICIAL WIFE" (VITAGRAPH)

JANE DARWELL, THOMAS W. ROSS
IN "THE ONLY SON" (LASKY)

BEVERLY BAYNE, FRANCIS X. BUSHMAN
IN "UNDER ROYAL PATRONAGE" (ESSANAY)

PHILLIPS SMALLEY, LOIS WEBER
IN "FALSE COLORS" (BOSWORTH)

JAMES MORRISON   CONSTANCE TALMADGE   ANTONIO MORENO   EDITH STOREY   WALLY VAN   MARGARET GIBSON

VITAGRAPH PLAYERS

CONSTANCE TALMADGE, ANTONIO MORENO IN "IN THE LATIN QUARTER" (VITAGRAPH)

LUCIEN MURATORE, LINA CAVALIERI IN "MANON LESCAUT" (PLAYGOERS)

CISSY FITZGERALD, WALLY VAN, L. ROGERS LYTTON, HUGHIE MACK IN "THE WIN(K)SOME WIDOW" (VITAGRAPH)

A SWAYNE GORDON, EARLE WILLIAMS, ANITA STEWART IN "TWO WOMEN" (VITAGRAPH)

DONALD HALL, MAURICE COSTELLO, S. RANKIN DREW IN "MR. BARNES OF NEW YORK" (VITAGRAPH)

NALD HALL, HARRY NORTHRUP, EDITH STOREY, ROSE LEY, and Above: EDITH STOREY, EARLE WILLIAMS, RY NORTHRUP IN "THE CHRISTIAN" (VITAGRAPH)

EARLE WILLIAMS, EDITH STOREY IN "THE CHRISTIAN" (VITAGRAPH)

SIDNEY DREW, JAMES LACKAYE, CLARA KIMBALL YOUNG, and Above: CLARA KIMBALL YOUNG, SIDNEY DREW, NED TINLEY IN "GOOD GRACIOUS!" (VITAGRAPH)

UGUSTUS CARNEY (ESSANAY) CLAIRE McDOWELL (BIOGRAPH)

THOMAS SANTSCHI (SELIG) MARY CHARLESON (VITAGRAPH)

ANDY CLARK (EDISON) ANNA Q. NILSSON (KALEM)

ALICE JOYCE
(KALEM)

HUGHIE MACK, LILLIAN WALKER, ALBERT ROCCARDI, FLORA FINCH
ETIENNE GIRARDOT, WALLY VAN IN "THE NEW SECRETARY"
(VITAGRAPH)

ETHEL CLAYTON IN
"MAZIE PUTS ONE OVER"
(LUBIN)

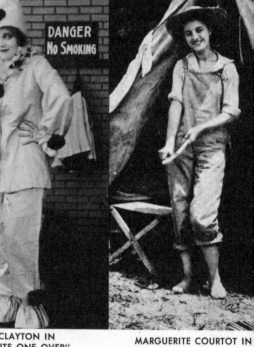

MARGUERITE COURTOT IN
"THE BAREFOOT BOY" (KALE

FREDERICK CHURCH
(ESSANAY)

CLAIRE WHITNEY
(SOLAX)

RAOUL WALSH
(MUTUAL)

DELLA CONNOR
(PATHÉ)

HUGHIE MACK
(VITAGRAPH)

1914 Lubin's bright stars were Ethel Clayton, Ar
Johnson, Ormi Hawley, Earle Metcalf and L
Briscoe. D. W. Griffith, who is given the credit for first u
the technique of the close-up, the fade-in, fade-out and
shots which he worked out with G. W. "Billy" Bitzer,
cameraman, was rushing through his filming of "The Battl
The Sexes" at Mutual in four days to meet the payroll.
was not smooth sailing prior to "The Birth of A Nati
Griffith also filmed "The Avenging Conscience" and "H
Sweet Home" during these anxious times. Most of his pla

HOBART BOSWORTH, ADELE FARRINGTON
IN "THE COUNTRY MOUSE" (BOSWORTH)

HAROLD LLOYD (left), JANE NOVAK IN
"FROM ITALY'S SHORE" (UNIVERSAL)

ALAN HALE IN
"THE CRICKET ON THE HEARTH" (BIOGRAPH)

ROSETTA BRICE, WILLIAM ELLIOTT, CHARLES BRANDT, ETHEL CLAYTON,
GEORGE SOULE SPENCER IN "THE FORTUNE HUNTER" (LUBIN)

"BILLIE" RITCHIE
(UNIVERSAL)

LOUISE GLAUM
(UNIVERSAL)

EARLE WILLIAMS
(VITAGRAPH)

1914 had worked for him at Biograph and included Lillian and Dorothy Gish, Henry B. Walthall, Blanche Sweet, Owen Moore, James Kirkwood, Mae Marsh, Jack Pickford, and Robert Harron who had started as a Biograph office boy. William S. Hart, who made his first appearance in "Two Gun Hicks," a two-reeler, was attracting public attention in a Mutual Master Picture "On The Night Stage" which was directed by Reginald Barker. Thomas H. Ince's first outstanding directorial and producing job was "The Wrath of The Gods," a 1914 release.

EDWARD J. PEIL   JOHN INCE   JACK STANDING   KEMPTON GREENE   JOSEPH SMILEY

LUBIN LEADING MEN

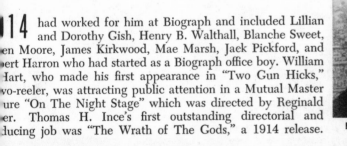

EVELYN NESBIT THAW
IN "THREADS OF DESTINY" (LUBIN)

HELEN BADGELY AND SHEP
IN "A DOG'S LOVE" (THANHOUSER)

ROSEMARY THEBY, HARRY C. MYERS
IN "BABY" (UNIVERSAL)

E. K. LINCOLN, MIMI YVONNE
IN "THE LITTLEST REBEL"

WELLINGTON PLAYTER, BERTHA KALICH IN
"MARTA OF THE LOWLANDS" (FAMOUS PLAYERS)

WINIFRED KINGSTON, ROBERT EDESON, J. W. JOH
THEODORE ROBERTS IN "WHERE THE TRAIL DIVIDES"

CARLYLE BLACKWELL
(KALEM)

Standing (L. to R.): MARC MacDERMOTT, BEN WILSON, BARRY O'MOORE,
WILLIAM WADSWORTH, Seated: MARY FULLER, ANDY CLARK
EDISON "SERIES" STARS

EDNA MAYO, CARLYLE BLACKWELL IN
"THE KEY TO YESTERDAY"

SESSUE HAYAKAWA, TSURU AOKI
"THE TYPHOON"

SAM LUCAS, MARIE ELINE AS UNCLE TOM AND
LITTLE EVA IN "UNCLE TOM'S CABIN" (PEERLESS)

IRVING CUMMINGS IN
"THE LAST VOLUNTEER" (PATHÉ)

JACOB ADLER IN
"MICHAEL STROGOFF" (LUBIN)

BLANCHE SWEET AND HENRY B. WALTHALL
IN "THE AVENGING CONSCIENCE"

LILLIAN GISH, FAY TINCHER, OWEN MOORE
IN "BATTLE OF THE SEXES"

LILLIAN GISH
IN "HOME SWEET HOME"

LILLIAN AND DOROTHY GISH

ALD CRISP, JACK PICKFORD, JAMES KIRKWOOD
IN "HOME SWEET HOME"

HENRY B. WALTHALL, LILLIAN GISH, JOSEPHINE CROWELL
IN "HOME SWEET HOME"

ROBERT HARRON, MAE MARSH
IN "HOME SWEET HOME"

D. W. GRIFFITH'S MUTUAL FILMS — 1914

LILLIAN GISH (top) and SCENES FROM
"THE BIRTH OF A NATION"

D. W. GRIFFITH

LILLIAN GISH and BIT-PLAYER

MIRIAM COOPER

HENRY B. WALTHALL, GEORGE SEIGMANN

in "THE BIRTH OF A NATION"

1915 The outstanding event of the year was D. W. Griffith's "The Birth of A Nation," probably the world's greatest silent motion picture, if greatness is measured by fame. The story was taken from a four act play "The Clansman" which ran for 51 performances on the stage of the Liberty Theatre, New York, in 1906, and which the Rev. Thomas Dixon had fashioned from his own novel of the same name. It had its world premiere at Clune's Auditorium in Los Angeles, February 8, 1915, under the title of "The Clansman," but Thomas Dixon, the author, thought the title was too tame, and at his suggestion, it opened at the same Liberty Theatre, New York, where it had been performed as a play, on March 3, 1915, as "The Birth of A Nation." In twelve reels it was released by the Epoch Film Corporation, an outfit newly formed by Mr. Griffith himself to exploit it independently as a road show. Following its New York success, twelve road showings of the film swept the country at two-dollar top prices and broke all theatre records, not only in the United States, but in all the world capitals where it was eventually shown. The cast, with names that were to become world famous, included Lillian Gish, Henry B. Walthall, Mae Marsh, Wallace Reid, Miriam Cooper, Robert Harron, Mary Alden, Elmer Clifton, Ralph Lewis, Donald Crisp, Josephine Crowell, Spottiswoode Aiken, Walter Long, George Seigmann, Jennie Lee, J. A. Beringer, John French, Joseph Henabery, Howard Gaye and Raoul Walsh, who later became a well-known director.

LILLIAN GISH
: JOSEPHINE CROWELL, HENRY B.
WALTHALL, LILLIAN GISH

HENRY B. WALTHALL
Top: MAE MARSH, HENRY B. WALTHALL

MAE MARSH

MAE MARSH

ELMER CLIFTON, MIRIAM COOPER, ROBERT HARRON

in "THE BIRTH OF A NATION"

MONROE SALISBURY, MARGUERITE CLARK IN
"THE GOOSE GIRL"

MADGE EVANS, DOROTHEA CAMDEN, GEORGIA FURNSTMAN,
JEAN STEWART, I. FEDER, SYDNEY MASON, LOLA BARCLAY,
MARGUERITE CLARK, MAYME LYNTON, EDWIN MORDANT,
CONWAY TEARLE IN "SEVEN SISTERS"

MARGUERITE CLARK

EDWIN MORDANT, MARGUERITE CLARK IN
"THE PRINCE AND THE PAUPER"

MARGUERITE CLARK, JACK PICKFORD IN
"THE PRETTY SISTER OF JOSÉ"

JACK PICKFORD

MARGUERITE CLARK, WILMUTH MERKYL, HELEN
LUTRELL, ARTHUR HOOPS IN "GRETNA GREEN"

FAMOUS PLAYERS FEATURES

GABY DESLYS

HARRY PILCER, GABY DESLYS IN
"HER TRIUMPH"

HAROLD LOCKWOOD

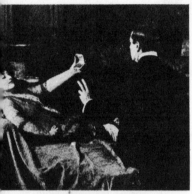

LORENCE REED, EUGENE ORMONDE
IN "THE DANCING GIRL"

1915

Since Adolph Zukor had stirred up the industry with his idea of famous players in famous plays, capturing stars of the stage was like big game hunting. The old established companies and newly formed outfits were after stage names. Famous Players itself engaged the theatre's Marie Doro, Gaby Deslys, William H. Crane, John Mason, Charles Cherry, Sam Bernard, Henry Ainley, William Elliott, Pauline Frederick, Maclyn Arbuckle, Florence Reed and Alice Dovey. Marie Doro made her film debut in "The Morals of Marcus," and followed this with "The White Pearl." Pauline Frederick appeared in "The Eternal City" (an eight-reeler filmed in Rome), also "Zaza," "Bella Donna" and "Sold." Both these stars attained screen prominence. Other stage stars who made their first screen appearances with Famous Players the year before and achieved great popularity were John Barrymore, who made five films, Hazel Dawn, who appeared in six, and Marguerite Clark who made seven. Mary Pickford, who was now called "America's Sweetheart" and was the biggest money-making star in the industry, appeared in eight films. Marguerite Clark was the only star who threatened this supremacy.

HAROLD LOCKWOOD, MACLYN ARBUCKLE IN
"THE COUNTY CHAIRMAN"

WILLIAM H. CRANE, KATE MEEKS
IN "DAVID HARUM"

WILLIAM
ELLIOTT

FLORENCE
REED

SAM
BERNARD

CHARLES
CHERRY

RUSSELL BASSETT, JOHN MASON
IN "JIM THE PENMAN"

PAULINE FREDERICK, THOMAS HOLDING IN
"THE ETERNAL CITY"

PAULINE FREDERICK

PAULINE FREDERICK, JULIAN L'ESTRANGE IN
"BELLA DONNA"

FAMOUS PLAYERS FEATURES

MARY PICKFORD, MARSHALL NEILAN IN
"MADAM BUTTERFLY"

OWEN MOORE

OWEN MOORE, MARY PICKFORD IN
"MISTRESS NELL"

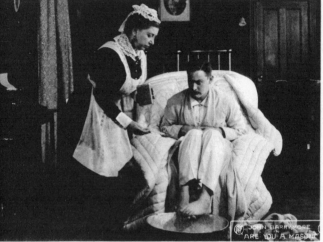

JOHN BARRYMORE IN
"ARE YOU A MASON?"

FAMOUS PLAYERS–CHARLES FROHMAN CO.
PRESENTS
JOHN BARRYMORE
IN THE CELEBRATED ADVENTUROUS ROMANCE,

BETWEEN TWO FIRES.

"THE DICTATOR"
BY
RICHARD HARDING DAVIS
A THRILLINGLY HUMOROUS PHOTO-ADAPTATION
OF THE FAMOUS MELODRAMATIC COMEDY.
RELEASED JUNE 21ST 1915
PRODUCED BY THE
FAMOUS·PLAYERS·FILM CO.
ADOLPH ZUKOR, President
DANIEL FROHMAN, Managing Director   EDWIN S. PORTER, General Manager

JOHN BARRYMORE, HELEN WEIR IN
"THE INCORRIGIBLE DUKANE"

MARIE DORO IN
"THE MORALS OF MARCUS".

MARIE DORO

THOMAS HOLDING, MARIE DORO IN
"THE WHITE PEARL"

FRANK LOSEE, HAZEL DAWN, ELLIOTT DEXTER
IN "THE MASQUERADERS"

HAZEL DAWN

HAZEL DAWN, CHARLES ABBE IN
"NIOBE"

MARY PICKFORD

ADDA GLEASON, DONALD BRIAN IN
"THE VOICE IN THE FOG"

THEODORE ROBERTS, MABEL VAN BUREN, HOUSE
PETERS IN "THE GIRL OF THE GOLDEN WEST"

WALLACE REID, CLEO RIDGELY IN
"THE CHORUS LADY"

BLANCHE SWEET

1915 Jesse L. Lasky scooped the industry when he signed opera star Geraldine Farrar to appear in three pictures to be filmed in eight weeks. For this work she was paid $20,000. Also she was furnished a house, servants, motor car and groceries during her sojourn in Hollywood, plus a private railroad car for her transportation to and from New York. Her first film was the opera "Carmen," and it was a great success. Wallace Reid played Don José and Pedro de Cordoba, Escamillo. The Lasky Company also announced the signing of film stars Blanche Sweet and Carlyle Blackwell and stage stars Fannie Ward, Lou Tellegen, Edna Goodrich, Victor Moore, Charlotte Walker, Edgar Selwyn, Laura Hope Crews, Ina Claire, Donald Brian, Edith Wynne Matthison, Theodore Roberts, Edith Taliaferro, Valeska Suratt and Rita Jolivet. It was the film debut for all of them, but only Fannie Ward, Victor Moore, Lou Tellegen and Theodore Roberts remained screen stars. Dustin Farnum, first star Lasky ever signed, made a film version of his stage play, "Cameo Kirby."

WALLACE REID

CLEO
RIDGELY

TOM
FORMAN

RITA
JOLIVET

LOU
TELLEGEN

LAURA HOPE
CREWS

HOUSE
PETERS

EDITH
TALIAFERRO

ANITA KING, VICTOR MOORE IN "SNOBS"

VALESKA SURATT
IN "THE IMMIGRANT"

DUSTIN FARNUM, FRED MONTAGUE, DICK LaRENO IN
"CAMEO KIRBY"

RO DE CORDOBA, GERALDINE FARRAR
IN "CARMEN"

GERALDINE FARRAR IN
"CARMEN"

ALLACE REID, GERALDINE FARRAR
IN "CARMEN"

GERALDINE FARRAR IN
"CARMEN"

GERALDINE FARRAR, WALLACE REID
IN "CARMEN"

CARLYLE
ACKWELL

EDITH WYNNE
MATTHISON

EARLE
FOXE

CHARLOTTE
WALKER

DONALD
BRIAN

INA
CLAIRE

THEODORE
ROBERTS

BLANCHE SWEET IN A DUAL ROLE WITH THOMAS
MEIGHAN IN "THE SECRET SIN"

EDGAR SELWYN
IN "THE ARAB"

INA CLAIRE, TOM FORMAN, THEODORE ROBERTS, HELEN
MARLBOROUGH IN "THE WILD GOOSE CHASE"

LASKY FEATURES

FANNIE WARD

FANNIE WARD, SESSUE HAYAKAWA IN
"THE CHEAT" (LASKY)

SESSUE HAYAKAWA

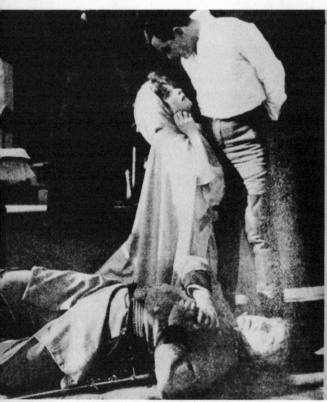

J. FARRELL MacDONALD, MRS. LESLIE CARTER,
WILLIAM SHAY IN "THE HEART OF MARYLAND"

LENORE ULRICH
(MOROSCO)

COURTENAY FOOTE, DUSTIN FARNUM IN
"CAPTAIN COURTESY" (BOSWORTH)

FORREST STANLEY, BLANCHE RING
IN "THE YANKEE GIRL" (BOSWORTH)

FRITZI SCHEFF (left), OWEN MOORE (center) IN
"PRETTY MRS. SMITH" (BOSWORTH)

GEORGE BEBAN IN
"THE ALIEN" (INCE)

MYRTLE STEDMAN

MYRTLE STEDMAN, CYRIL MAUDE IN
"PEER GYNT" (MOROSCO)

CYRIL MAUDE

1915 Oliver Morosco, California theatrical producer, entered the motion picture business, and, associating himself with Bosworth, they both released their films through Paramount. Among Morosco's output were Cyril Maude in the title role of Ibsen's "Peer Gynt," Charlotte Greenwood making her film debut in "Jane," and Lenore Ulric (spelled Ulrich at this time) in her first starring picture, "Kilmeny." Bosworth brought Fritzi Scheff, Blanche Ring and Elsie Janis to the screen for their initial appearances in "Pretty Mrs. Smith," "The Yankee Girl," and "The Caprices of Kitty" respectively. Miss Janis also filmed "Betty In Search of A Thrill" and "Nearly A Lady," while Dustin Farnum made "Captain Courtesy." Thomas H. Ince presented George Beban in "The Alien" independently. Mrs. Leslie Carter made two independent films of her stage successes, "Du Barry" and "The Heart of Maryland," and Jane Cowl made her screen debut in "The Garden of Lies."

JANE COWL, WILLIAM RUSSELL IN
"THE GARDEN OF LIES"

OWEN MOORE, ELSIE JANIS IN
"NEARLY A LADY" (BOSWORTH)

FRITZI SCHEFF

MRS. LESLIE CARTER

CHARLOTTE GREENWOOD

BLANCHE RING

W. C. FIELDS IN
"POOL SHARKS"

RICHARD BENNETT IN
"DAMAGED GOODS"

FRANCINE LARRIMORE IN
"THE DEVIL'S DARLING"

TWO MORE STARS IN REGULAR SERVICE

WALTER HAMPDEN
STAR OF "THE SERVANT IN THE HOUSE" and "THE CITY"
AND
MARION LEONARD
THE POPULAR SCREEN FAVORITE
IN
"THE DRAGON'S CLAW"
AN UNUSUALLY GRIPPING
PHOTODRAMA

RELEASED
SEPTEMBER 29th

WRITTEN AND PRODUCED BY
STANNER E. V. TAYLOR

STAR THREE REELERS
EVERY OTHER WEDNESDAY ON
GENERAL FILM COMPANY
REGULAR PROGRAM

Knickerbocker Star Features
NEW YORK

1915 J. Forbes-Robertson, the greatest Hamlet of his time, filmed the tragedy in three reels with his wife, Gertrude Elliott, playing Ophelia.

MOTOGRAPHY
EQUITABLE
PRESENTS
The MAGIC MISTRESS of a THOUSAND EMOTIONS
LENORE ULRIC

THE TALE OF A WOMAN
IN WHOSE HEART DEADENS ALL
SENSE OF RIGHT AND HONOR
WHOSE DEVOTION WINS THE
MAN OF HER CHOICE

"The BETTER WOMAN
RELEASED NOVEMBER

Produced by TRIUMPH FILM CORPORATION

EQUITABLE MOTION PICTURES CORPORATION
LEWIS J. SELZNICK, VICE PRES. AND ADVISORY DIRECTOR
WORLD FILM CORPORATION

LOUISE
VALE

HAROLD
LLOYD

"Nothing Succeeds Like SUCCESS"

"COMEDIES THAT ARE"

This is

HAROLD C. LLOYD

Our Double-Jointed Rubber Comedian with Two of the Many

See Him Fall and Get Tossed in

PHUNPHILMS

Released Through Pathé Exchange, Inc.

Hal Roach Is Directing
Some Company

ROLIN FILM COMPANY
Los Angeles
D. Whiting, Gen. Mgr. 907 Brockman Bldg.

The advertising in the "News" is the gateway to a wise purchase.

FRANKLIN
RITCHIE

FLORENCE
LaBADIE

CLAUDE COOPER, FLORENCE LaBADIE, JUSTUS D. BARNES, CAREY L. HASTINGS IN "THE COUNTRY GIRL" (THANHOUSER)

ALAN HALE

WALKER WHITESIDE, VALENTINE GRANT, FLETCHER HARVEY IN "THE MELTING POT"

RICHARD BENNETT

MABEL TALIAFERRO

J. FORBES-ROBERTSON

GERTRUDE ELLIOTT

TRUE BOARDMAN IN "STINGAREE" (KALEM)

CREIGHTON HALE, MABEL TALIAFERRO IN "THE THREE OF US"

1915 Other independent releases included stage star Walter Hampden with film favorite Marion Leonard in "The Dragon's Claw," Francine Larrimore in "The Devil's Darling," Mr. and Mrs. Vernon Castle in "The Whirl of Life," Walker Whiteside in "The Melting Pot," Richard Bennett in his stage success, "Damaged Goods," and Mabel Taliaferro in "The Three of Us." W. C. Fields, a comedian who was tasting his first success in the "Ziegfeld Follies," made his first film for Gaumont, a one-reeler called "Pool Sharks." Harold Lloyd, who had worked as an extra in "Samson" at Universal, met Hal Roach, a young man with ambition to direct. Roach inherited $3,000, and with it produced a one-reel comedy, "Just Nuts," with Lloyd in the lead. It was the beginning of a profitable film assocation, the Rolin Film Company and Harold Lloyd's characterization "Lonesome Luke."

LOUISE VALE, ALAN HALE IN "JANE EYRE" (BIOGRAPH)

RUTH ROLAND, WILLIAM ELLIOTT, LEW CODY IN "COMRADE JOHN"

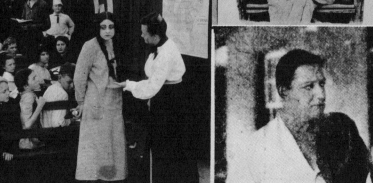

VALENTINE GRANT IN "THE BRUTE" (KALEM)

VERNON AND IRENE CASTLE IN "THE WHIRL OF LIFE"

MAX FIGMAN, BURR McINTOSH, LOLITA ROBERTSON IN "ADVENTURES OF WALLINGFORD" (PATHÉ)

WILLIAM FARNUM IN
"THE PLUNDERER"

WILLIAM FARNUM (center), CLAIRE WHITNEY (extreme right) IN
"THE NIGGER"

NANCE O'NEIL IN
"THE KREUTZER SONATA"

1915 Fox was forging ahead as one of the leading film companies, and this year their prestige soared when in January they released "A Fool There Was" with Theda Bara in the leading role. She became famous overnight. "A Fool There Was" had been a stage play which had been evolved from Kipling's poem "The Vampire." The word "vamp" became a household word and Theda Bara became the most famous vampire on the screen and a great box office attraction. She made 40 pictures for Fox in three years, or more than one a month. A legend, built in a press agent's mind, had Miss Bara born in the shadow of the Sphinx, the daughter of a French artist and his Arab mistress. She was born Theodosia Goodman in Cincinnati of a nice middle-class family. As Theodosia De Coppett she had some stage experience and played a small part in Pathé's film "The Stain" before shooting to stardom. She appeared also this year in a version of "Carmen" in direct competition with Geraldine Farrar, and "The Two Orphans" with Jean Sothern and Herbert Brenon who subsequently became a famous director. Another Fox star who was on the ascent was William Farnum. Fox also contracted Nance O'Neil and Robert B. Mantell, famous stage stars, Betty Nansen, well-known Danish actress, and Valeska Suratt who had made her film debut for Lasky earlier in the year. Biograph Company was nearing the end of its existence. It was still releasing one- and two-reelers with an occasional three-reel feature such as "Under Two Flags," "Jane Eyre" and "Dora." Their players included Alan Hale, Louise Vale, Franklin Ritchie and Gretchen Hartman. Thanhouser, besides "Zudora" its serial, was still releasing mostly one- and two-reel pictures. Florence LaBadie, Marguerite Snow, James Cruze and Harry Benham were their top stars.

VALESKA SURATT, JANE LEE IN
"SOUL OF BROADWAY"

VALESKA SURATT

WILLIAM FARNUM

BETTY NANSEN   NANCE O'NEIL   ROBERT MANTELL

THEDA BARA IN
"THE TWO ORPHANS"

THEDA BARA, EINAR LINDEN IN
"CARMEN"

HERBERT BRENON, JEAN SOTHERN IN "THE TWO ORPHANS"
Right: THEDA BARA IN "SIN"

THEDA BARA IN
"A FOOL THERE WAS"

THEDA BARA
(FOX)

THEDA BARA

JAMES CRUZE, MARGUERITE SNOW, HARRY BENHAM
IN "ZUDORA" (THANHOUSER)

MARY CHARLESON, CRANE WILBUR IN
"ROAD O' STRIFE" (LUBIN)

ANNA LITTLE, HERBERT RAWLINSON (cen
IN "THE BLACK BOX" (UNIVERSAL)

LILLIAN LORRAINE, WILLIAM
COURTLEIGH, JR. IN
"NEAL OF THE NAVY" (PATHÉ)

"RUNAWAY JUNE" COMPANY (RELIANCE-MUTUAL)
(center) OSCAR EAGLES, DIRECTOR, NORMA PHILLIPS (right), J. W.
JOHNSTON (left)

NORMA PHILLIPS
(MUTUAL)

CREIGHTON HALE, PEARL WHITE IN
"THE EXPLOITS OF ELAINE"

PEARL WHITE, ARNOLD DALY IN
"THE EXPLOITS OF ELAINE"
(PATHÉ)

LIONEL BARRYMORE, CREIGHTON HALE, PEA
WHITE IN "THE EXPLOITS OF ELAINE"

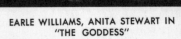

ANITA STEWART, EARLE WILLIAMS IN
"THE GODDESS"

EARLE WILLIAMS

ANITA STEWART

EARLE WILLIAMS, ANITA STEWART IN
"THE GODDESS"

(VITAGRAPH)

WILLIAM RUSSELL (left), IRVING CUMMINGS (right) IN "THE DIAMOND FROM THE SKY"

LOTTIE PICKFORD

IRVING CUMMINGS

(AMERICAN-MUTUAL)

WILLIAM RUSSELL, IRVING CUMMINGS, LOTTIE PICKFORD IN "THE DIAMOND FROM THE SKY"

1915 The serial, with its "continued next week" policy which took the country by storm in 1914, was at the height of its popularity in 1915. There were over a dozen serials thrilling the public. Pearl White, after her phenomenal success in "The Perils of Pauline," continued her harrowing escapes each week in "The Exploits of Elaine" for Pathé and became the greatest serial queen of all time. In her Elaine ventures she was ably assisted by Sheldon Lewis, Creighton Hale and Arnold Daly, a noted stage star. Lionel Barrymore appeared in the later episodes. Pathé also was responsible for the "Who Pays?" serial with Ruth Roland and Henry King, "Neal of The Navy" with Lillian Lorraine, an ex-Follies Beauty, and William Courtleigh, Jr., and "Who's Guilty?" with stage actress Emmy Wehlen and Howard Estabrook. Thanhouser's contribution was "Zudora" with Marguerite Snow and James Cruze. Universal was well represented with "The Black Box" starring Herbert Rawlinson and Anna Little, "The Broken Coin" exploiting the brave deeds of Grace Cunard and Francis Ford, and "The Master Key" with Robert Leonard and Ella Hall. Vitagraph and Lubin got into the swim with Anita Stewart and Earle Williams in "The Goddess" and Crane Wilbur and Mary Charleson in "Road O' Strife." Reliance released a popular serial, "Runaway June," starring "Our Mutual Girl" Norma Phillips and J. W. Johnston. The American Film Company tried to lure Mary Pickford away from Famous Players with an offer of $4,000 a week to star in their serial "The Diamond From The Sky," but settled for her sister Lottie. Irving Cummings, who later became a famous director, played the hero and the cast featured William Russell, Charlotte Burton, Eugenie Forde and George Periolat. The director was William Desmond Taylor whose murder in 1921 is still an unsolved Hollywood mystery.

RUTH ROLAND, MOLLIE McCONNELL, HENRY KING IN "WHO PAYS?" (PATHÉ) CENTER: RUTH ROLAND

HENRY KING, DANIEL GILFETHER, ED J. BRADY, RUTH ROLAND IN "WHO PAYS?" (PATHÉ) Center: HENRY KING

GRACE CUNARD, HARRY MANN, FRANCIS FORD IN "THE BROKEN COIN"

GRACE CUNARD, FRANCIS FORD IN "THE BROKEN COIN"

(UNIVERSAL)

GRACE CUNARD IN "THE BROKEN COIN"

EDWARD BOULDEN

MABEL TRUNNELLE

YALE BOSS

MARY FULLER

MARC MacDERMOTT

MIRIAM NESBITT

SALLY CRUTE

HERBERT PRI

EDISON PLAYERS

SYDNEY GRANT, SYD de GREY, CHARLOTTE GREENWOOD,
FORREST STANLEY IN "JANE" (MOROSCO)

KATHERINE LEE, NAT C. GOODWIN
IN "THE MASTER HAND" (FOX)

THOMAS MEIGHAN, CHARLOTTE WALKER
IN "KINDLING" (LASKY)

HARRY MILLARDE, ALICE HOLLISTER IN
"DON CAESAR DE BAZAN" (KALEM)

VIOLA DANA IN
"THE BLIND FIDDLER" (EDISON)

RICHARD TUCKER, SALLY CRUTE IN
"WHILE THE TIDE WAS RISING" (EDISON)

OWEN MOORE, ROBERT HARRON, BLANCHE SWEET
IN "THE ESCAPE" (D. W. GRIFFITH)

HELEN HOLMES, J. P. McGOWAN AND
"THE HAZARDS OF HELEN" COMPANY
(KALEM)

TOM TRENT, HELEN GIBSON IN
"THE HAZARDS OF HELEN" SERIES (KALEM)

ALICE HOLLISTER

WILMUTH MERKYL

MARGUERITE COURTOT

PAT O'MALLEY

HELEN HOLMES

HARRY MILLARDE

HELEN GIBSON

ROLAND BOTTO

KALEM PLAYERS

COGHLAN
(LUBIN)

BOBBY CONNELLY
(VITAGRAPH)

GRACE DARMOND
(SELIG)

WEBSTER CAMPBELL
(KAY-BEE)

MAE MARSH
(MUTUAL)

DONALD CRISP
(MUTUAL)

MARY ALDEN
(MUTUAL)

THOMAS CHATTERTON
(KAY-BEE)

TYRONE POWER, SR., IN
"A TEXAS STEER" (SELIG)

1915 The five-reel or more feature had a firm grip on the industry as well as the public. Vitagraph, Essanay, Lubin, Kalem, Selig, Universal, Pathé, Mutual, were still releasing two-reelers, but the handwriting was on the wall. It was the beginning of the end of two-reel features. To buck competition, Vitagraph, Lubin, Selig and Essanay incorporated for releasing purposes and were known as "V. L. S. E." They released features with their own important stars and also joined the parade in signing stage stars. Vitagraph signed Frank Daniels, Edison contracted Mrs. Fiske, Lubin got Marie Dressler and Rose Coghlan, Selig snared Tyrone Power, and Essanay captured Viola Allen. Kalem was about ready to quit. Their biggest box office star was still Alice Joyce. True Boardman's "Stingaree" series and Helen Holmes' railroad series, "Hazards of Helen," were popular. Later, Helen Gibson replaced Miss Holmes who with J. H. McGowan formed the Signal Film Corporation. Francis X. Bushman and Beverly Bayne were Essanay's fair-haired team. Vitagraph's outstanding favorites were Norma Talmadge, Anita Stewart, Earle Williams, Edith Storey and Antonio Moreno. World War I had been in progress a year before the motion picture industry took much cognizance of it. Vitagraph started the parade of war pictures with their pretentiously produced "The Battle Cry of Peace," a filmization of Hudson Maxim's book "Defenseless America." Box office favorites were commanding larger salaries. Mary Pickford demanded and received $104,000 a year when she re-signed with Famous Players. Charles Chaplin signed with Essanay for a $1,250 weekly salary just fourteen months after making his first film at Keystone for $150 per week.

MARIE DRESSLER IN
"TILLIE'S TOMATO SURPRISE" (LUBIN)

INA ROBBINS, FRANK DANIELS, ANNA LAUGHLIN
IN "CROOKY SCRUGGS" (VITAGRAPH)

FRANKIE MANN, ALLEN QUINN, ROSE COGHLAN, GEORGE
SOULE SPENCER, CHARLES BRANDT, FERDINAND TIDMARSH
IN "THE SPORTING DUCHESS" (LUBIN)

BOSWORTH IN
ODYSSEY OF THE
(BOSWORTH)

MRS. FISKE IN "VANITY FAIR" WITH
RICHARD TUCKER (extreme right)
(EDISON)

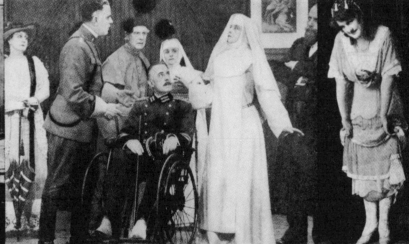

CAMILLE D'ARCY, RICHARD TRAVERS, THOMAS COMMERFORD,
SYDNEY AINSWORTH, VIOLA ALLEN IN "THE WHITE SISTER"
(ESSANAY)

NORMA PHILLIPS
"OUR MUTUAL GIRL"

LEIGHTON
(SELIG)

GLADDEN JAMES
(VITAGRAPH)

FLORENCE LAWRENCE
(UNIVERSAL)

S. RANKIN DREW
(VITAGRAPH)

HELEN BADGELY
(THANHOUSER)

TYRONE POWER, SR.
(SELIG)

JUSTINA HUFF
(LUBIN)

GEORGE FIELD
(MUTUAL)

EDITH STOREY, ANTONIO MORENO
IN "THE ISLAND OF REGENERATION"

ANITA STEWART, EARLE WILLIAMS, JOSEPH KILGOUR
IN "MY LADY'S SLIPPER"

EDITH STOREY IN
"DUST OF EGYPT"

EARLE WILLIAMS IN
"MY LADY'S SLIPPER"

SIDNEY DREW

HARRY S. NORTHUP, LUCILLE HAMIL, LOUISE BEAUDET, JAMES
LACKAYE, NORMA TALMADGE, CHARLES RICHMAN. Above: CHARLES
RICHMAN, MARY MAURICE, JAMES MORRISON, NORMA TALMADGE

Above: JAMES MORRISON, MARY MAURICE,
CHARLES RICHMAN, NORMA TALMADGE
SCENES FROM "THE BATTLE CRY OF PEACE"

LUCILE McVEY
(MRS. SIDNEY DREW)

ADMIRALS SIGSBEE, MARIX
AND GENERAL HORATIO C. KING

DONALD HALL, NAOMI CHILDERS, ANTONIO MORENO
IN "ANSELO LEE"

MAURICE COSTELLO, LEAH BAIRD
IN "TRIED FOR HIS OWN MURDER"

SIDNEY DREW, MRS. DREW, EDITH STOREY
IN A DREW COMEDY

VITAGRAPH RELEASES

VERLY BAYNE, FRANCIS X. BUSHMAN, THOMAS COMMERFORD, HELEN DUNBAR,
LESTER CUNEO IN "GRAUSTARK"

FRANCIS X. BUSHMAN, NELL CRAIG
IN "THE RETURN OF RICHARD NEAL"

RUTH STONEHOUSE

VICTOR POTEL, MARGARET JOSLIN, HARRY TODD
IN "SNAKEVILLE COMEDY"

RICHARD TRAVERS, NELL CRAIG IN
"IN THE PALACE OF THE KING"

BEVERLY BAYNE

BILLY MASON

RICHARD TRAVERS

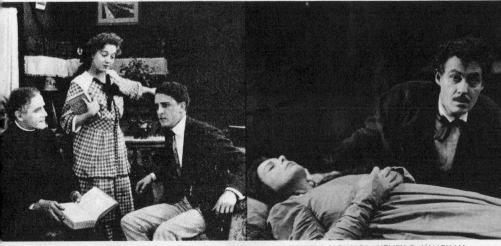

EDNA MAYO, BRYANT WASHBURN
IN "THE BLINDNESS OF VIRTUE"

WANDA HOWARD, HENRY B. WALTHALL
IN "THE RAVEN"

ESSANAY RELEASES

JOHN JUNIOR, E. H. CALVERT, CAMILLE D'ARCY,
MARGUERITE CLAYTON IN "A DAUGHTER
OF THE CITY"

85

1915 With a great exploitation campaign by Essan Charles Chaplin's career was well on the ascent January he filmed his first Essanay two-reel comedy, "His I Job," at their Chicago studio in three weeks. He disliked (cago's cold climate, so "A Night Out," his second Essanay and subsequent ones were shot at their Niles, California, stu The casts of these comedies included a former burlesque musical comedy actor, Ben Turpin. Edna Purviance, a blo Nevada girl Chaplin had met at a social gathering, became leading lady in "The Champion," his third Essanay picture. appeared in many other Chaplin comedies and theirs was association of many years.

"SHANGHAIED"

WITH BEN TURPIN IN "HIS NEW JOB"   "HIS NEW JOB"   "A WOMAN"   "THE CHAMPION"   "THE BANK"

CHARLES CHAPLIN
ESSANAY 1915 RELEASES

CHARLES CHAPLIN

WINIFRED
GREENWOOD

WALLACE REID, LILLIAN GISH
IN "ENOCH ARDEN"

ED COXEN

MARY ALDEN, HENRY B. WALTHALL
IN "GHOSTS"

WILLIAM GARWOOD, CHARLOTTE BURTON
IN "A MAN'S WAY"

ED COXEN, WINIFRED GREENWOOD
IN "THE PROFLIGATE"

WILLIAM FRAWLEY, FRANK BORZAGE (center)
IN AN AMERICAN BEAUTY COMEDY

JOSEPH HARRIS, FRED GAMBLE, VIRGINIA KIRTLEY,
WEBSTER CAMPBELL IN "OH, DADDY"

CHARLES CLARY, FRANCELIA BILLINGTON, WILLIAM HAMMO
IN "CHILDREN OF THE SEA"

WILLIAM HINCKLEY, DOROTHY GISH
IN "OUT OF BONDAGE"

MARGARITA FISCHER, HARRY POLLARD
IN "THE PEACOCK FEATHER FAN"

MARGARITA FISCHER

WILLIAM GARWOOD, VIVIAN RICH
IN "BUSINESS VS. LOVE"

WINIFRED GREENWOO
GEORGE FIELD IN
"THE DERELICT"

1915 PHOTOPLAYS AND PLAYERS

LOUISE FAZENDA
KEYSTONE COMEDIES

SYD CHAPLIN
KEYSTONE COMEDIES

MINTA DURFEE
KEYSTONE COMEDIES

LOUISE FAZENDA

SYDNEY CHAPLIN

MINTA DURFEE

ROSCOE ARBUCKLE
IN "REBECCA'S WEDDING DAY"

1915 Mabel Normand and Roscoe Arbuckle were still the chief laugh provokers at Keystone, and Charles Chaplin had been replaced on their roster by his brother, Sydney Chaplin. Also signed were Louise Fazenda and Minta Durfee. Margarita Fischer who was near the top of various popularity contests joined Mutual with her husband Harry Pollard. Harold Lockwood and May Allison were cast together in Mutual features and were acquiring many fans. Other Mutual players recognized as good drawing cards were Ed Coxen, Vivian Rich and William Garwood. Henry B. Walthall had left Mutual and D. W. Griffith for Essanay. Griffith himself withdrew from Mutual in May taking with him Lillian and Dorothy Gish. Wallace Reid and Thomas Meighan had signed with Lasky where they soon became important leading men.

MABEL NORMAND
IN "A MISPLACED FOOT"

MABEL NORMAND, ROSCOE ARBUCKLE
IN "FATTY AND MABEL ADRIFT"

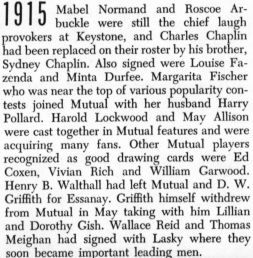

ROSCOE "FATTY" ARBUCKLE

JIMMY FINLAYSON, CHESTER CONKLIN, MACK SWAIN, CLYDE COOK, FORD
STERLING, BOBBY VERNON, HANK MANN
MACK SENNETT'S KEYSTONE COMEDIES AND COMEDIANS

PHYLLIS ALLEN, ROSCOE ARBUCKLE, MINTA DURFEE
IN "FICKLE FATTY'S FALL"

LOIS MEREDITH
(FAMOUS PLAYERS)

ARTHUR HOUSMAN
(EDISON)

MARGARET WYCHERLY
(WORLD)

ROBERT WALKER
(KALEM)

MAY ALLISON
(AMERICAN)

TOM TERRIS
(KINETOPHONE)

FRANCELIA BILLINGTON
(THANHOUSER)

RAPLEY HOLMES
(ESSANAY)

SIDNEY C
(KALI

ORMI HAWLEY, EARLE METCALF
IN "THE INSURRECTION"

LOTTIE BRISCOE IN
"THE BELOVED ADVENTURER"
(LUBIN)

HOUSE PETERS, ETHEL CLAYTON
IN "THE GREAT DIVIDE"

FLORENCE HACKETT, JAMES CASSADY, LILIE LESLIE
IN "SIREN OF CORSICA"

MAE HOTELY, BILLIE REEVES
IN "THE NEW BUTLER"
(LUBIN)

ETHEL CLAYTON IN
"THE COLLEGE WIDOW"

ETHEL CLAYTON
(LUBIN)

THOMAS MEIGHAN
(PARAMOUNT)

ORMI HAWLEY
(LUBIN)

ROBERT HARRON
(MUTUAL)

90

RT EDESON
(ASKY)

EDNA MAISON
(UNIVERSAL)

RAY GALLAGHER
(UNIVERSAL)

EUGENIE FORDE
(AMERICAN)

FRED C. TRUESDELL
(ECLAIR)

WILTON LACKAYE
(WORLD)

FANIA MARINOFF
(WORLD)

ARTHUR HOOPS
(FAMOUS PLAYERS)

LILIE LESLIE
(LUBIN)

SCENES FROM "DAMON AND PYTHIAS" (UNIVERSAL) WITH HERBERT RAWLINSON, ANN LITTLE, WILLIAM
WORTHINGTON, CLEO MADISON AND FRANK LLOYD

KING BAGGOT IN THE DUAL ROLE
IN "THE CORSICAN BROTHERS" (UNIVERSAL)

ROBERT LEONARD
(UNIVERSAL)

ETHEL GRANDIN
(SMALLWOOD)

ELLA HALL
(REX)

FRANK LLOYD
(UNIVERSAL)

BETTY SHADE, DOUGLAS GERRARD, RUPERT JULIAN, ANNA PAVLOWA
IN "THE DUMB GIRL OF PORTICI"

ANNA PAVLOWA

ANNA PAVLOWA, RUPERT JULIAN
IN "THE DUMB GIRL OF PORTICI"

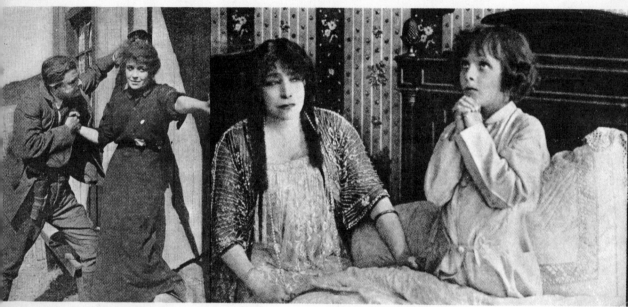

HARRY CARTER, JULIA DEAN
IN "JUDGE NOT"

SARAH BERNHARDT
IN "JEANNE DORÉ"

JACK HOLT, PHILLIPS SMALLEY IN
"A CIGARETTE—THAT'S ALL"

1915 Universal took Mary Fuller away from Edison. They also signed a great array of stage stars including Marie Cahill, Henry E. Dixey, Marie Tempest, Lewis Waller, Julia Dean and ballerina Anna Pavlowa. J. Warren Kerrigan and King Baggot were still kingpins on the Universal lot. Among the money-makers were a spectacle, "Damon and Pythias" with Herbert Rawlinson, Anna Little, William Worthington and Cleo Madison, and a French film, "Jeanne Doré," starring Sarah Bernhardt which they released. Metro Pictures Corporation was formed with Richard Rowland as president and Louis B. Mayer, secretary. Olga Petrova was their first star. Also signed were Ethel and Lionel Barrymore, Mary Miles Minter and Francis X. Bushman.

HOBART HENLEY

LOIS WEBER

VERA SISSON

MATT MOORE

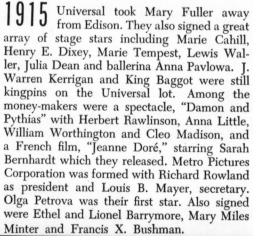

EDDIE LYONS, W. GRAHAM BROWNE, VIOLET
MacMILLAN, MARIE TEMPEST IN
"MRS. PLUMB'S PUDDING"

MARIE CAHILL
IN "JUDY FORGOT"
UNIVERSAL PICTURES AND PLAYERS

GEORGE PERIOLAT, J. WARREN KERRIGAN
IN "THE ADVENTURES OF TERENCE O'ROURKE"

ANN LITTLE
(REX)

MARIE CAHILL

MARY FULLER

J. WARREN KERRIGAN
(UNIVERSAL)

JULIA DEAN

WILLIAM FAVERSHAM   ETHEL BARRYMORE

ETHEL BARRYMORE
IN "THE FINAL JUDGEMENT"

NILES WELCH   MARY MILES MINTER

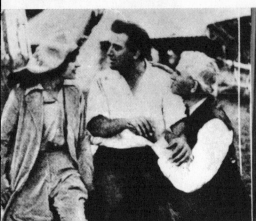

MARGUERITE SNOW, FRANCIS X. BUSHMAN,
FRANK BACON IN "THE SILENT VOICE"

EMILY STEVENS, GEORGE LA GUERE
IN "THE SOUL OF A WOMAN"
METRO PICTURES AND PLAYERS

MARY MILES MINTER, MRS. THOMAS WHIFFEN, GUY
COOMBS, WALLACE SCOTT IN "BARBARA FRIETCHIE"

HOLBROOK BLINN, ALICE BRADY
IN "THE BOSS"

HOLBROOK BLINN, FANIA MARINOFF
IN "McTEAGUE"

CHESTER BARNETT, VIVIAN MARTIN
IN "THE WISHING RING"

FANIA MARINOFF
IN "McTEAGUE"

WORLD FILM COMPANY
Standing: ALBERT CAPELLINI, FRANK CRANE, EMIL CHAUTARD, HOLBROOK BLINN,
MAURICE TOURNEUR, ALICE BRADY, JAMES YOUNG, CLARA KIMBALL YOUNG
Seated: DOROTHY FAIRCHILD, WILTON LACKAYE, ELAINE HAMMERSTEIN

HOLBROOK BLINN, VIVIAN MA
IN "THE BUTTERFLY ON THE WH

ALEC B. FRANCIS, EDWARD M. KIMBALL, MARY MOORE,
CLARA KIMBALL YOUNG IN "LOLA"

CLARA KIMBALL YOUNG
IN "TRILBY"

CLARA KIMBALL YOUNG, MILTON SILLS
IN "THE DEEP PURPLE"

CLARA KIMBALL YOUNG
IN "CAMILLE"

WILTON LACKAYE, CLARA KIMBALL YOUNG
IN "TRILBY"

CLARA KIMBALL YOUNG, VERNON STEELE
IN "HEARTS IN EXILE"

CLARA KIMBALL YOUNG, CHESTER BARN
IN "THE HEART OF THE BLUERIDGE'

WORLD FEATURES

CLARA BEYERS, BEATRIZ MICHELENA, HOUSE
PETERS IN "MIGNON" (WORLD)

LILLIAN RUSSELL IN "WILDFIRE" (WORLD)

ROBERT WARWICK IN
"THE FACE IN THE MOONLIGHT" (WORLD)

1915 In February, World Film Corporation was formed. It included the theatrical interests of the Shuberts and William A. Brady. Arthur Spiegel, head of a mail order house, became president and Lewis J. Selznick, a former small-time jeweler, was vice-president and general manager. Their first major move was the acquisition of Clara Kimball Young, Vitagraph star with sensational box office power. Alice Brady, Robert Warwick, Vivian Martin and Holbrook Blinn, all stage personalities, were signed and became important in the film realm. California, and especially Hollywood, on the then outskirts of Los Angeles, was coming into the spotlight as a film producing center. Selig was the first company to make films in California in the early days, and in 1908 G. M. Anderson established a Western branch of Essanay at Niles, California. Because the climate was better for out-door filming, soon Vitagraph, Biograph, Kalem and most of the established companies opened branch studios in California. By 1915 about fifty percent of American films were being made in the Golden State.

O. A. C. LUND, BARBARA TENNANT IN
"WHEN BROADWAY WAS A TRAIL" (WORLD)

HAROLD LOCKWOOD, MAY ALLISON
IN "SHOPGIRLS" (MUTUAL)

EDWARD DILLON, FAY TINCHER
IN "FAITHFUL TO THE FINISH" (KOMIC)

VIVIAN MARTIN, GEORGE HASSELL, CHARLES JUDELL, MARIE
EMPRESS, CHARLES BARNETT, LEW FIELDS IN
"OLD DUTCH" (WORLD)

CHARLES RAY, LOUISE GLAUM IN
"THE LURE OF WOMAN" (BRONCHO)

HOLBROOK BLINN   VIVIAN MARTIN   ROBERT WARWICK   CLARA KIMBALL YOUNG   **95**

RAYMOND HITCHCOCK, OWEN MOORE, MABEL
NORMAND BETWEEN SHOTS OF "MY VALET"

LOUISE GLAUM, DUSTIN FARNUM, ENID MARKEY
IN "THE IRON STRAIN"

MARY BOLAND, ROBERT McKIM IN
"THE EDGE OF THE ABYSS"

DOUGLAS FAIRBANKS IN
"HIS PICTURE IN THE PAPERS"

TULLY MARSHALL, DE WOLF HOPPER, DOUGLAS FAIRBANKS, JANE GREY, ORRIN JOHNSON
STAGE STARS SIGNED BY TRIANGLE

DOUGLAS FAIRBANKS
IN "THE LAMB"

CHARLES K. FRENCH, FRANK KEENAN, CHARLES RAY IN "THE COWARD"
Above: GERTRUDE CLAIRE, CHARLES RAY IN "THE COWARD"

BILLIE BURKE
Above: DOUGLAS FAIRBANKS
TRIANGLE PRODUCTIONS

WILLIAM DESMOND, BILLIE BURKE IN "PEGGY"
Above: WILLIAM DESMOND, WILLIAM H. THOMPSON, BILLIE B
IN "PEGGY"

SCENES FROM "DON QUIXOTE" STARRING DE WOLF HOPPER
WITH FAY TINCHER AND GEORGE WALSH

WILLIAM S. HART

1915
D. W. Griffith, Thomas H. Ince and Mack Sennett formed the Triangle Film Corporation. Triangle stock was listed on the New York Curb and motion pictures had joined America's important industries. They announced an imposing array of names which included Billie Burke, William Collier, Eddie Foy, Weber and Fields, Mary Boland, Frank Keenan, De Wolf Hopper, Raymond Hitchcock, Louise Dresser, Douglas Fairbanks, Constance Collier, Dustin Farnum, Sir Herbert Tree, H. B. Warner, Lillian and Dorothy Gish, Henry Woodruff, Sam Bernard, Julia Dean and William S. Hart. Of all this array, the most important, as history was to prove, were Douglas Fairbanks and William S. Hart. Hart became the screen's greatest cowboy star. Douglas Fairbanks was one of Broadway's youngest stars when he appeared in his first film, "The Lamb." His success was instantaneous and he became one of the greatest figures of filmdom. Billie Burke was paid $40,000 for five weeks' work. It was the largest salary paid to any artist who had so far appeared in pictures. "Peggy," her first picture, was the beginning of a long and successful film career. Triangle announced that it would make two-dollar-a-seat pictures, which was unheard of at this time. On September 23, 1915, the threat became a fact with its first Triangle offering at the Knickerbocker Theatre with the regular Broadway scale of prices from two dollars to fifty cents and some especially deluxe seats at three dollars. The program consisted of "The Lamb," "The Iron Strain" and "My Valet," products of Griffith's, Ince's and Sennett's supervision.

MARGERY WILSON, JOHN GILBERT
IN "THE MOTHER INSTINCT"

MACK SENNETT

D. W. GRIFFITH

THOMAS H. INCE

MOND WELLS, DOROTHY GISH, WALLACE REID (Also Above)
IN "OLD HEIDELBERG"

WALLACE REID IN
"OLD HEIDELBERG"
TRIANGLE PRODUCTIONS

WILLIAM COLLIER

WEBER AND FIELDS IN "THE BEST OF ENEMIES"
Above: EDDIE FOY AND THE SEVEN LITTLE FOYS
IN "A FAVORITE FOOL"

97

MONROE SALISBURY, ADDA GLEASON
IN "RAMONA" (W. H. CLUNE)

ELEONORA DUSE IN
"CENERE" (AMBROSIO-CAESAR)

FREDERICK WARDE, LORRAINE HULING, BOYD MAR
IN "KING LEAR" (THANHOUSER)

SCENES FROM THOMAS H. INCE'S
"CIVILIZATION"

1916 The price of two dollars a seat for a motion picture, which Triangle had inaugurated, was now becoming an established price for films that were shown in legitimate theatres about the country. "Intolerance," "Ramona," "Civilization," "The Fall of A Nation" and "A Daughter of The Gods" were all in this category. "Intolerance," which was D. W. Griffith's second large-scale production, was not a worthy successor to his "Birth of A Nation." It opened at the same Liberty Theatre, New York, on September 6, 1916, and its critical reception was decidedly mixed. The cast included Lillian Gish, Robert Harron, Mae Marsh, Elmer Clifton, Seena Owen (then known as Signe Auen), Constance Talmadge, Alfred Paget, Sam de Gross, George Siegmann, Bessie Love, Ralph Lewis, Tully Marshall, Joseph Hennaberry, George Walsh and Eric Von Stroheim. Among the bit players who later achieved prominence were Coleen Moore, Elmo Lincoln, Alma Rubens, Monte Blue, Carmel Myers, Pauline Starke, Mildred Harris, Carol Dempster, Jewel Carmen, Winifred Westover and Natalie Talmadge. Constance Talmadge had her first success as the Mountain Girl and Von Stroheim, who had been acting as stunt man and bit player in other Griffith films, played the second Pharisee. The film took twenty months to make and ran three and one-half hours on the screen.

ARTHUR SHIRLEY, LORRAINE HULING
SCENES FROM THOMAS DIXON'S
"THE FALL OF A NATION"

ANNETTE KELLERMANN

MARK PRICE, ANNETTE KELLERMANN, STUART HOLMES
SCENES FROM "A DAUGHTER OF THE GODS" (FOX)

ANNETTE KELLERMANN

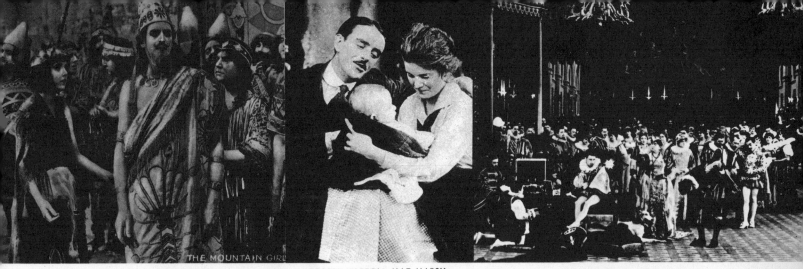

CONSTANCE TALMADGE, ALFRED PAGET   ROBERT HARRON, MAE MARSH   THE COURT OF CHARLES IX

SCENES FROM D. W. GRIFFITH'S "INTOLERANCE"

ONSTANCE TALMADGE   ALFRED PAGET, SEENA OWEN   SCENE OF ANCIENT BABYLON

Above: LILLIAN GISH   IN "INTOLERANCE"

SCENES FROM "INTOLERANCE"

GERALDINE FARRAR, WALLACE REID   ERNEST JOY, PEDRO DE CORDOBA, GERALDINE FARRAR, WALLACE REID

SCENES FROM "MARIA ROSA" (LASKY)

WALLACE REID

CHARLES CLARY, RAYMOND HATTON, HOBART BOSWORTH, GERALDINE FARRAR
IN "JOAN THE WOMAN"

GERALDINE FARRAR

WALLACE REID, HOBART BOSWORTH, GERALDINE FARRAR

WALLACE REID, GERALDINE FARRAR

SCENES FROM "JOAN THE WOMAN"

WALLACE REID, GERALDINE FARRAR

| EDWARD ARNOLD (ESSANAY) | MADGE EVANS (WORLD) | HARRY POLLARD (MUTUAL) | EUGENIE BESSERER (SELIG) | BOYD MARSHALL (THANHOUSER) | ADELE FARRINGTON (BOSWORTH) | RALPH LEWIS (MUTUAL) | STELLA RAZETO (SELIG) | MURDOCK MacQU... (UNIVERSAL) |

Jesse L. Lasky Presents
Theodore Roberts
In Mark Twain's
"Pudd'nhead Wilson"
Arrangement with The Mark Twain Co.
On the Paramount Program.

Tom afraid to fight.

ALAN HALE, THEODORE ROBERTS, THOMAS MEIGHAN
IN "PUDD'NHEAD WILSON"

MAE MURRAY, WALLACE REID
IN "TO HAVE AND TO HOLD"

MARIE DORO, ELLIOTT DEXTER
IN "THE HEART OF NORA FLYNN"

LASKY FEATURES

THEODORE ROBERTS, BLANCHE SWEET, THOMAS MEIGHAN
IN "THE SOWERS"

MARIE DORO
AS OLIVER TWIST

MARIE DORO, TULLY MARSHALL, HOBART BOSWORTH,
RAYMOND HATTON IN "OLIVER TWIST"

1916 Lasky's company was forging ahead as one of the most important in the industry. Geraldine Farrar, now one of his top stars, made "Maria Rosa" and "Joan The Woman" which Cecil B. de Mille directed. It was made on an elaborate scale with thousands of extras participating, and it was a forerunner of many of the de Mille spectacles to come. Mae Murray, a Follies beauty, was signed and made her screen debut in "To Have and To Hold." Blanche Sweet, Fannie Ward and Marie Doro were bright stars on the Lasky lot and Miss Doro re-created the title role of her stage success, "Oliver Twist." Wallace Reid was leading man to most of the important stars and was building a fan following that soon led to stardom. At Famous Players, Marguerite Clark, Pauline Frederick, Hazel Dawn and John Barrymore were emoting for their public, and Ann Pennington, another Follies dimpled doll, made her film debut in "Susie Snowflakes."

BELLE BENNETT, TOM FORMAN, MAE MURRAY
IN "SWEET KITTY BELLAIRS"

WALLACE REID, CLEO RIDGELY, EARLE FOXE
IN "THE LOVE MASK"

RTENAY
FOOTE
US PLAYERS)

JESSALYN
VAN TRUMP
(MUTUAL)

MATTY ROUBERT
(UNIVERSAL)

RHEA MITCHELL
(MUTUAL)

EUGENE PALLETTE
(MUTUAL)

EDNA MAYO
(ESSANAY)

O. A. C. LUND
(WORLD)

MYRTLE GONZALEZ
(VITAGRAPH)

DOUGLAS GERRARD
(UNIVERSAL)

JACK DEAN, FANNIE WARD
IN "TENNESSEE'S PARDNER"

MABEL VAN BUREN, LOU TELLEGEN
IN "THE VICTORIA CROSS"
LASKY FEATURES

CHARLOTTE WALKER, EARLE FOXE
IN "THE TRAIL OF THE LONESOME PINE"

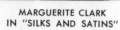

MARGUERITE CLARK, NILES WELCH
IN "MISS GEORGE WASHINGTON"

WILLIAM COURTLEIGH, JR., ALBERT GRAN, ROBERT CONVILLE,
MARGUERITE CLARK, IVAN SIMPSON IN "OUT OF THE DRIFTS"

MARGUERITE CLARK
IN "SILKS AND SATINS"

WILLIAM COURTLEIGH, JR., ANN PENNINGTON
IN "SUSIE SNOWFLAKE"

JOHN BARRYMORE
IN "THE LOST BRIDEGROOM"

IRVING CUMMINGS, HAZEL DAWN
IN "THE SALESLADY"

LOUISE HUFF, JACK PICKFORD
IN "GREAT EXPECTATIONS"

JOHN BARRYMORE, FLORA ZABELLE
IN "THE RED WIDOW"

KATE LESTER, OWEN MOORE, IRENE FENWICK
IN "A CONEY ISLAND PRINCESS"

ALAN HALE, PAULINE FREDERICK
IN "THE WOMAN IN THE CASE"

FRANK LOSEE, PAULINE FREDERICK
IN "ASHES OF EMBERS".

JACK CURTIS, PAULINE FREDERICK
IN "LYDIA GILMORE"

PAULINE FREDERICK, THOMAS HOLDING
IN "THE MOMENT BEFORE"

AMOUS PLAYERS FEATURES

RUSSELL BASSETT, FRANK LOSEE, JOHN BOWERS,
MARY PICKFORD IN "HULDA FROM HOLLAND"

MARY PICKFORD
IN "THE ETERNAL GRIND"

MARY PICKFORD, DAVID POWELL
IN "LESS THAN THE DUST"

ALMA TELL, DONALD BRIAN
IN "THE SMUGGLERS"

VERNON STEELE, ETHEL CLAYTON
IN "FOR THE DEFENSE"

MARIE DORO, ELLIOTT DEXTER
IN "DIPLOMACY"

MARY PICKFORD
IN "POOR LITTLE PEPPINA"
FAMOUS PLAYERS FEATURES

ROBERT CAIN, HAZEL DAWN
IN "MY LADY INCOG"

BLANCHE SWEET IN
"THE RAGAMUFFIN"

CLEO RIDGELY, WALLACE REID
IN "THE YELLOW PAWN"

VICTOR MOORE, JEROLD WARD
IN "THE CLOWN"
LASKY FEATURES

MAE MURRAY, EARLE FOXE
IN "THE DREAM GIRL"

MARIE DORO, ELLIOTT DEXTER
IN "THE LASH"

FRANCIS X. BUSHMAN, BEVERLY BAYNE   BEVERLY BAYNE, FRANCIS X. BUSHMAN   FRANCIS X. BUSHMAN, ROBERT CUMMINGS, BEVERLY BAYN

SCENES FROM "ROMEO AND JULIET"

FRANCIS X. BUSHMAN, BEVERLY BAYNE   BEVERLY BAYNE, JOHN DAVIDSON, FRANCIS X. BUSHMAN

SCENES FROM "ROMEO AND JULIET"

WARNER OLAND, OLGA PETROVA, Also above:
MAHLON HAMILTON, OLGA PETROVA IN
"THE ETERNAL QUESTION"

OLGA PETROVA

METRO FEATURES

NORMAN KERRY, OLGA PETROVA IN "THE BLACK BUTTERL
Above: OLGA PETROVA IN "THE SOUL MARKET"

HARRY HILLIARD, THEDA BARA, JOHN WEBB DILLON

THEDA BARA, HARRY HILLIARD

THEDA BARA, HARRY HILLIARD

SCENES FROM "ROMEO AND JULIET"

916 Mary Pickford was still queen of the Famous Players lot and Adolph Zukor ned her for two more years at a guarantee of 040,000 and in August formed the Artcraft Pic-s Corporation to distribute Pickford Pictures. r days after the Pickford contract was signed, kor announced the merger of Famous Players-ky Corporation which included also the Bos-th, Morosco and Pallas companies. Zukor had solidated production for Paramount distribution. ine, Edison, Selig and Essanay of the old guard panies united as K. E. S. E., trying desperately orestall their eventual downfall. Metro was be-ing an important company. The Fox Company stige increased yearly. Both these companies ed lavish productions of "Romeo and Juliet." signed stage star Bertha Kalich and George lsh, a Fordham University athlete who had been ring minor roles in Griffith and Triangle produc-s. The press releases stated that by "public and" Metro had signed Beverly Bayne and re-ed her with Francis X. Bushman. They also tracted Harold Lockwood and May Allison se popularity as a team was threatening the hman-Bayne supremacy. Ethel Barrymore, her Lionel, Olga Petrova, Mabel Taliaferro, a Dana and Valli Valli were other Metro stars.

ALICE GALE, HARRY HILLIARD, THEDA BARA, JOHN WEBB DILLON, EDWIN HOLT, HELEN TRACY
IN "ROMEO AND JULIET"

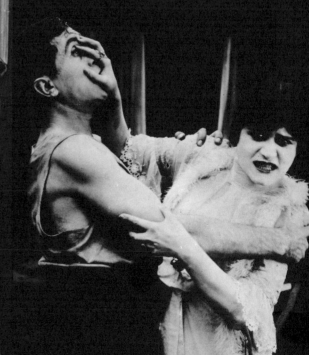

CARL VON SCHILLER, GLADYS BROCKWELL
IN "SINS OF THE PARENTS"

ANNA LUTHER, GEORGE WALSH
IN "THE BEAST"

THEDA BARA
IN "DESTRUCTION"

FOX FEATURES

May Allison, Harold Lockwood
in "The Secret Wire" (Mutual-American)

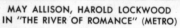

Harold Lockwood
(Metro)

Harold Lockwood

May Allison, Harold Lockwood
in "The River of Romance" (Metro)

May Allison

Lionel Barrymore
in "The Quitter"
(Metro)

Grace Valentine, Lionel Barrymore
in "The Brand of Cowardice" (Metro)

May Allison
(Metro)

Mabel Taliaferro
in "A Magdalene of
the Hills" (Metro)

Edwin Carewe, Mabel Taliaferro
in "The Snowbird" (Metro)

SEPH GRANBY, VALESKA SURATT
IN "JEALOUSY" (FOX)

DOROTHY BERNARD, WILLIAM FARNUM
IN "A MAN OF SORROW" (FOX)

EARLE FOXE, TSURU AOKI
IN "ALIEN SOULS" (LASKY)

ETHEL BARRYMORE
IN "THE KISS OF HATE" (METRO)

VICTOR MOORE
(LASKY)

MARY BOLAND
(TRIANGLE)

GEORGE WALSH
(FOX)

VIOLA DANA
(METRO)

MARSHALL NEILAN
(LASKY)

MARGARITA FISCHER
(MUTUAL)

MR. AND MRS. SIDNEY DREW
IN "CHILDHOOD'S HAPPY DAYS" (METRO)

1916 Keystone Comedies with their cops, custard pies and bathing beauties continued to cheer the country. Harold Lloyd, with Bebe Daniels as his leading lady, was finding a receptive public with his "Lonesome Luke" comedies released by Pathé. Al Christie, who had been successful as producer of the Nestor comedies, formed the Al E. Christie Comedies and became the nearest competitor Mack Sennett ever had. His first release, on September 18, 1916, was "A Seminary Scandal" with Billie Rhodes and Harry Ham. Lloyd V. Hamilton and Bud Duncan were successful with their "Ham and Bud" series for Kalem. Mr. and Mrs. Sidney Drew were making their delightful domestic comedies at Metro. Biograph's last gasp was a series of two-reelers starring Bert Williams, famous colored stage comedian. Frank Daniels, Kolb and Dill, Harry Watson, Jr. and George Ovey were other stage comics making films.

ROBERT B. MANTELL, GENEVIEVE HAMPER
IN "A WIFE'S SACRIFICE" (FOX)

VALLI VALLI
IN "THE TURMOIL" (METRO)

GEORGE WALSH
IN "THE ISLAND OF DESIRE" (FOX)

BERTHA KALICH, JEROME LAWLER
IN "SLANDER" (FOX)

OLLIE KIRKBY (KALEM) **FRANK CAMPEAU** (TRIANGLE) **GERDA HOLMES** (ESSANAY) **ALFRED VOSBURGH** (MUTUAL) **ALICE TERRY** (TRIANGLE) **JOSEPH KAUFMAN** (LUBIN) **VALLI VALLI** (METRO) **WILLIAM STOW** (MUTUAL)

PATHÉ

Bebe Daniels the charming little comedienne of the "LUKE" COMEDIES, supporting HAROLD

ROLIN COMEDIES are the bright spot on the program of every exhibitor who shows them. BOOK THEM and you'll see why Current release

SCENES FROM "LONESOME LUKE" COMEDIES (PATHÉ)
WITH HAROLD LLOYD AND BEBE DANIELS

JOHNNY HINES (WORLD) **IRENE WARFIELD** (ESSANAY) **HAL COOLEY** (SIGNAL) **BARBARA TENNANT** (WORLD) **HARRY BEAUMONT** (ESSANAY) **MADELINE TRAVERSE** (PATHÉ) **ELMER CLIFTON** (TRIANGLE) **NELL CRAIG** (ESSANAY)

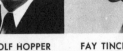

ANDER GADEN
(UNIVERSAL)

MARGARET THOMPSON
(TRIANGLE)

THOMAS HOLDING
(FAMOUS PLAYERS)

MARGUERITE CLAYTON
(ESSANAY)

DE WOLF HOPPER
(TRIANGLE)

FAY TINCHER
(TRIANGLE)

RAYMOND McKEE
(EDISON)

GRACE VALENTINE
(METRO)

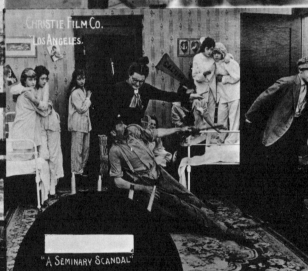

KEYSTONE-TRIANGLE COMEDIES
Center: KEYSTONE BATHING GIRLS, Top: CHARLES MURRAY, LOUISE FAZENDA,
Top Right: ROSCOE ARBUCKLE, AL ST. JOHN

"A SEMINARY SCANDAL" WITH BILLIE RHODES, STELLA ADAMS,
EDDIE BARRIE, HARRY HAM
Above: EDDIE LYONS, BETTY COMPSON IN AN EARLY CHRISTIE COMEDY

WARD EARLE
(EDISON)

VIVIAN RICH
(MUTUAL)

ART ACORD
(MUTUAL)

ANNA HELD
(MOROSCO)

HOBART BOSWORTH
(BOSWORTH)

VIRGINIA PEARSON
(VITAGRAPH)

FORREST STANLEY
(MOROSCO)

WINIFRED KINGSTON
(PALLAS)

BETTY COMPSON IN
"HIST AT 6 O'CLOCK"
(CHRISTIE)

SALLY CRUTE IN
"HELEN OF THE CHORUS"
(EDISON)

EUGENE O'BRIEN IN
"THE CHAPERON"
(ESSANAY)

KATHLYN WILLIAMS IN
"SWEET LADY PEGGY"
(SELIG)

VIRGINIA HAMMOND
IN "THE DISCARD"
(ESSANAY)

TYRONE POWER, SR
"JOHN NEEDHAM'S DO
(SELIG)

EUGENE O'BRIEN, EDWARD MAWSON, EDNA MAYO
IN "RETURN OF EVE"

HUGH THOMPSON, EDWARD ARNOLD, NELL CRAIG
IN "THE PRIMITIVE STRAIN"

HENRY B. WALTHALL, THOMAS COMMERFORD, JOHN WAL
ANTOINETTE WALKER IN "THE STING OF VICTORY"

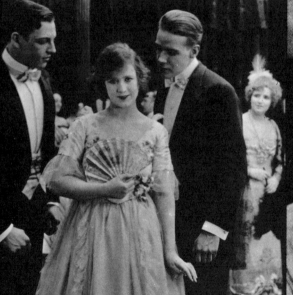

FRANCINE LARRIMORE IN
"THE PRINCESS FROM THE POORHOUSE"

WILLIAM GILLETTE
AS SHERLOCK HOLMES

BRYANT WASHBURN, EDNA MAYO IN
"THE PRINCE OF GRAUSTARK"

BRYANT WASHBURN, LEWIS STONE, GLADYS HANSON
IN "THE HAVOC"

WILLIAM GILLETTE, MARJORIE KAY
IN "SHERLOCK HOLMES"
ESSANAY RELEASES

ANN MURDOCK, RICHARD TRAVERS IN
"CAPTAIN JINKS OF THE HORSE MARINES"

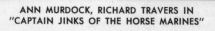

BESSIE EYTON
IN "THE CRISIS"
(SELIG)

FLORENCE REED, FORREST WINANT
IN "NEW YORK"
(PATHÉ)

RUTH STONEHOUSE IN
"PEG O' THE RING"
(UNIVERSAL)

ORMI HAWLEY
IN "TEMPTATION"
(LUBIN)

TOM TERRISS, JILL WOODWARD
IN "MY COUNTRY FIRST"
(PATHÉ)

TOM MIX
(SELIG)

BERT WILLIAMS IN
"A NATURAL BORN GAMBLER" (BIOGRAPH)

PEARL WHITE, BRUCE McREA, WILLIAM RILEY HATCH
IN "HAZEL KIRKE" (PATHÉ)

ROSE MELVILLE AS SIS HOPKINS IN
"SHE CAME, SHE SAW, SHE CONQUERED" (KALEM)

1916 Of the old guard, Vitagraph, Essanay and Pathé were the only companies showing signs of surviving the onrush of the powerful and vastly expanding newer companies. Essanay signed William Gillette to film his famous "Sherlock Holmes"; also Ann Murdock, Eugene O'Brien, Sallie Fisher, Lewis Stone, Gladys Hanson and Virginia Hammond from the stage. Vitagraph signed such stage luminaries as E. H. Sothern, Edna May, May Robson and Barney Bernard, and filmdom's own Alice Joyce. Jeanne Eagels, prior to her stage fame, made her film debut in "The World and The Woman" for Pathé, but it was the numerous serials with popular Pearl White and Ruth Roland that saved Pathé from oblivion. Lewis J. Selznick was branching out. Under his banner he formed the Clara Kimball Young Film Corporation. He also contracted Norma Talmadge and the famous Russian actress, Nazimova, who made her screen debut in "War Brides." A youngster named Richard Barthelmess, whose mother had taught Nazimova English, had a small role in this film.

MATT SNYDER, MARSHALL NEILAN
IN "THE CRISIS" (SELIG)

LLOYD V. HAMILTON AND BUD DUNCAN OF
"HAM AND BUD" COMEDIES (KALEM)

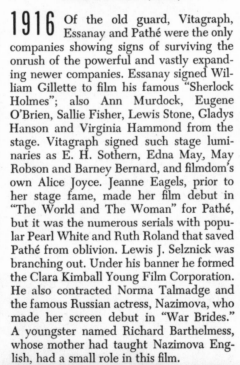

MABEL TRUNNELLE, EDWARD EARLE, MARC
MacDERMOTT IN "RANSON'S FOLLY"
(EDISON)

ROBERT EDESON, JOSE COLLINS IN
"THE LIGHT THAT FAILED"
(PATHÉ)

WHEELER OAKMAN, HARRY LONSDALE, KATHLYN
WILLIAMS IN "THE NE'ER-DO-WELL"
(SELIG)

111

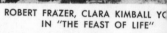

CLARA KIMBALL YOUNG, EDWIN AUGUST
IN "THE YELLOW PASSPORT"

LESLIE STOWE, CHESTER BARNETT, PAUL CAPELLANI, ALICE BRADY,
ZENA KEEFE, JUNE ELVIDGE IN "LA BOHEME"

ROBERT FRAZER, CLARA KIMBALL YO
IN "THE FEAST OF LIFE"

JACK SHERRILL, HELEN ARNOLD, MARIE SHOTWELL,
C. AUBREY SMITH, ETTA DE GROFF IN
"THE WITCHING HOUR"

CLARA KIMBALL YOUNG, CONWAY TEARLE
IN "THE COMMON LAW"

ELEANOR WOODRUFF, HOLBROOK BLINN, ALMA HA
IN "THE WEAKNESS OF MAN"

ARTHUR ASHLEY, MOLLIE KING
IN "THE SUMMER GIRL"

MADGE EVANS, HOLBROOK BLINN,
ETHEL CLAYTON IN "HUSBAND AND WIFE"

CARLYLE BLACKWELL, ETHEL CLAYTON
MONTAGUE LOVE IN "A WOMAN'S WAY"

ROBERT WARWICK
IN "HUMAN DRIFTWOOD"

NAZIMOVA, RICHARD BARTHELMESS

THEODORA WARFIELD, NILA MAC, NAZIMOVA, ROBERT WHITWORTH, GERTRUDE BERKELEY
SCENES FROM "WAR BRIDES"
WORLD-SELZNICK FEATURES

NAZIMOVA

CLARA KIMBALL YOUNG

CISSY FITZGERALD   L. ROGERS LYTTON   NAOMI CHILDERS   BARNEY BERNARD   MAY ROBSON   PAUL KELLY   EDNA MAY   CHARLES RIC

HARRY MOREY, EDNA MAY
IN "SALVATION JOAN"

EDITH STOREY, E. H. SOTHERN
IN "AN ENEMY TO THE KING"

PEGGY HYLAND, E. H. SOTHERN
IN "THE CHATTEL"

ELEANOR WOODRUFF, ANDERS RANDOLPH, CHARLES
RICHMAN, JAMES MORRISON, ZENA KEEFE IN
"THE HERO OF SUBMARINE D2"

BOBBY CONNELLY, EDNA HUNTER, CHARLOTTE IVES,
BARNEY BERNARD IN "A PRINCE IN A PAWNSHOP"

BILLIE BILLINGS, JAMES MORRISON, PEGGY HYLAN
EVART OVERTON IN "THE ENEMY"

ANITA STEWART, WILFRED LYTELL
IN "THE COMBAT"

CHARLES KENT, MURIEL OSTRICHE, ANTONIO MORENO
IN "KENNEDY SQUARE"
VITAGRAPH PLAYS AND PLAYERS

LILLIAN WALKER, ADOLPHE MENJOU
IN "THE BLUE ENVELOPE"

SETTA BRICE (LUBIN)   GEORGE PERIOLAT (UNIVERSAL)   ENID BENNETT (TRIANGLE)   WILLIAM S. HART (TRIANGLE)   MOLLIE KING (WORLD)   EDWARD ABELES (LASKY)   CONSTANCE COLLIER (TRIANGLE)   JOHN BARRYMORE (FAMOUS PLAYERS)

EDNA PURVIANCE, CHARLES CHAPLIN
IN "CARMEN" (ESSANAY)

CHARLES CHAPLIN
IN "CARMEN"

CHARLES CHAPLIN
IN "THE FLOORWALKER" (MUTUAL)

1916 Shortly before celebrating his twenty-seventh birthday, Charles Chaplin signed a contract with the Mutual Film Corporation at $10,000 per week and a bonus of $150,000 for signing the contract, or a total of $675,000 for a year's work. He made twelve two-part pictures for them during the next year and a half. His first for Mutual was "The Floorwalker." "Easy Street," which was considered one of his best, was in the series of comedies he made at this time. "Carmen Burlesque," a film he had made for Essanay, was also released this year. He was now the highest priced film star in the industry.

CHARLES CHAPLIN
IN "ONE A. M." (MUTUAL)

EDNA PURVIANCE, CHARLES CHAPLIN
IN "THE VAGABOND" (MUTUAL)

HARRY WATSON, JR.
IN "THE MISHAPS OF MUSTY SUFFER" (KLEINE)

JEANNE EAGELS

VIVIAN RICH, ALFRED VOSBURGH
IN "ENCHANTMENT" (MUTUAL)

115

FORREST STANLEY, ANNA HELD, PAGE PETERS
IN "MADAME LA PRESIDENTE" (MOROSCO)

CONSTANCE COLLIER, FORREST STANLEY
IN "THE CODE OF MARCIA GRAY" (MOROSCO)

LENORE ULRICH IN "INTRIGUE" (PALLAS)
KING VIDOR (left) AS AN EXTRA

ALFRED VOSBURGH, VIVIAN MARTIN
IN "HER FATHER'S SON" (PALLAS)

VIVIAN MARTIN, EDWARD PEIL, JACK LIVINGSTON
IN "THE STRONGER LOVE" (PALLAS)

LENORE ULRICH, HOWARD DAVIES, FORREST STAN
IN "THE HEART OF PAULA" (PALLAS)

CONSTANCE COLLIER, SIR HERBERT
BEERBOHM TREE IN "MACBETH"

ON THE "MACBETH" SET WITH SIR HERBERT BEERBOHM TREE,
CONSTANCE COLLIER, D. W. GRIFFITH (FINE ARTS-TRIANGLE)

WINIFRED KINGSTON, DUSTIN FARN
IN "DAVID GARRICK" (PALLAS)

DOROTHY DONNELLY, JOHN BOWERS
IN "MADAME X" (PATHÉ)

MAURICE, JULIAN L'ESTRANGE, FLORENCE WALTON
IN "THE QUEST OF LIFE" (FAMOUS PLAYERS)

JACK NELSON, HELEN JEROME EDDY, GEORGE BEB
IN "PASQUALE" (MOROSCO)

LOUISE GLAUM, WILLIAM S. HART
IN "THE ARYAN"

WILLIAM S. HART
IN "THE DESERT MAN"

MARGERY WILSON, WILLIAM S. HART, ROBERT McKIM
IN "THE PRIMAL LURE"

ENID MARKEY, WILLIAM S. HART

ENID MARKEY
SCENES FROM "THE CAPTIVE GOD"

DOROTHY DALTON, WILLIAM DESMOND

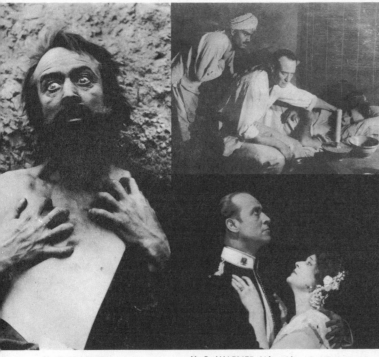

H. B. WARNER
IN "THE BEGGAR OF CAWNPORE"

H. B. WARNER (Also Above), LOLA MAY
IN "THE BEGGAR OF CAWNPORE"

BESSIE BARRISCALE (Also Above with
CHARLES RAY), LOUISE GLAUM IN "HOME"

NORMA TALMADGE
IN "GOING STRAIGHT"

THOMAS GUISE, WILLIAM COLLIER, JR.
IN "THE BUGLE CALL"

WARNER RICHMOND, OWEN MOORE, LEONORE HARRIS,
DOROTHY GISH IN "BETTY OF GRAYSTONE"
TRIANGLE PRODUCTIONS

BESSIE LOVE, WILFRED LUCAS, MARY ALDEN
IN "ACQUITTED"

117

ENID MARKEY, WILLARD MACK
IN "ALOHA OE"

ON THE LOT
JOHN EMERSON, CONSTANCE COLLIER, DE WOLF HOPPER, DOROTHY GISH,
SIR HERBERT BEERBOHM TREE (IN MACBETH COSTUME) DOUGLAS FAIRBANKS

MARY BOLAND, ROBERT McKIM
IN "THE STEPPING STONE"

LF BREED"   WITH BESSIE LOVE IN "REGGIE MIXES IN" (Also Above)   WITH JEWEL CARMEN IN "MANHATTAN MADNESS"   DOUGLAS FAIRBANKS
DOUGLAS FAIRBANKS FEATURES   Above: IN "THE AMERICANO"

1916 Triangle's greatest attractions were Douglas Fairbanks and William S. Hart, now on their way to world-wide fame. Charles Ray, Dorothy Dalton, Bessie Barriscale, William Desmond and Enid Markey were becoming important screen personalities under the Triangle banner. H. B. Warner, Dustin Farnum and Robert Warwick, matinee idols of the theatre, were now established screen stars. At Universal, actress Lois Weber became the first important woman producer of the industry. Shakespeare's plays, filmed as one-reelers earlier, were being made on elaborate scales. Besides the two versions of "Romeo and Juliet," Pathé released a Thanhouser production of "King Lear," and Triangle released the Fine Arts production of "Macbeth."

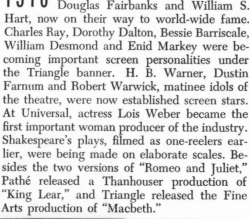

HOWARD HICKMAN, JULIA DEAN, THELMA SALTER
IN "MATRIMONY"

CHARLES RAY, RITA STANWOOD, WEDGEWOOD NOW
IN "THE DESERTER"

WILLIAM DESMOND, ALICE TERRY, BESSIE BARRISCALE
IN "NOT MY SISTER"

MARIE DORO
IN "THE WOOD NYMPH"

DE WOLF HOPPER
IN "CASEY AT THE BAT'

DOROTHY DALTON, H. B. WARNER
IN "THE VAGABOND PRINCE"

TRIANGLE PRODUCTIONS

CLEO MADISON, WILLIAM V. MONG
IN "THE SEVERED HAND"

A. D. BLAKE, RENE ROGERS, TYRONE POWER, HELEN RIAVME
IN "WHERE ARE MY CHILDREN?"

RUPERT JULIAN, ELLA HALL, KINGSLEY BENEDICT
IN "THE BUGLER OF ALGIERS"

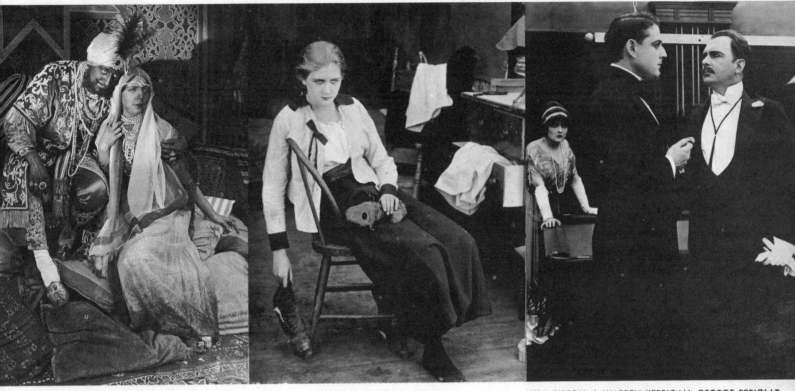

ALAN HOLUBAR, JANE GAIL IN
"TWENTY THOUSAND LEAGUES UNDER THE SEA"

MARY MacLAREN IN "SHOES"
UNIVERSAL PICTURES

VERA SISSON, J. WARREN KERRIGAN, GEORGE PERIOLAT
IN "LANDON'S LEGACY"

RANK BORZAGE, ANN LITTLE
IN "THAT GAL OF BURKE'S"

HELEN HOLMES ON HORSEBACK ON STAGE OF SIGNAL STUDIOS

VALKYRIEN
IN "HIDDEN VALLEY" (PATHÉ)

MARGARITA FISCHER, HARRY POLLARD
IN "SUSIE'S NEW SHOES" (MUTUAL)

LOIS WEBER, (Center) DISCUSSING "THE MYSTERIOUS MRS.
MUSSLEWHITE" WITH ARTHUR FORD, MARY MacLAREN,
AL SIEGLER AND HARRISON FORD

LOUISE HUFF, JACK PICKFORD IN
"SEVENTEEN" (FAMOUS PLAYERS)

OLLIE KIRKBY, MARIN SAIS, TRUE BOARDMAN
IN SCENES FROM "THE SOCIAL PIRATES" (KALEM)

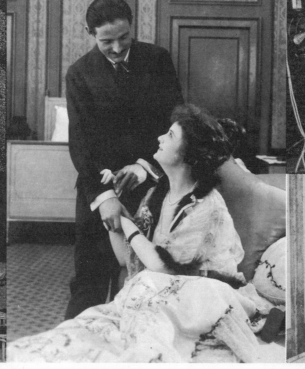

DAVID POWELL, BILLIE BURKE
IN "GLORIA'S ROMANCE" (KLEINE)

JEAN SOTHERN, HOWARD ESTABROOK IN SCENES
FROM "THE MYSTERIES OF MYRA" (PATHÉ)

TOM MOORE, ANNA Q. NILSSON
IN "WHO'S GUILTY?" (PATHÉ)

1916 The serial was still a potent factor for bringing an audience into a theatre. Pearl White made two serials, "The Iron Claw" and "Pearl of The Army," for Pathé. Other Pathé serials included "The Red Circle" with Ruth Roland, "The Grip of Evil" with Jackie Saunders, "Who's Guilty?," "The Mysteries of Myra" and "The Shielding Shadow." Billie Burke appeared in "Gloria's Romance" for Kleine, and Maurice Costello and Ethel Grandin made "The Crimson Stain Mystery." Universal starred Grace Cunard in "Peg O' The Ring" and Marie Walcamp and Eddie Polo in "For Liberty." Metro joined the easy-money parade with "The Great Secret" starring Francis X. Bushman and Beverly Bayne. Kalem made "The Social Pirates" with Ollie Kirkby and Marin Sais. Essanay contributed "The Strange Case of Mary Page" and American made "The Secrets of The Submarine." There were others too numerous to mention.

HENRY B. WALTHALL, EDNA MAYO, ERNEST COSSA
IN "THE STRANGE CASE OF MARY PAGE" (ESSAN

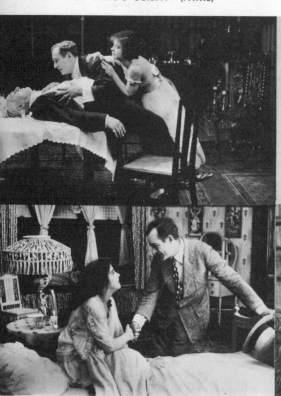

ETHEL GRANDIN, MAURICE COSTELLO IN
SCENES FROM "THE CRIMSON STAIN MYSTERY"

GRACE DARMOND, LEON BARY IN SCENES
FROM "THE SHIELDING SHADOW" (PATHÉ)

PHILO McCULLOUGH, RUTH ROLAND IN "THE RED CIR
Above: JACKIE SAUNDERS, ROLAND BOTTOMLEY IN
"THE GRIP OF EVIL" (PATHÉ)

HOWARD ESTABROOK IN
"THE MYSTERIES OF MYRA" (PATHÉ)

FRANCIS X. BUSHMAN, BEVERLY BAYNE
IN "THE GREAT SECRET" (METRO)

PEARL WHITE IN
"PEARL OF THE ARMY" (PATHÉ)

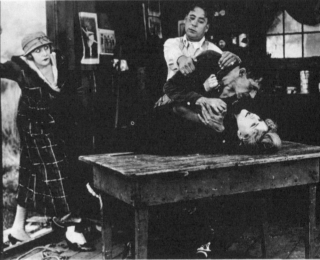

JUANITA HANSEN, LAMAR JOHNSTONE
IN "THE SECRET OF THE SUBMARINE" (AMERICAN)

GRACE CUNARD IN
"PEG O' THE RING" (UNIVERSAL)

GRACE DARLING, HARRY FOX, ROBIN TOWNLEY, MAE HOPKINS
IN "BEATRICE FAIRFAX" (WHARTON)

CREIGHTON HALE, PEARL WHITE IN
SCENES FROM "THE IRON CLAW"
(PATHÉ)

MARIE WALCAMP, EDDIE POLO AND DIRECTOR HENRY McRAE
REHEARSING A SCENE FOR "LIBERTY, A DAUGHTER OF THE U.S.A."
(UNIVERSAL)

PEARL WHITE, RALPH KELLARD, MARIE WAYNE IN
SCENES FROM "PEARL OF THE ARMY"
(PATHÉ)

121

MABEL NORMAND
(GOLDWYN)

MAE MARSH
(GOLDWYN)

HELEN FERGUSON
(ESSANAY)

EDDIE LYONS
(UNIVERSAL)

TEDDY SAMSON
(TRIANGLE)

JACK SHERRILL
(FROHMAN)

ANN PENNINGTON
(PARAMOUNT)

FRANKLYN FARNUM
(UNIVERSAL)

DORIS KENYON
(WORLD)

WILLIAM
COURTLEIGH, JR.
(PARAMOUNT)

ANN MU
(MUTU

LIONEL BARRYMORE
(METRO)

MR. AND MRS. SIDNEY DREW
(METRO)

WILLIAM GARWOOD
(TRIANGLE)

ETHEL GRANDIN
(SMALLWOOD)

PLAYERS OF THE PERIOD

MARIE DRESSLER
(GOLDWYN)

NAZIMOVA
(METRO)

J. BARNEY SHERRY
(TRIANGLE)

DOROTHY KELLY
(VITAGRAPH)

E. K. LINCOLN
(WORLD)

GLADYS BROCKWELL
(FOX)

EDMUND BREESE
(PATHÉ)

JEAN SOTHERN
(PATHÉ)

ELMO LINCOLN
(TRIANGLE)

MARIN SAIS
(KALEM)

GEORGE BEBAN
(PARAMOUNT)

H. B. WARNER
(TRIANGLE)

BESSIE BARRISCALE
(TRIANGLE)

WILLIAM RUSSELL
(MUTUAL)

CORINNE GRIFFITH
(VITAGRAPH)

PLAYERS OF THE PERIOD

123

DOUGLAS FAIRBANKS

WALLACE REID

RAYMOND HATTON, THEODORE KOSLOFF, GERALDINE FARRAR, WALLACE REID
SCENES FROM "THE WOMAN GOD FORGOT"

GERALDINE FARRAR

1917 Triangle lost its most important personnel when D. W. Griffith, Thomas H. Ince, Douglas Fairbanks and William S. Hart signed with Artcraft, and Mack Sennett agreed to film his Keystone comedies for Paramount. Artcraft also signed stage stars George M. Cohan and Elsie Ferguson. In May, Adolph Zukor announced that Paramount had gained control of Artcraft. He also became a partner of Lewis J. Selznick's enterprises. With his various combinations, Zukor controlled the output of half the important stars of the industry. Thomas L. Tally, a leading pioneer California showman, was annoyed at the rising cost of big star pictures, and especially those controlled by Zukor. With J. D. Williams, who had large theatre interests in Australia, and twenty-seven other theatre operators about the country, he formed the First National Exhibitors Circuit. The first star signed was Charles Chaplin who received $1,075,000 for eight two-reel pictures. Ironic that Tally who had never run a Chaplin comedy in his theatres and did not think him funny handled the details in the signing of the contract.

DOUGLAS FAIRBANKS
IN "DOWN TO EARTH"

ARLINE PRETTY, DOUGLAS FAIRBANKS
IN "IN AGAIN—OUT AGAIN"

DOUGLAS FAIRBANKS
IN "WILD AND WOOLLY"

FRANK CAMPEAU, EUGENE ORMONDE, DOUGLAS
FAIRBANKS IN "REACHING FOR THE MOON"
Above: DOUGLAS FAIRBANKS, EILEEN PERCY
IN "DOWN TO EARTH"

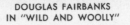

PARAMOUNT-ARTCRAFT PRODUCTIONS

KENNETH HARLAN
(TRIANGLE)

EDNA PURVIANCE
(MUTUAL)

CREIGHTON HALE
(PATHÉ)

FLORENCE LA BADIE
(THANHOUSER)

RALPH KELLARD
(PATHÉ)

FAIRBANKS TWIN
MADELEINE AND MA
(THANHOUSER)

MARY PICKFORD, JACK HOLT IN "THE LITTLE
AMERICAN" (Also Center)
Top: ZASU PITTS, MARY PICKFORD IN "THE LITTLE PRINCESS"

MARY PICKFORD IN
"REBECCA OF SUNNYBROOK FARM"

MARY PICKFORD IN "THE POOR LITTLE RICH GIRL"
Top: WITH ELLIOTT DEXTER IN "A ROMANCE OF THE REDW
Center: WITH MATT MOORE IN "THE PRIDE OF THE CLA

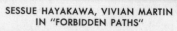

PAUL WILLIS, VIVIAN MARTIN
IN "THE TROUBLE BUSTER"

JAMES NEILL, SESSUE HAYAKAWA
IN "THE BOTTLE IMP"
PARAMOUNT-ARTCRAFT PICTURES

SESSUE HAYAKAWA, VIVIAN MARTIN
IN "FORBIDDEN PATHS"

126

MARY FULLER
(PARAMOUNT)

BERT LYTELL
(SELZNICK)

ROSEMARY THEBY
(UNIVERSAL)

HARRY C. MYERS
(UNIVERSAL)

BEBE DANIELS
(PATHÉ)

ANTONIO MORENO
(VITAGRAPH)

MARGUERITE CLARK (Also Above), ELSIE LAWSON,
HELEN GREENE IN "THE AMAZONS"
ANK LOSEE, MARGUERITE CLARK IN "THE VALENTINE GIRL"

MARGUERITE CLARK
IN COSTUME FOR "SNOW WHITE"

MARGUERITE CLARK, RICHARD BARTHELMESS
IN "THE SEVEN SWANS" AND ABOVE IN
"BAB'S BURGLAR" Top: IN "SNOW WHITE"

ITH CHAPMAN, BLANCHE SWEET, WALTER LONG,
TOM FORMAN IN "THE EVIL EYE"

KATHLYN WILLIAMS, THOMAS HOLDING
IN "REDEEMING LOVE"
PARAMOUNT-ARTCRAFT PICTURES

OWEN MOORE, HAZEL DAWN
IN "UNDER COVER"

127

MARIE DORO
(PARAMOUNT)

ARLINE PRETTY
(ARTCRAFT)

ETHEL MARY OAKLAND, JACK PICKFORD
IN "THE DUMMY"

WALLACE REID, KATHLYN WILLIAMS, ALFRED PAGET
IN "BIG TIMBER"

1917 Mary Pickford maintained her high box office status. Marguerite Clark, Pauline Frederick, Marie Doro, Blanche Sweet, Geraldine Farrar and Vivian Martin continued as popular Paramount stars. Billie Burke and Lina Cavalieri joined the Paramount fold. Margaret Illington made her film debut in "The Inner Shrine" for Zukor, and Lasky signed Julian Eltinge, famous female impersonator. "A Tale of Two Nations," an independent film, was one of the earliest all-color feature films ever made in this country. It starred Edwin August, pioneer film actor.

VOLA VALE
(BALBOA)

CHESTER BARNETT
(WORLD)

TSURU AOKI
(PARAMOUNT)

WILFRED LUCAS
(TRIANGLE)

MINTA DURFEE
(KEYSTONE)

MONTAGU
(WORLD

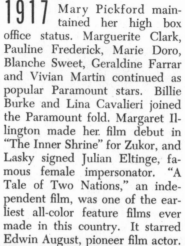

ANTRIM SHORT, JACK PICKFORD (Also Above WITH CLARA
HORTON , ROBERT GORDON IN "TOM SAWYER"

JACK PICKFORD
IN "TOM SAWYER"

JULIAN ELTINGE IN TWO SCENES
FROM "THE COUNTESS CHARMING"

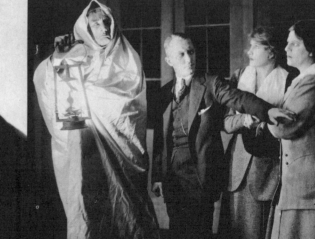

GEORGE M. COHAN, MARGUERITE SNOW
IN "BROADWAY JONES"

GEORGE M. COHAN

GEORGE M. COHAN, ANNA Q. NILSSON
IN "SEVEN KEYS TO BALDPATE"

LOU TELLEGEN, MARY FULLER
IN "THE LONG TRAIL"

GEORGE LE GUERE   HELEN JEROME EDDY

MARIE DORO, ELLIOTT DEXTER
IN "CASTLES FOR TWO"

RY HILLIARD (FOX)   LOUISE LOVELY (FOX)   NIGEL BARRIE (WORLD)

1917 Herbert Brenon, now an important director, capitalized on the Russian revolution with his independently produced "The Fall of The Romanoffs." "The Submarine Eye," made by the Williamson Brothers and with many scenes filmed under water, was another production that caused comment. Both these pictures had their first runs at "legit" theatres. Brenon was also responsible for J. Forbes-Robertson filming his famous stage success, "The Passing of The Third Floor Back." Other independent films included "Raffles" starring John Barrymore and Benjamin Chapin's Lincoln Cycle.

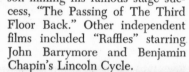

MARJORIE DAW (PARAMOUNT)   WINDHAM STANDING (PARAMOUNT)   EVELYN GREELEY (WORLD)

GEORGE BEBAN AND SON
IN "LOST IN TRANSIT"

WILLIAM S. HART AND FRITZ
IN "THE NARROW TRAIL"

BILLIE BURKE, THOMAS MEIGHAN
IN "THE LAND OF PROMISE"

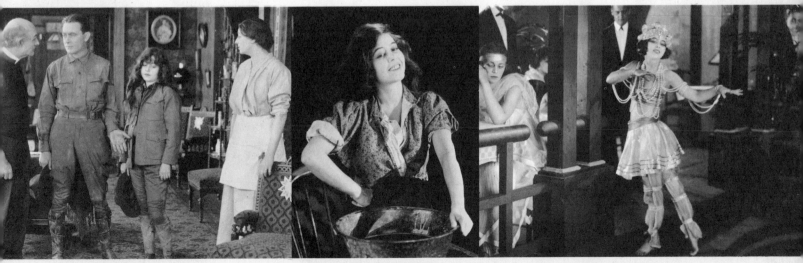

OWEN MOORE, ANN PENNINGTON
IN "THE LITTLE BOY SCOUT"

ANN PENNINGTON
IN "SUNSHINE NAN"
PARAMOUNT-ARTCRAFT PRODUCTIONS

ANN PENNINGTON
IN "THE ANTICS OF ANN"

PAULINE FREDERICK
(PARAMOUNT)

FANNIE WARD
IN "THE SCHOOL FOR HUSBANDS" (LASKY)

GERALDINE FARRAR
(PARAMOUNT)

JAMES COOLEY, ALICE HAYES, EDWIN AUGUST
IN "A TALE OF TWO NATIONS" (INDEPENDENT)

LINA CAVALIERI
IN "THE ETERNAL TEMPTRESS" (PARAMOUNT)

ADOLPH ZUKOR VISITS MARGARET ILLINGTON ON TH
SET OF "THE INNER SHRINE," HER PICTURE DEBUT

CHARLES RAY
(TRIANGLE)

MAE MURRAY
(PARAMOUNT)

COLLEEN MOORE
(TRIANGLE)

LLOYD V. HAMILTON
(KALEM)

130

HENRY B. WALTHALL
(ESSANAY)

ALFRED HICKMAN, NANCE O'NEIL IN
"THE FALL OF THE ROMANOFFS" (BRENON)

DUSTIN FARNUM
(FOX)

ELLIOTT DEXTER, ELSIE FERGUSON IN
"THE RISE OF JENNIE CUSHING" (ARTCRAFT)

KOLB AND DILL WITH JUANITA HANSEN
IN "GLORY" (INDEPENDENT)

UNDERWATER SCENE FROM
"THE SUBMARINE EYE" (WILLIAMSON BROS.)

PEDRO de CORDOBA, ELSIE FERGUSON
IN "BARBARY SHEEP" (ARTCRAFT)

ELSIE FERGUSON
(ARTCRAFT)

BENJAMIN CHAPIN AS LINCOLN IN
"THE LINCOLN CYCLE" (INDEPENDENT)

The
Great Big
Splashes
of
Fun and Beauty

Are YOU
Wearing
The
Keystone
Smile?

1917 Mack Sennett bathing beauties were pin-up g
for the doughboys of the First World War. Gl
Swanson, Marie Prevost, Phyllis Haver and Mary Thurr
were Sennett bathing girls at this time. Roscoe Arbuc
now more familiarly known as "Fatty" Arbuckle, left S
nett to make his own comedies at Paramount. With Arbu
in this setup were two clever acrobatic comedians, Bu
Keaton and Al St. John. Before the year was out, Senn
was making his Keystone comedies for Paramount. Cha
Murray, Ben Turpin, Louise Fazenda, Chester Conklin,
Teddy and Pepper, a dog and cat, were now the ch
Keystone comics.

GLORIA SWANSON

CHESTER CONKLIN WITH MACK
SENNETT BATHING BEAUTIES

GLORIA SWANSON, PHYLLIS HAVER

PHYLLIS HAVER

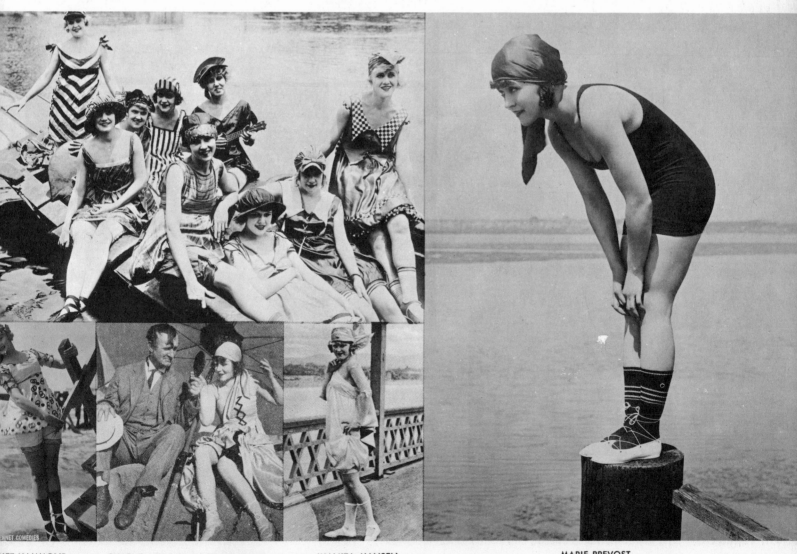

IET HAMMOND

CHARLIE MURRAY, MARY THURMAN

JUANITA HANSEN

MARIE PREVOST

MACK SENNETT BATHING BEAUTIES

133

CHARLIE MURRAY SYDNEY CHAPLIN BEN TURPIN LOUISE FAZENDA AL ST. JOHN SLIM SUMMERVIL

MACK SENNETT COMEDIANS

BEN TURPIN AND BATHING BEAUTIES

TEDDY AND LOUISE FAZENDA IN
"THE SUMMER GIRLS"
KEYSTONE COMEDIES

GLORIA SWANSON, BOBBY VERNON AND
MACK SENNETT BATHING BEAUTIES

TEDDY
(KEYSTONE)

CHESTER CONKLIN, GLORIA SWANSON, MACK
SWAIN IN A KEYSTONE COMEDY

GLORIA SWANSON, BOBBY VERNON
IN A KEYSTONE COMEDY

PEPPER
(KEYSTONE)

EVART OVERTON
(VITAGRAPH)

ORA CAREW
(KEYSTONE)

BERTRAM GRASSBY
(UNIVERSAL)

NEVA GERBER
(MUTUAL)

HARRY GRIBBON
(KEYSTONE)

FRANCES NELSON
(METRO)

J. FRANK GLENDON
(VITAGRAPH)

LILLIAN TUCKER
(WORLD)

CHARLES G
(TRIANG

ROSCOE ARBUCKLE, LUKE, JOSEPHINE STEVENS
IN "THE BUTCHER BOY"

ROSCOE ARBUCKLE, ALICE MANN, AL ST. JOHN
IN "HIS WEDDING NIGHT"
ARBUCKLE-PARAMOUNT COMEDIES

ROSCOE ARBUCKLE, AL ST. JOHN
IN "FATTY IN CONEY ISLAND"

MARIE CAHILL
IN "GLADYS' DAY DREAMS" (MUTUAL)

BILLIE RHODES, JAY BELASCO
IN "SOME NURSE" (MUTUAL)

VICTOR MOORE IN
"HOME DEFENSE" (PARAMOUNT)

CHARLIE MURRAY
(KEYSTONE)

BERT LYTELL, HAZEL DAWN IN
"THE LONE WOLF" (HERBERT BRENON)

DORIS KENYON, FRANK McINTYRE IN
"THE TRAVELING SALESMAN" (PARAMOUNT)

AL ST. JOHN
(KEYSTONE)

D WHITE
UTUAL)

EDITH JOHNSON
(VITAGRAPH)

TAYLOR HOLMES
(ESSANAY)

MARGUERITE MARSH
(GOLDWYN)

C. AUBREY SMITH
(WORLD)

OLIVE FULLER
GOLDEN
(UNIVERSAL)

VICTOR POTEL
(KEYSTONE)

GRETCHEN LEDERER
(VITAGRAPH)

STUART HOLMES
(FOX)

135

JOHN BARRYMORE IN
"RAFFLES, THE AMATEUR CRACKSMAN"
(INDEPENDENT)

JEANNE EAGELS, FREDERICK WARDE
IN "UNDER FALSE COLORS" (PATHÉ)

FRANCINE LARRIMORE, MAX LINDER
IN "MAX WANTS A DIVORCE" (ESSANAY)

J. FORBES-ROBERTSON IN
"THE PASSING OF THE THIRD FLOOR

THOMAS SANTSCHI, HELEN WARE, HARRY LONSDALE
IN "THE GARDEN OF ALLAH" (SELIG)

TAYLOR HOLMES, VIRGINIA VALLI, ROD LA ROCQUE
IN "EFFICIENCY EDGAR'S COURTSHIP" (ESSANAY)

DERWENT HALL CAINE, LYDIA KNOTT, CARL GERARD,
COLEMAN, MARGUERITE COURTOT IN "CRIME AND PUNISH
(PATHÉ)

WEBSTER CAMPBELL, MARGUERITE CLAYTON IN
"THE CLOCK STRUCK ONE" (ESSANAY)

JACK GARDNER, HELEN FERGUSON
IN "GIFT O' GAB" (ESSANAY)

ALICE BRADY
(WORLD)

HAZEL DALY, BRYANT WASHBURN IN
"SKINNER'S DRESS SUIT" (ESSANAY)

MARY McALISTER
(ESSANAY)

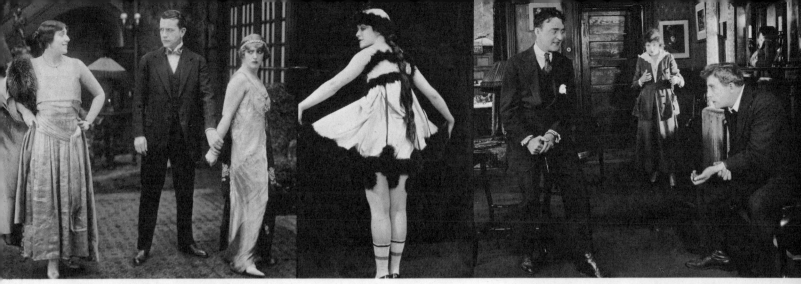

LEONORE HARRIS, FRANK MILLS, FLORENCE REED
IN "TODAY" (PATHÉ)

VIRGINIA VALLI
(ESSANAY)

WILLIAM COURTENAY, MOLLIE KING, JOHN BOYLE
IN "KICK IN" (PATHÉ)

BOB McGOWAN, BETTY COMPSON
IN "A BOLD BAD NIGHT" (CHRISTIE)

1917 The famous pioneer companies, Biograph, Kalem, and Lubin, had shut down. Vitagraph and Essanay were still active. George Ade's "Fables In Slang" were popular two-reel Essanay comedies. Max Linder, famous French comic, made several films for Essanay but they flopped and he returned to France. Anita Stewart, Alice Joyce, Earle Williams and Antonio Moreno were Vitagraph's drawing cards, and a young New Orleans beauty-contest winner named Corinne Griffith was creating interest. Marion Davies, an ingenue in "Oh, Boy," a Broadway musical, was starred in her first picture, "Runaway Romany."

MARION DAVIES, PEDRO de CORDOBA
IN "RUNAWAY ROMANY" (PATHÉ)

H. B. WARNER, W. LAWSON BUTT
IN "THE DANGER TRAIL" (SELIG)

MARIE OSBORNE, HENRY KING
IN "JOY AND THE DRAGON" (PATHÉ)

SARAH BERNHARDT
IN "MOTHERS OF FRANCE" (WORLD)

MARION DAVIES
(PATHÉ)

RUDOLPH CAMERON, ANITA STEWART IN "CLOVERS REBELLION" Top: ANITA STEWART, S. RANKIN DREW IN "THE GIRL PHILIPPA"

ANITA STEWART

ETHEL GRAY TERRY, EARLE WILLIAMS (Also Above W BRINSLEY SHAW), BILLIE BILLINGS IN "ARSENE LUPI

ANDERS RANDOLF, ALICE JOYCE, JOE DONOHUE IN "WITHIN THE LAW"

WALTER McGRAIL, ALICE JOYCE, HARRY MOREY IN "WITHIN THE LAW"

WILLIAM DESMOND TAYLOR, MYRTLE GONZALES IN "CAPTAIN ALVAREZ"

ANTONIO MORENO, MARY ANDERSON IN "THE MAGNIFICENT MEDDLER" Above: ANTONIO MORENO, EDITH STORY IN "ALADDIN FROM BROADWAY"

LILLIAN WALKER (Also Above), DONALD CAMERON IN "KITTY MACKAY"

VITAGRAPH PHOTOPLAYS

TEMPLE SAXE, BOBBY CONNELLY, PEGGY HYLAND, MAR MacDERMOTT IN "INTRIGUE" Above: MILDRED MANNIN CLEO AYERS, J. FRANK GLENDON IN "THE THIRD JUDGEME

T. CARLETON, EDNA GOODRICH IN "A DAUGHTER OF MARYLAND" Top: EDNA GOODRICH, WILLIAM HINCKLEY IN "REPUTATION"

MARY MILES MINTER

CLIFFORD CALLIS, GEORGE AHERN, MARY MILES MINTER IN "CHARITY CASTLE" Top: MARY MILES MINTER, GEORGE FISHER IN "ENVIRONMENT"

1917 Pathé was still releasing numerous serials, Harold Lloyd's Luke comedies, and features starring Irene (Mrs. Vernon) Castle, Florence LaBadie and Gladys Hulette. Mutual lost Chaplin and was on the decline. Marjorie Rambeau, Ann Murdock, Gail Kane, Edna Goodrich, Olive Tell and Juliette Day, stage personalities, all made Mutual features. Julia Sanderson filmed one picture, "The Runaway," and Marie Cahill made three two-reel comedies. Mary Miles Minter, William Russell and Margarita Fischer were also Mutual stars. Francis X. Bushman with Beverly Bayne, and Harold Lockwood with May Allison were popular Metro teams. Ethel Barrymore, Lionel Barrymore, Viola Dana, Emmy Wehlen and Emily Stevens were on the Metro roster. Universal stars included Dorothy Phillips, Harry Carey, Ella Hall.

NANCE O'NEIL IN "HEDDA GABLER"

WILLIAM RUSSELL, ANTRIM SHORT IN "PRIDE AND THE MAN"

GAIL KANE, ALFRED WHITMAN IN "THE SERPENT'S TOOTH" Above: GAIL KANE, DOUGLAS MacLEAN IN "SOULS IN PAWN"

MARJORIE RAMBEAU, AUGUSTA BURMASTER IN "MARY MORELAND" Above: MARJORIE RAMBEAU IN "THE GREATER WOMAN" MUTUAL PHOTOPLAYS

CARL SAUERMAN, ANN MURDOCK, DAVID POWELL IN "THE BEAUTIFUL ADVENTURE" Above: ANN MURDOCK, REX McDOUGALL IN "PLEASE HELP EMILY" **139**

MONROE SALISBURY
(UNIVERSAL)

MARIE OSBORNE
(PATHE)

FRANK KEENAN
(TRIANGLE)

JACKIE SAUNDERS
(MUTUAL)

WILLIAM COURTENAY
(PATHE)

EMMY WEHLEN
(METRO)

WILLIAM D. TA
(FOX)

EMILY STEVENS, WALTER MILLER
IN "THE SLACKER" (METRO)

CHARLES CHAPLIN
IN "EASY STREET" (MUTUAL)

CHARLES CHAPLIN IN
"THE ADVENTURER" (MUTUAL)

BEVERLY BAYNE, FRANCIS X. BUSHM.
IN "RED, WHITE AND BLUE BLOOD" (MI

EDNA PURVIANCE, ERIC CAMPBELL, CHARLES CHAPLIN
IN "THE ADVENTURER"

CHARLES CHAPLIN, EDNA PURVIANCE
IN "THE IMMIGRANT"

CHAPLIN-MUTUAL RELEASES

CHARLES CHAPLIN
IN "THE CURE"

IRVING CUMMINGS, ETHEL BARRYMORE, CHARLES DIXON,
DUDLEY HAWLEY IN "AN AMERICAN WIDOW"

ETHEL BARRYMORE
IN "THE LIFTED VEIL"

METRO FEATURES

ETHEL BARRYMORE, ROBERT WHITTIER, WILLIAM B. DAVIDSO
IN "THE CALL OF HER PEOPLE"

ANE NOVAK
(UNIVERSAL)

HAMILTON REVELLE
(METRO)

PEGGY HYLAND
(VITAGRAPH)

CRANE WILBUR
(MUTUAL)

CARMEL MYERS
(UNIVERSAL)

JACK MULHALL
(UNIVERSAL)

GRACE DARLING
(PATHE)

UGUSTUS PHILLIPS, HENRY HALLAM, ROBERT
ER, VIOLA DANA IN "GOD'S LAW AND MAN'S"
(METRO)

MAX LINDER
(ESSANAY)

DOROTHY PHILLIPS
(UNIVERSAL)

JACK MULHALL, LOUISE LOVELY, CARMEL MYERS
IN "SIRENS OF THE SEA" (UNIVERSAL)

UTH CLIFFORD, EMORY JOHNSON, RUPERT JULIAN
GRETCHEN LEDERER IN "A KENTUCKY CINDERELLA"

F. S. KELSEY DIRECTS LEAH BAIRD IN A
SCENE FROM "A SUNSET"
UNIVERSAL FEATURES

LON CHANEY, DOROTHY PHILLIPS, WILLIAM
STOWELL IN "TRIUMPH"

HAROLD LOCKWOOD
IN "THE HAUNTED PAJAMAS"

MAY ALLISON, HAROLD LOCKWOOD
IN "THE PROMISE"

PAULINE CURLEY, HAROLD LOCKWOOD
IN "THE SQUARE DECEIVER"

HAROLD LOCKWOOD, MAY ALLISON
IN "BIG TREMAINE"

METRO FEATURES

THEDA BARA

SCENES FROM "CLEOPATRA" WITH THEDA BARA AS CLEOPATRA, FRITZ LEIBER AS
JULIUS CAESAR, THURSTON HALL AS ANTONY AND ALBERT ROSCOE, HERSCHEL MAYALL, HENRI DE VRIES

THEDA BARA AS CIGARETTE
IN "UNDER TWO FLAGS"

THEDA BARA, ALBERT ROSCOE
IN "CAMILLE"

FOX PRODUCTIONS

THEDA BARA
IN "DU BARRY"

VALKYRIEN
(FOX)

EDWARD SUTHERLAND
(KEYSTONE)

JEWEL CARMEN, WILLIAM FARNUM

JEWEL CARMEN, WILLIAM FARNUM
SCENES FROM "A TALE OF TWO CITIES"

WILLIAM FARNUM, FLORENCE VIDOR

JANE GREY
(PARAMOUNT)

TULLY MARSHALL
(TRIANGLE)

KITTENS REICHERT, STUART HOLMES, MARY
MARTIN IN "THE SCARLET LETTER"

VALESKA SURATT

JUNE CAPRICE, FRANK MORGA
IN "A MODERN CINDERELLA"

IRENE FENWICK
(PARAMOUNT)

WALTER MILLER
(FOX)

WINIFRED KINGSTON, DUSTIN FARNUM
IN "THE SCARLET PIMPERNEL"

1917 Vampires were "box-office." Theda Bara, the most famous, was portraying such historical and fictional characters as Cleopatra, Camille, Du Barry and Cigarette. Fox also had Valeska Suratt and Virginia Pearson working their wiles. At Triangle Louise Glaum was building a reputation as a home-wrecker. The ludicrous costumes these shady ladies wore were considered alluring and seductive. With the loss of their most important stars, Triangle was exploiting Charles Ray, Dorothy Dalton, William Desmond, Enid Bennett, Belle Bennett, Bessie Love, Roy Stewart, and a former Ziegfeld beauty, Olive Thomas. World stars included Alice Brady, Carlyle Blackwell, Ethel Clayton, Robert Warwick and Kitty Gordon. Selznick's Select Company released films starring Clara Kimball Young, Norma and Constance Talmadge and Bert Lytell, a stage juvenile who co-starred with Hazel Dawn in his first film, "The Lone Wolf."

VIRGINIA LEE CORBIN, JIM TA
FRANCIS CARPENTER IN "JA
AND THE BEANSTALK"

ROBERT CONNESS
(WORLD)

JOSÉ COLLINS
(WORLD)

DOUGLAS MacLEAN
(WORLD)

BUDDY AND GERTRUDE MESSINGER, VIRGINIA CORBIN, VIOLET
RADCLIFFE IN "ALADDIN AND HIS WONDERFUL LAMP"

EVA TANGUAY
(SELZNICK)

RAYMOND HITC
(TRIANGL

FOX PHOTOPLAYS

RVING CUMMINGS, VIRGINIA PEARSON
IN "A ROYAL ROMANCE" (FOX)

JANE AND KATHERINE LEE
(FOX)

WILLIAM S. HART
IN "THE GUN FIGHTER" (TRIANGLE)

PAUL WILLIS
(PARAMOUNT)

JULIA FAYE
(KEYSTONE)

LOUISE GLAUM IN SOME OF HER "VAMPING" COSTUMES

LOUISE GLAUM, GEORGE WEBB
IN "IDOLATERS" (TRIANGLE)

GEORGE WEBB
(TRIANGLE)

LOUISE GLAUM
(TRIANGLE)

LIVINGSTON, BESSIE BARRISCALE
"WOODEN SHOES" (TRIANGLE)

COLLEEN MOORE, ROBERT HARRON
IN "THE BAD BOY" (TRIANGLE)

NICHOLAS DUNAEW
(UNIVERSAL)

BILLIE WEST
(KING-BEE)

RY WILSON
IANGLE)

ROY STEWART
(TRIANGLE)

CHARLES RAY IN SCENES FROM "THE CLODHOPPER"
WITH MARGERY WILSON (TRIANGLE)

POLLY MORAN
(KEYSTONE)

MARY THURMAN
(KEYSTONE)

ED KENNEDY
(KEYSTONE)

DOROTHY DALTON IN
"THE FLAME OF THE YUKON" (TRIANGLE)

NORMAN TREVOR, JULIA SANDERSON
IN "THE RUNAWAY" (MUTUAL)

ROY STEWART, JOHN GILBERT
IN "THE DEVIL DODGER" (TRIANGLE)

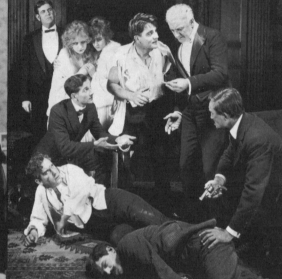

ALFRED VOSBURG, JOHN GILBERT, ENID BENNETT
IN "PRINCESS IN THE DARK"

OLIVE THOMAS IN
"BETTY TAKES A HAND"
TRIANGLE RELEASES

WILLIAM DESMOND, J. BARNEY SHERRY
IN "FLYING COLORS"

BELLE BENNETT

WILLIAM DESMOND

OLIVE THOMAS

DOROTHY DALTON

JOHN GILBERT

BESSIE LOVE

TRIANGLE PLAYERS

BELLE BENNETT, J. BARNEY SHERRY
IN "FUEL OF LIFE"

CHARLES GUNN, ALMA RUBENS
IN "THE FIREFLY OF TOUGH LUCK"

CLARA WILLIAMS, WILLIAM DESMOND
IN "PAWS OF THE BEAR"

BESSIE LOVE, KENNETH HARLAN
IN "CHEERFUL GIVERS"

TRIANGLE RELEASES

CLARA KIMBALL YOUNG, ALAN HALE
IN "THE PRICE SHE PAID"

CLARA KIMBALL YOUNG, NIGEL BARRIE, EDWARD M.
KIMBALL IN "THE MARIONETTES"
CLARA KIMBALL YOUNG PRODUCTIONS

EDWARD M. KIMBALL, CLARA KIMBALL YOUNG,
THOMAS HOLDING IN "MAGDA"

Joseph M. Schenck presents
Norma Talmadge in
"Panthea"

L. ROGER LYTTON, EARLE FOXE, NORMA TALMADGE
IN "PANTHEA" (SELECT)

EUGENE O'BRIEN, NORMA TALMADGE
IN "POPPY" (SELECT)

ROCKLIFFE FELLOWES, CLARA KIMBALL YOUNG, JOSEPH
KILGOUR IN "THE EASIEST WAY"

CONSTANCE TALMADGE, EARLE FOXE
IN "THE HONEYMOON" (SELECT)

GEORGE MacQUARRIE, ALICE BRADY
IN "BETSY ROSS" (WORLD)

CARLYLE BLACKWELL, MADGE EVANS
IN "THE BURGLAR" (WORLD)

Herbert Brenon
presents
Florence Reed
in
"The Eternal Sin"

RICHARD BARTHELMESS, FORENCE REED, WILLIAM SHAY
IN "THE ETERNAL SIN" (SELECT)

MADGE EVANS, HENRY HULL
IN "THE VOLUNTEER" (WORLD)

MONTAGU LOVE, JULIA DEAN IN
"RASPUTIN, THE BLACK MONK" (WORLD)

147

ALICE JOYCE
(VITAGRAPH)

ROBERT HARRON
(GOLDWYN)

BLANCHE SWEET
(PARAMOUNT)

ETHEL CLAYTON
(WORLD)

JULIAN ELTINGE
(PARAMOUNT)

RUTH STONEHO
(UNIVERSAL

MAXINE ELLIOTT, HENRY CLIVE
IN "THE FIGHTING ODDS"

MABEL JULIENE SCOTT, MITCHELL LEWIS, EDWARD ROSEMAN
IN "THE BARRIER"

RUBYE DE REMER, TOM POWERS
IN "THE AUCTION BLOCK"

JOHN CUMBERLAND, KATHRYN ADAMS, MADGE
KENNEDY IN "BABY MINE"

GOLDWYN STARS
MAXINE ELLIOTT, MAE MARSH, MADGE KENNEDY, JANE COWL

TOM MOORE, MAE MARSH, GEORGE FAWCET
IN "THE CINDERELLA MAN"

MAE MARSH
IN "POLLY OF THE CIRCUS"

MADGE KENNEDY
IN "NEARLY MARRIED"

JANE COWL
IN "THE SPREADING DAWN"

MARIE DRESSLER
IN "THE SCRUBLADY"

GOLDWYN RELEASES

MAXINE ELLIOTT   TOM MOORE   MADGE KENNEDY   JANE COWL   VERNON STEELE   MARY GARDEN

GOLDWYN PLAYERS

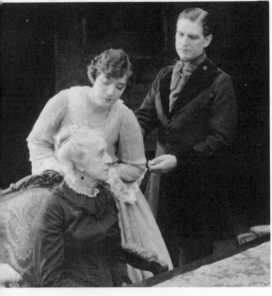

MRS. EDITH McALPIN, JANE COWL, ORME CALDARA
IN "THE SPREADING DAWN"

1917 Samuel Goldfish, who later changed his name legally to Goldwyn, left the Lasky Company. With Edgar Selwyn, former actor and an established theatrical producer, and Margaret Mayo, a playwright, he formed the Goldwyn Pictures Corp. With much fanfare, he announced the signing of film favorites Mae Marsh and Mabel Normand, stage stars Maxine Elliott, Jane Cowl and Madge Kennedy, and from opera, Mary Garden. They also signed "eminent authors" and exploited them with the idea of creating a demand for authors' films. These included Rex Beach, Rupert Hughes, Mary Roberts Rinehart, Sir Gilbert Parker and Elinor Glyn. This proved that the stars, and not the authors, were profit providers. On September 9, they released their first picture, "Polly of The Circus," from Margaret Mayo's famous play, starring Mae Marsh.

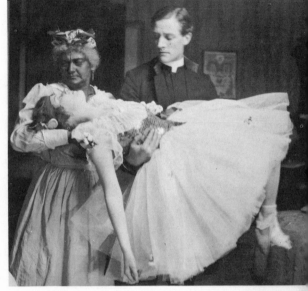

LUCILLE LAVERNE, MAE MARSH, VERNON STEELE
IN "POLLY OF THE CIRCUS"

MARY GARDEN
IN "THAIS"

-AT ALL LEADING THEATRES THROUGHOUT THE WORLD-

Jane Cowl. Madge Kennedy. Mary Garden. Maxine Elliott. Mabel Normand. Mae Marsh.

APPEARING EXCLUSIVELY IN

Goldwyn Pictures

RUBYE DE REMER
IN "THE AUCTION BLOCK"

HAMILTON REVELLE, MARY GARDEN
IN "THAIS"

MARY GARDEN IN "THAIS"

HAMILTON REVELLE, MARY GARDEN
IN "THAIS"

GOLDWYN RELEASES

PEARL WHITE, EARLE FOXE
IN "THE FATAL RING"

PEARL WHITE
(PATHÉ)

PEARL WHITE, WARNER OLAND
IN "THE FATAL RING"

HELEN HOLMES IN "THE LOST EXPRESS"
(SIGNAL)

MARIE WALCAMP, LARRY PEYTON IN
"THE RED ACE" (UNIVERSAL)

CREIGHTON HALE, MOLLIE KING IN
"THE SEVEN PEARLS" (PATHÉ)

1917 Serials were still money makers, but with the passing of the nickelodeon era and the dominance now of the neighboring theatre, the great serial days were over. "Patria," starring Irene Castle, was an outstanding serial of the year, and so was the ever popular Pearl White's "The Fatal Ring." Others included "The Purple Mask" with Grace Cunard and Francis Ford, "The Seven Pearls" with Mollie King, "Who Is 'Number One'?" with Kathleen Clifford, "The Red Ace" with Marie Walcamp, "The Neglected Wife" with Ruth Roland, "The Hidden Hand" with Doris Kenyon, "The Lost Express" with Helen Holmes, "The Fighting Trail" with William Duncan and Carol Holloway, "The Mystery Ship" with Ben Wilson and Neva Gerber, and many others. McClure Pictures, an independent company, produced "Seven Deadly Sins," a series of seven five-reel films under the titles "Envy," "Pride," "Greed," "Sloth," "Wrath," "Passion" and "The Seventh Sin." Shirley Mason and George Le Guere appeared in all seven while Ann Murdock, Holbrook Blinn, Nance O'Neil, H. B. Warner and Charlotte Walker appeared in one of the features.

WARNER OLAND, IRENE CASTLE IN
"PATRIA" Above: IRENE CASTLE

SHIRLEY MASON, NANCE O'NEIL IN "GREED"
Above: GEORGE LE GUERE IN "PRIDE"

SHIRLEY MASON, CLIFFORD BRUCE
IN "PASSION" Above: GEORGE
LE GUERE, ANN MURDOCK IN "ENVY"

KATHLEEN CLIFFORD, CULLEN LAND
"WHO IS 'NUMBER ONE'?" (PARAMO
Above: KATHLEEN CLIFFORD

SCENES FROM "SEVEN DEADLY SINS" IN WHI

WILLIAM S. HART

JULIAN ELTINGE, THEODORE ROBERTS, WILLIAM S. HART, DOUGLAS FAIRBANKS,
MARY PICKFORD IN "WAR RELIEF" (PROPAGANDA PICTURE)

CLARA KIMBALL YOUNG IN SAN FRANCISCO IN THE
INTEREST OF NAVY RECRUITING

EDWARD GRIFFITH DIRECTS PAUL KELLY IN "FIT TO
FIGHT" A GOVERNMENT PROPAGANDA FILM

LT. TOM FORMAN

MARIE DRESSLER IN A
WAR-TIME COMEDY

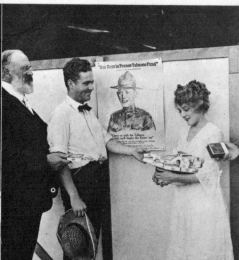

MARY PICKFORD PRESENTING WALLACE REID OF THE
LASKY HOME GUARD WITH THE REGIMENT'S COLORS

THEODORE ROBERTS, MARSHALL NEILAN, MARY
PICKFORD, NORMAN KERRY

SGT. BERT LYTELL   CAPT. RICHARD TRAVERS

CAPT. ROBERT WARWICK   MARY PICKFORD HONORARY COLONEL

JULIA ARTHUR AS ITALY IN PROLOGUE OF "THE COMMON CAUSE" (VITAGRAPH)

1918 "Mothers of France," a French propaganda film starring Sarah Bernhardt, had been circulating in the United States in 1917 when we entered World War I, but it was nearly a year later before our entry into the war was reflected in our films. The country became flooded with such propaganda films as "To Hell With The Kaiser," "The Kaiser's Finish," "Lafayette, We Come," "The Woman The Germans Shot" (later changed to "The Cavell Case"), "The Beast of Berlin," and a parody of it called "The Geezer of Berlin." Germany was our enemy. Margarita Fischer dropped the "c" from her name, Alfred Vosburgh changed his to Alfred Whitman, and Norman Kaiser became Norman Kerry. The U. S. Government also made propaganda pictures. The Treasury Department asked the stars to help sell Liberty Loans. Such major screen personalities as Pickford, Hart and Fairbanks became active salesmen for Uncle Sam. Clara Kimball Young and Pearl White gave their time for recruiting purposes. Film actors who had "joined up" included Robert Warwick, Bert Lytell, Tom Forman, Richard Travers, S. Rankin Drew, Kenneth Harlan, Norman Kerry, Earle Metcalf, Rex Ingram and others. D. W. Griffith went abroad during the war and in France filmed "Hearts of the World," a tale of a village behind the lines. While the industry was contributing patriotism and propaganda, it was also providing the populace with entertainment. Metro proudly announced it had signed "The Great Nazimova." Edith Storey, the Dolly Sisters, and Bert Lytell became Metro stars.

LAWRENCE GRANT AS THE KAISER IN "TO HELL WITH THE KAISER" (METRO)

E. K. LINCOLN, DOLORES CASSINELLI IN "LAFAYETTE, WE COME" (INDEPENDENT)

ROBERT HARRON (Right)   BEN ALEXANDER, LILLIAN GISH   LILLIAN GISH, NOEL COWARD   DOROTHY AND LILLIAN GISH, ROBERT HARRON

SCENES FROM D. W. GRIFFITH'S "HEARTS OF THE WORLD"

ALICE JOYCE IN
"A WOMAN BETWEEN FRIENDS"
(VITAGRAPH)

EDDIE POLO IN
"THE LURE OF THE CIRCUS"
(UNIVERSAL)

NAZIMOVA IN
"EYE FOR EYE"
(METRO)

CARLYLE BLACKWELL IN
"HIS ROYAL HIGHNESS"
(WORLD)

PAULINE FREDERICK I
"LA TOSCA"
(PARAMOUNT)

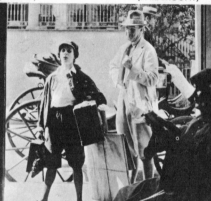

LUCILLE LEE STEWART, WILFRED LYTELL, JOHN DALY MURPHY,
HUNTLEY GORDON, ETHEL BARRYMORE IN
"OUR MRS. McCHESNEY" (METRO)

THE DOLLY SISTERS (YANCSI AND ROZSIKA)
IN "THE MILLION DOLLAR DOLLIES"
(METRO)

NAZIMOVA IN "REVELATION"
(METRO)

BERT LYTELL, ANNA Q. NILSSON
IN "THE TRAIL TO YESTERDAY" (METRO)

HAROLD LOCKWOOD, MARTHA MANSFIELD, CORNISH BECK
IN "BROADWAY BILL" (METRO)

FRANCIS X. BUSHMAN, BEVERLY BAYNE
IN "SOCIAL QUICKSANDS" (METRO)

RUDOLPH
CAMERON
(VITAGRAPH)

VIOLET
HEMING
(PARAMOUNT)

RAYMOND
HATTON
(PARAMOUNT)

BILLIE RHODES
(MUTUAL)

RALPH GRAVES
(TOURNEUR)

MARGUERITE
CLAYTON
(ARTCRAFT)

ALFRED
HICKMAN
(BRENON)

CATHERINE
CALVERT
(KEENEY)

HAROL
LOCKV
(METRO)

KATHLYN WILLIAMS IN "THE HIGHWAY OF HOPE" (PARAMOUNT)

JOHN BARRYMORE IN "HERE COMES THE BRIDE" (PARAMOUNT)

GEORGE WALSH IN "I'LL SAY SO" (FOX)

WALLACE REID IN "BELIEVE ME, XANTIPPE" (PARAMOUNT)

CLARA KIMBALL YOUNG IN "THE SAVAGE WOMAN" (SELECT)

RAYMOND McKEE, JOSEPH BURKE IN "KIDNAPPED" (EDISON)

MARY MILES MINTER, ALAN FORREST IN "ROSEMARY CLIMBS THE HEIGHTS" (MUTUAL)

COLLEEN MOORE, THOMAS JEFFERSON, FRANK HAYES IN "A HOOSIER ROMANCE" (SELIG)

1918 Select Pictures Corporation, which had become the brand name of Selznick productions when Zukor became a partner, was releasing the films of Clara Kimball Young, Alice Brady, and Norma and Constance Talmadge, who were becoming potent box-office stars. World Film Company had lost prestige since Selznick's withdrawal. Mutual features starred Mary Miles Minter, William Russell, Margarita Fisher, Olive Tell and Ann Murdock. But Mutual's days were numbered. Essanay and Selig too were floundering. Edison Company quit. Its last film was "The Unbeliever," a six-part war drama starring Marguerite Courtot and Raymond McKee. The old order was passing. Both Vitagraph and Pathé were putting up a fight to survive. Vitagraph released several serials. Their features starred Alice Joyce, Corinne Griffith, Earle Williams, Gladys Leslie and Bessie Love. Pearl White was still serial queen of the Pathé lot. Fannie Ward, Irene Castle and Frank Keenan emoted for their feature films, while Toto, a clown from the Hippodrome extravaganza, was making comedies for them.

HALE HAMILTON, MAY ALLISON IN "THE WINNING OF BEATRICE" (METRO)

LAWRENCE D'ORSAY, TAYLOR HOLMES IN "RUGGLES OF RED GAP" (ESSANAY)

...Y HAM ...GRAPH)

FLORENCE DESHON (VITAGRAPH)

HALE HAMILTON (METRO)

SEENA OWEN (TRIANGLE)

TOM MIX (FOX)

DOROTHY GISH (PARAMOUNT)

LEW CODY (PARAMOUNT)

LILLIAN GISH (ARTCRAFT)

GEORGE FAWCETT (TRIANGLE)

RUBY LAFAYETTE IN
"MY MOTHER" (UNIVERSAL)

ROBERT WARWICK, ANN LITTLE
IN "THE SILENT MASTER" (SELECT)

NORMA TALMADGE IN
"THE FORBIDDEN CITY" (SELECT)

CHARLES RAY IN
"THE LAW OF THE NORTH" (PARA

EARLE WILLIAMS, BOBBY CONNELLY
IN "THE SEAL OF SILENCE" (VITAGRAPH)

GUY EMPEY IN
"OVER THE TOP" (VITAGRAPH)

J. FRANK GLENDON, GLADYS LESLIE IN
"THE WOOING OF PRINCESS PAT" (VITAGRAPH)

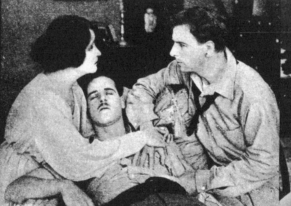

LILLIAN HALL, GEORGE KELSON, DOROTHY BERNARD, FLORENCE
FLIMM, KATE LESTER, ISABEL LAMON IN "LITTLE WOMEN"
(WORLD)

CLARA KIMBALL YOUNG, JACK HOLT, MILTON SILLS
IN "THE CLAW" (SELECT)

HARRISON FORD, CONSTANCE TALMADGE IN
"A PAIR OF SILK STOCKINGS" (SELECT)

CARLYLE BLACKWELL, EVELYN GREELEY
IN "THE ROAD TO FRANCE" (WORLD)

KITTY GORDON, FRANK MAYO
IN "THE INTERLOPER" (WORLD)

EUGENE O'BRIEN, NORMA TALMADGE
IN "THE SAFETY CURTAIN" (SELECT)

ALICE BRADY, ELLIOTT DEX
IN "WOMAN AND WIFE" (SE

BEBE DANIELS
(PATHÉ)

MILDRED HARRIS, LEW CODY
IN "FOR HUSBANDS ONLY" (JEWEL)

DORALDINA, WARNER OLAND
IN "THE NAULAHKA" (PATHÉ)

ANTONIO MORENO IN
"THE IRON TEST" (VITAGRAPH)

1918 Many independent companies were formed, but most of them folded fast. Paralta Plays, Inc., during their short existence, released starring vehicles of J. Warren Kerrigan, Bessie Barriscale, Henry B. Walthall and Louise Glaum. Crest Pictures signed Lillian Walker. Edgar Rice Burroughs' famous Tarzan stories first appeared on the screen when National Film Corporation released "Tarzan of The Apes," and a sequel, "The Romance of Tarzan." Catherine Calvert starred in a "Frank A. Keeney Picture" and George Larkin appeared in "Zongar," a Bernarr MacFadden Physical Culture Play. Jewel Productions made "Price of A Good Time," "Borrowed Clothes" and "For Husbands Only" under Lois Weber's supervision. They featured Mildred Harris, but after her marriage to Chaplin she was billed as "Mrs. Charles Chaplin."

IRENE CASTLE, RALPH KELLARD IN
"THE HILLCREST MYSTERY" (PATHÉ)

PEARL WHITE
IN "HOUSE OF HATE" (PATHÉ)

GABY DESLYS
IN "INFATUATION" (PATHÉ)

LYDIA YEAMANS TITUS, CARMEL MYERS, RUDOLPH
VALENTINO IN "ALL NIGHT" (UNIVERSAL)

FRANK KEENAN, LOIS WILSON, ED COXEN, IDA LEWIS
IN "THE BELLS" (PATHÉ)

CORINNE GRIFFITH, BETTY BLYTHE
IN "MISS AMBITION" (VITAGRAPH)

ALICE JOYCE, MAURICE COSTELLO
IN "CAP'N ABE'S NIECE"

WILLIAM STOWELL, DOROTHY PHILLIPS
IN "THE HEART OF HUMANITY" (UNIVERSAL)

CARMEL MYERS, EDWIN AUGUST IN
"CITY OF TEARS" (UNIVERSAL)

IRENE CASTLE
(PATHÉ)

IRVING CUMMINGS
(WORLD)

ANNA Q. NILSSON
(GOLDWYN)

LILA LEE
(PARAMOUNT)

BRYANT WASHBURN
(PARAMOUNT)

KATHLYN WILLIA
(PARAMOUNT)

EDNA PURVIANCE, CHARLES AND SYDNEY CHAPLIN
IN "SHOULDER ARMS" (MUTUAL)

CHARLES CHAPLIN
IN "A DOG'S LIFE" (MUTUAL)

CHARLES CHAPLIN, SYDNEY CHAPLIN (Right)
IN "SHOULDER ARMS" (MUTUAL)

CHARLES CHAPLIN
IN "SHOULDER ARMS" (MUTUAL)

CHARLES CHAPLIN
IN "PAY DAY" (MUTUAL)

GEORGE OVEY
(CUB)

BETTY COMPSON
(CHRISTIE)

BOBBY VERNON
(CHRISTIE)

MILDRED HARRIS
(JEWEL)

NEAL BURNS
(CHRISTIE)

LINA CA
(PARAM

BETTY COMPSON IN
"BETTY MAKES UP" (CHRISTIE)

BILLIE RHODES, CULLEN LANDIS IN
"BEWARE OF BLONDES" (MUTUAL)

AGNES AYRES
(VITAGRAPH)

CHARLES RAY
(PARAMOUNT)

JUNE CAPRICE
(FOX)

JACK HOLT
(PARAMOUNT)

JUNE ELVIDGE
(WORLD)

EUGENE O'BRIEN
(SELECT)

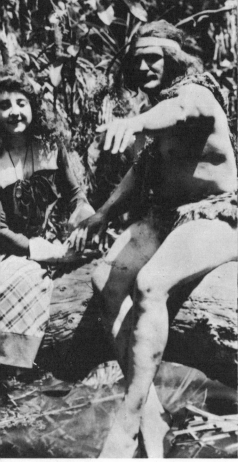

ENID MARKEY, ELMO LINCOLN IN
"ROMANCE OF TARZAN" (NATIONAL)

ENID MARKEY, ELMO LINCOLN (Also Above
WITH TRUE BOARDMAN, Left) IN
"TARZAN OF THE APES" (NATIONAL)

ELMO LINCOLN
AS TARZAN

TO,
THÉ)

HEDDA NOVA
(VITAGRAPH)

FRANCIS McDONALD
(TRIANGLE)

EDITH ROBERTS
(UNIVERSAL)

GEORGE CHESEBRO
(TRIANGLE)

MIRIAM COOPER
(FOX)

CULLEN LANDIS
(MUTUAL)

ISABEL RAE
(UNIVERSAL)

RUPERT JULIAN
(UNIVERSAL)

LOIS WILSON, HENRY B. WALTHALL IN
"HIS ROBE OF HONOR" (PARALTA)

DAVID POWELL, EUGENE O'BRIEN, CATHERINE CALVERT
IN "A ROMANCE OF THE UNDERWORLD" (KEENEY)

LOIS WILSON, J. WARREN KERRIGAN, ED COXEN
IN "A MAN'S MAN" (PARALTA)

159

DOROTHY BERNARD, WILLIAM FARNUM, JEWEL CARMEN
Above: WILLIAM FARNUM, GEORGE MOSS
SCENES FROM "LES MISERABLES"

WILLIAM FARNUM
IN "LES MISERABLES"

HUGH THOMPSON, ANNETTE KELLERMANN, BETH
Above: WALTER LONG, ANNETTE KELLERMA
SCENES FROM "QUEEN OF THE SEA"

1918 First National made an auspicious beginning with Chaplin's comedies, "A Dog's Life," "Shoulder Arms" and "Pay Day." Universal was making serials with Marie Walcamp and Eddie Polo, and new stars on their payroll included Priscilla Dean, Monroe Salisbury and Edith Roberts. On the Triangle lot, Gloria Swanson was playing leads in dramatic pictures. Fox films were starring Theda Bara, William Farnum, June Caprice, George Walsh, Virginia Pearson and Tom Mix. Goldwyn's major stars continued to be Mae Marsh, Mabel Normand, and Madge Kennedy. Mary Garden made one more picture, but Jane Cowl and Maxine Elliott dropped out. Goldwyn signed Geraldine Farrar, Will Rogers, and starred Tom Moore. With Moore in "Thirty A Week," Tallulah Bankhead, a young Southern society belle, made her first professional appearance anywhere as leading lady. The first film Will Rogers ever appeared in was as the star of "Laughing Bill Hyde."

JUNE CAPRICE
IN "THE HEART OF ROMANCE"

TOM MIX
IN "WESTERN BLOOD"

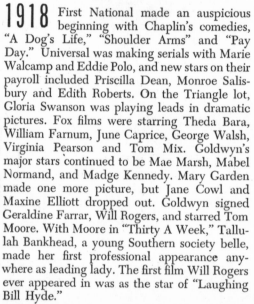

ALBERT ROSCOE, THEDA BARA
IN "SALOME"

THEDA BARA (Also Above)
IN "SALOME"
FOX PRODUCTIONS

THEDA BARA
IN "SALOME"

TOM MOORE, MADGE KENNEDY
IN "THE DANGER GAME"

WILL ROGERS IN
"LAUGHING BILL HYDE"

ANNA LEHR, WILL ROGERS
IN "LAUGHING BILL HYDE"

GERALDINE FARRAR, HASSARD SHORT
IN "THE TURN OF THE WHEEL"

BILLIE RHODES, "SMILING BILL" PARSONS
IN "DAD'S KNOCKOUT"

ANDERS RANDOLPH, MARY GARDEN
IN "THE SPLENDID SINNER"

MABEL NORMAND, ROD LA ROCQUE IN "THE
VENUS MODEL" Above: MABEL NORMAND,
TOM MOORE IN "THE FLOOR BELOW"

TALLULAH BANKHEAD, TOM MOORE
IN "THIRTY A WEEK"
GOLDWYN RELEASES

CHESTER MORRIS, MAE MARSH IN "THE BELOVED
TRAITOR" Above: WARNER BAXTER,
MAE MARSH IN "ALL WOMAN"

WILLIAM DESMOND, WILLIAM FRANEY
IN "AN HONEST MAN"

WILLIAM DESMOND
IN "THE SUDDEN GENTLEMAN"
TRIANGLE FEATURES

JACK RICHARDSON, GLORIA SWANSON
IN "YOU CAN'T BELIEVE EVERYTHING"

DAVID POWELL, OLIVE TELL, WARBURTON GAMBLE
IN "THE UNFORESEEN" (METRO)

HARRY MESTAYER, PAULINE STARKE
IN "THE ATOM" (TRIANGLE)

JOHN LINCE, WALLACE McDONALD, ALMA RUBENS
IN "MADAME SPHINX" (TRIANGLE)

MABEL NORMAND
IN "MICKEY"

TEXAS GUINAN, FRANCIS McDONALD
IN "THE GUN WOMAN" (TRIANGLE)

GLORIA SWANSON, WILLIAM DESMOND
IN "SOCIETY FOR SALE" (TRIANGLE)

JACK MULHALL, MABEL NORMAND, MRS. WARD, ALBERT HACKETT
IN "MICKEY" (MABEL NORMAND FEATURE FILM CO.)

BELLE BENNETT IN
"A SOUL IN TRUST" (TRIANGLE)

162

ORMI HAWLEY, ENRICO CARUSO
IN "THE SPLENDID ROMANCE"

ENRICO CARUSO

(PARAMOUNT-ARTCRAFT)

ENRICO CARUSO, CAROLINA WHITE
IN "MY COUSIN"

JULIAN ELTINGE
IN "OVER THE RHINE" (INDEPENDENT)

MARGUERITE CLAYTON, RUSSELL BASSETT,
RICHARD BARTHELMESS, GEORGE M. COHAN IN
"HIT THE TRAIL HOLIDAY" (ARTCRAFT)

W. H. FORESTELLE, FRANK LOSEE, JULES RAUCOURT,
PAULINE FREDERICK IN "LA TOSCA" (PARAMOUNT)

1918 Adolph Zukor was still trying his old "famous player" idea when he signed Enrico Caruso of opera fame. He starred him in two films, "My Cousin" and "The Splendid Romance." His first film was a financial flop so the second stayed on the shelf. Paramount acquired Ethel Clayton and Bryant Washburn and elevated Wallace Reid to stardom. Zukor received a bitter blow toward the year's end when Mary Pickford signed to make three pictures for First National for $1,050,000. As an added inducement for Mary to leave Artcraft, they gave her mother a $50,000 bonus and signed her brother Jack for a series of pictures at $50,000 each.

SYLVIA BREMMER, ROBERT GORDON
IN "MISSING" (PARAMOUNT)

JOHN BARRYMORE
IN "ON THE QUIET" (PARAMOUNT)

ZASU PITTS

EDITH DAY, RAMSEY WALLACE, LILLIAN WALKER
IN "THE GRAIN OF DUST" (CREST)

BRYANT WASHBURN, MONTE BLUE IN
"TILL I COME BACK TO YOU" (ARTCRAFT)

GEORGE LARKIN
IN "ZONGAR"
(MACFADDEN) **163**

FRANK CAMPEAU, DOUGLAS FAIRBANKS, PAULINE CURLEY
IN "BOUND IN MOROCCO" (ARTCRAFT)

KATHERINE MacDONALD, DOUGLAS FAIRBANKS
IN "HEADIN' SOUTH" (ARTCRAFT)

LOUISE HUFF
(PARAMOUNT)

SESSUE HAYAKAWA
(PARAMOUNT)

CHARLES ELDRIDGE, CONSTANCE AND FAIRE BINNEY,
WARNER RICHMOND IN "SPORTING LIFE" (PARAMOUNT-ARTCRAFT)

RUTH ROLAND
(PATHÉ)

SYDNEY CHAPLIN
(MUTUAL)

ROBERT GORDON, JACK PICKFORD
IN "HUCK AND TOM" (PARAMOUNT)

THOMAS MEIGHAN, MARY PICKFORD
IN "M'LISS" (ARTCRAFT)

JACK PICKFORD IN
"HIS MAJESTY BUNKER BEAN"

CONWAY TEARLE, MARY PICKFORD
IN "STELLA MARIS" (ARTCRAFT)

ELLA HALL, FRED STONE IN
"UNDER THE TOP" (PARAMOUNT-ARTCRAFT)

ROBIN MacDOUGALL, GERTRUDE McCOY, TULA BELLE (Center)
IN "THE BLUE BIRD" (ARTCRAFT)

IOLET AND CLAIRE
MERSEREAU
(UNIVERSAL)

MARGUERITE CLARK
(PARAMOUNT)

LON CHANEY, KATHERINE MacDONALD, WILLIAM S. HART
IN "RIDDLE GAWNE" (PARAMOUNT-ARTCRAFT)

BEVERLY BAYNE
(METRO)

TALLULAH BANKHEAD
(GOLDWYN)

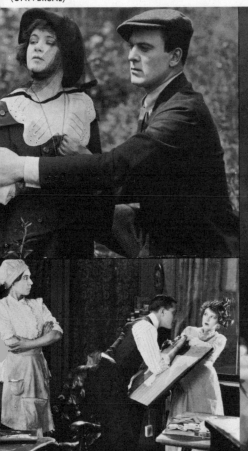

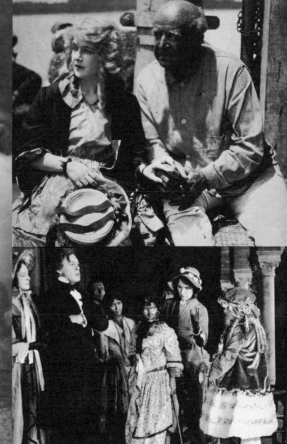

RICHARD BARTHELMESS, MARGUERITE CLARK IN
I MAN, POOR MAN" (PARAMOUNT) Above: MARGUERITE
LARK, THOMAS MEIGHAN IN "OUT OF A CLEAR SKY"

VIVIAN MARTIN
(PARAMOUNT)

MARGUERITE CLARK IN DUAL ROLE OF TOPSY AND
LITTLE EVA, And Above WITH FRANK LOSEE
IN "UNCLE TOM'S CABIN" (PARAMOUNT)

THOMAS SANTSCHI (GOLDWYN)   EMILY STEVENS (METRO)   ALBERT ROSCOE (FOX)   DOROTHY GREEN (FOX)   WALLACE MacDONALD (VITAGRAPH)   ENID MARKEY (NATIONAL)   MONTE BLUE (PARAMOUNT)   GLADYS BROCKWELL (FOX)   JOHN B... (WO...

ETHEL CLAYTON
(PARAMOUNT)

OLLIE KIRKBY

NIGEL BARRIE

NORMA TALMADGE

HARRISON FORD, LILA LEE IN
"SUCH A LITTLE PIRATE" (PARAMOUNT)

BUSTER KEATON, ROSCOE ARBUCKLE, AL ST. JOHN (PARAMOUNT)
Above: SCENES FROM KEYSTONE COMEDIES

MARIE WALCAMP (UNIVERSAL)   ALAN FORREST (MUTUAL)   JEANNE EAGELS (PATHÉ)   CRAWFORD KENT (PARAMOUNT)   LOIS WILSON (PARALTA)   SHELDON LEWIS (PATHÉ)   KITTY GORDON (WORLD)   ED COXEN (PATHÉ)   ANITA K... (PARAMOU...

N NESBIT
OX)

LEWIS STONE
(WORLD)

WILLETTE KERSHAW
(ARTCRAFT)

ALLEN HOLLUBAR
(UNIVERSAL)

EDNA GOODRICH
(MUTUAL)

FRANK MAYO
(WORLD)

OLIVE TELL
(METRO)

WARNER OLAND
(PATHÉ)

DOROTHY BERNARD
(FOX)

ARAGARET THOMPSON

HAROLD LOCKWOOD

DOROTHY DALTON

BILLIE BURKE
(PARAMOUNT)

NDHAM STANDING, ELSIE FERGUSON IN "ROSE
OF THE WORLD" Above: ELSIE FERGUSON,
ENE O'BRIEN IN "UNDER THE GREENWOOD TREE"

ANN LITTLE, WALLACE REID IN "LESS THAN KIN"
Above: WALLACE REID IN "BELIEVE ME, XANTIPPE"
PARAMOUNT FEATURES

WALLACE REID
(PARAMOUNT)

DE GARDE
GRAPH)

PEDRO deCORDOBA
(PARAMOUNT)

FLORENCE VIDOR
(PARAMOUNT)

SIDNEY DREW
(METRO)

MARJORIE RAMBEAU
(MUTUAL)

MAHLON HAMILTON
(METRO)

VIRGINIA KIRTLEY
(MUTUAL)

BEN ALEXANDER
(GRIFFITH)

GAIL KANE
(MUTUAL)

167

THOMAS MEIGHAN, GLORIA SWANSON
(Also Above)

GLORIA SWANSON, BEBE DANIELS, THOMAS MEIGHAN, SAM SEARLE
Above: JULIA FAYE, GLORIA SWANSON, EDNA MAE COOPER
SCENES FROM "MALE AND FEMALE"

GLORIA SWANSON, THOMAS MEIGHA
Above: THOMAS MEIGHAN, LILA LEE

GLORIA SWANSON, TOM FORMAN, ELLIOTT DEXTER
IN "FOR BETTER, FOR WORSE"

LON CHANEY, SEENA OWEN, JACK HOLT
IN "VICTORY"

JACK HOLT, KATHERINE MacDONALD
IN "THE WOMAN THOU GAVEST ME"

GLORIA SWANSON, JULIA FAYE, LEW CODY

LEW CODY, SYLVIA ASHTON, GLORIA SWANSON, ELLIOTT DEXTER
SCENES FROM "DON'T CHANGE YOUR HUSBAND"

ELLIOTT DEXTER, GLORIA SWANSON

PARAMOUNT-ARTCRAFT PRODUCTIONS

RUBY LAFAYETTE, LON CHANEY
: BETTY COMPSON, JOSEPH DOWLING,
THOMAS MEIGHAN

LON CHANEY, FRANKIE LEE, JOSEPH DOWLING, BETTY COMPSON, THOMAS MEIGHAN,
J. M. DUMONT, LUCILLE HUTTON, W. LAWSON BUTT
Above: LON CHANEY, J. M. DUMONT, BETTY COMPSON
SCENES FROM "THE MIRACLE MAN"

LON CHANEY, JOSEPH DOWLING
Above: J. M. DUMONT, BETTY COMPSON,
JOSEPH DOWLING, LON CHANEY

LINA CAVALIERI, LUCIEN MURATORE
IN "THE HOUSE OF GRANADA"

1919 The most influential man in films was still Adolph Zukor. To his enterprises he added a new concern, Realart Pictures Corp. He also combined with William Randolph Hearst, newspaper tycoon, who had organized Cosmopolitan Productions to produce Marion Davies pictures. Realart signed Mary Miles Minter and Alice Brady and elevated Constance Binney and later Bebe Daniels to stardom. The Triangle Film Co. and Mutual Film Corp. ceased to exist, and so did the old Thanhouser Company which had been releasing through Pathé. The Selznick name was saved from obscurity when Lewis J. Selznick's son Myron formed a company, Selznick Pictures. He signed Olive Thomas, Eugene O'Brien, Elaine Hammerstein and Owen Moore, but he was under age and his mother had to sign all the contracts he made.

DOUGLAS McLEAN, MARY PICKFORD
IN "CAPTAIN KIDD JUNIOR"

ORMAN KERRY, DOROTHY GREEN, MARION DAVIES
IN "THE DARK STAR"

BILLIE BURKE, JAMES CRANE, FRANK MILLS
IN "THE MISLEADING WIDOW"

WALTER HIERS, BRYANT WASHBURN, LOIS WILSON
IN "IT PAYS TO ADVERTISE"

PARAMOUNT-ARTCRAFT PRODUCTIONS

WITH HARRISON FORD
IN "THE THIRD KISS"

WITH NILES WELCH IN
"JANE GOES A-WOOING"

WITH RALPH GRAVES IN
"THE HOME TOWN GIRL"

WITH TOM FORMAN
IN "LOUISIANA"

VIVIAN MARTIN FEATURES

WITH ANN LITTLE, THEODORE ROBERTS
IN "THE ROARING ROAD"

WITH SYLVIA ASHTON AND HARRISON FORD
IN "THE LOTTERY MAN"
WALLACE REID FEATURES

IN "THE ROARING ROAD"

EUGENE O'BRIEN, MARGUERITE CLARK
IN "COME OUT OF THE KITCHEN"

MARGUERITE CLARK, NIGEL BARRIE, BROWNIE VERNON
IN "WIDOW BY PROXY"

MARGUERITE CLARK, CHARLES MEREDITH
IN "LUCK IN PAWN"

JEROME PATRICK, RICHARD BARTHELMESS,
MARGUERITE CLARK IN "THREE MEN AND A GIRL"

WITH JULES RAUCOURT IN "PRUNELLA"
MARGUERITE CLARK FEATURES

WITH JULES RAUCOURT IN "PRUNELLA"

WITH MONTE BLUE
IN "IN MIZZOURA"

WITH ANN LITTLE
IN "TOLD IN THE HILLS"
ROBERT WARWICK FEATURES

WITH IRVING CUMMINGS
IN "SECRET SERVICE"

JOHN BARRYMORE
"TEST OF HONOR" (PARAMOUNT)

1919 When Gloria Swanson was appearing in Triangle dramas she attracted the attention of Cecil B. De Mille, so when Triangle folded he cast her in his production "For Better, For Worse." "Don't Change Your Husband" and "Male and Female" followed. It was the beginning of a prosperous association, and a few years later Miss Swanson was Paramount's most valuable star and was drawing a salary of $20,000 a week. "The Miracle Man," a George Loane Tucker production released by Paramount, started Lon Chaney, Thomas Meighan and Betty Compson on their road to stardom. The Paramount-Artcraft star system now included Marguerite Clark, Douglas Fairbanks, William S. Hart, Elsie Ferguson, Wallace Reid, Billie Burke, Vivian Martin, Ethel Clayton, Charles Ray, Dorothy Gish, Robert Warwick, Dorothy Dalton, Bryant Washburn, Lila Lee, Enid Bennett, and the comedy team of Douglas MacLean and Doris May. On the Fox lot William Farnum was the big money-maker while Tom Mix and George Walsh were gaining in popularity. Theda Bara was losing out and toward the end of the year she left Fox to appear on the stage in "The Blue Flame." Colleen Moore, who appeared in Selig, Christie and Triangle films, became Tom Mix's leading lady. Blanche Bates, famous Belasco stage star, made a film appearance in "The Border Legion" produced by an independent company.

ELSIE FERGUSON
IN "THE AVALANCHE" (ARTCRAFT)

LLOYD HUGHES, ENID BENNETT
IN "THE HAUNTED BEDROOM"

LILA LEE, TOM FORMAN
IN "THE HEART OF YOUTH"
PARAMOUNT FEATURES

RICHARD BARTHELMESS, DOROTHY GISH
IN "I'LL GET HIM YET"

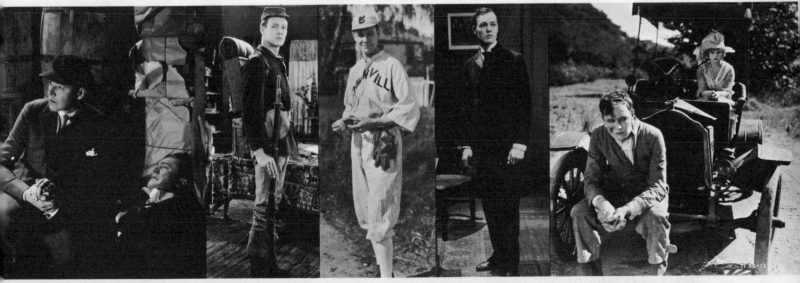

IN "CROOKED STRAIGHT"

IN "HAYFOOT, STRAWFOOT"

IN "THE BUSHER"

IN "THE SHERIFF'S SON"

CHARLES RAY FEATURES

WITH WANDA HAWLEY
IN "GREASED LIGHTNING"

DOUGLAS MacLEAN, DOROTHY DALTON
IN "THE HOME BREAKER" (PARAMOUNT)

ETHEL CLAYTON, ELLIOTT DEXTER
IN "MAGGIE PEPPER"

ERNEST TRUEX, LOUISE HUFF
IN "OH, YOU WOMEN"

NORMA TALMADGE
(FIRST NATIONAL)

RICHARD BARTHELMESS
(PARAMOUNT)

OLGA PETROVA
(PETROVA)

DOUGLAS MacLEAN
(PARAMOUNT)

ALMA RUBENS
(TRIANGLE)

PERCY MARMONT
(VITAGRAPH)

KATHERINE MacDONALD, ELLIOTT DEXTER, PAT MOORE
Above: ELLIOTT DEXTER, JACK HOLT
IN "THE SQUAW MAN"

DORIS MAY, DOUGLAS MacLEAN (Also Above)
IN "23½ HOURS LEAVE"
PARAMOUNT FEATURES

IRVING CUMMINGS, MONTE BLUE, THEODORE RO[...]
VIOLET HEMING, WANDA HAWLEY. Above: VIOLET H[...]
BEBE DANIELS, THEODORE ROBERTS IN "EVERYWO[...]

CAROL HALLOWAY
(VITAGRAPH)

HENRY HULL
(WORLD)

JEWEL CARMEN
(FOX)

KENNETH HARLAN
(SELECT)

HARRIET HAMMOND
(SENNETT)

HERBERT RAWLINSON
(GOLDWYN)

CLARA HORTON
(GOLDWYN)

GEORGE WALSH
(FOX)

ORMI HAW[...]
(PARAMOU[...]

AN KERRY IN
RS OF FORTUNE"
(PATHÉ)

MARGUERITE CLARK
IN "PRUNELLA"
(PARAMOUNT)

FRANK MAYO IN
"THE BRUTE BREAKER"
(PATHÉ)

BESSIE BARRISCALE IN
"A TRICK OF FATE"

TOM MOORE IN
"LORD AND LADY ALGY"
(GOLDWYN)

MABEL NORMAND
AS "SIS HOPKINS"
(GOLDWYN)

WILLIAM S. HART
IN "JOHN PETTICOATS"
(ARTCRAFT)

MARY MILES MINTER, PAUL KELLY
IN "ANNE OF GREEN GABLES" (REALART)

JAMES CRANE, ALICE BRADY
IN "A DARK LANTERN" (REALART)

BRADLEY BARKER, ANDERS RANDOLPH, GEORGE RENAVENT,
CONSTANCE BINNEY IN "ERSTWHILE SUSAN" (REALART)

ARJORIE DAW, DOUGLAS FAIRBANKS (Also Above)
I "THE KNICKERBOCKER BUCKAROO" (ARTCRAFT)

TOM MIX
(FOX)

DOUGLAS FAIRBANKS (Also Above)
IN "HIS MAJESTY, THE AMERICAN" (ARTCRAFT)

HIPMAN
GRAPH)

JULES RAUCOURT
(PARAMOUNT)

ZENA KEEFE
(SELZNICK)

ROCKCLIFEE FELLOWES
(SELECT)

MABEL JULIENNE
SCOTT
(BEACH)

GEORGE B. SEITZ
(ASTRA)

KATHLEEN CLIFFORD
(PARAMOUNT)

EARL RODNEY
(PARAMOUNT)

HELENE CHADWICK
(GOLDWYN)

GEORGE WALSH
(FOX)

WILLIAM FARNUM IN
"THE LONE STAR RANGER"

MIRIAM COOPER
IN "EVANGELINE"

THEDA BARA
IN "KATHLEEN MAVOURNEN"

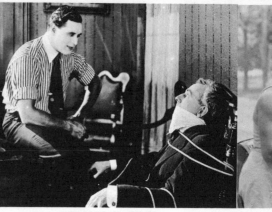

GEORGE WALSH IN
"PUTTING ONE OVER"

FOX PRODUCTIONS

GEORGE WALSH, JANE McALPINE
IN "THE WINNING STROKE"

COLLEEN MOORE, TOM MIX IN
"THE WILDERNESS TRAIL" (FOX)

1919 D. W. Griffith's productions included "The Girl Who Stayed At Home," "Scarlet Days," "Trueheart Susie" and one of his most famous, "Broken Blossoms." In this Lillian Gish had great success, and it put Richard Barthelmess on the road to fame and fortune. Clarine Seymour, another Griffith discovery, who scored a great success in "The Girl Who Stayed At Home," was on that same road when she died a year later during an emergency operation. Carol Dempster and Ralph Graves were two other Griffith discoveries of the year. Alice Joyce, Earle Williams and Corinne Griffith continued as top Vitagraph stars. Marie Doro was making successful films in England and Italy.

ALBERT ROSCOE, MIRIAM COOPER
IN "EVANGELINE" (FOX)

ALMA RUBENS, JACK CONWAY
IN "RESTLESS SOULS" (TRIANGLE)

HOBART BOSWORTH, BLANCHE BATES
IN "THE BORDER LEGION" (INDEPENDENT)

LILLIAN GISH, ROBERT HARRON IN
"THE GREATEST THING IN LIFE" (ARTCRAFT)

LLIAN GISH, RICHARD BARTHELMESS (Also Above)

LILLIAN GISH, DONALD CRISP
SCENES FROM "BROKEN BLOSSOMS"

RICHARD BARTHELMESS

CLARINE SEYMOUR IN
"THE GIRL WHO STAYED AT HOME"

LILLIAN GISH, ROBERT HARRON
IN "TRUE HEART SUSIE"

CLARINE SEYMOUR, ROBERT HARRON
IN "THE GIRL WHO STAYED AT HOME"

D. W. GRIFFITH PRODUCTIONS

RALPH GRAVES, RICHARD BARTHELMESS, CAROL DEMPSTER
Above: CLARINE SEYMOUR, RICHARD BARTHELMESS
IN "SCARLET DAYS"

MAURICE COSTELLO, ALICE JOYCE
IN "THE CAMBRIC MASK"

EARLE WILLIAMS, RUDOLPH VALENTINO
IN "A ROGUE'S ROMANCE"
VITAGRAPH PRODUCTIONS

HATTIE DELARO, ANITA STEWART
IN "THE MIND-THE-PAINT GIRL"

ALICE JOYCE
IN "THE THIRD DEGREE"
(VITAGRAPH)

ANTONIO MORENO
IN "PERILS OF THUNDER MOUNTAIN"
(VITAGRAPH SERIAL)

EDITH JOHNSON, WILLIAM DUNCA
(VITAGRAPH)

LARRY SEMON
IN "SIMPLE LIFE" (VITAGRAPH)

BEN TURPIN, CHESTER CONKLIN, MARIE PREVOST
A BURLESQUE OF "UNCLE TOM'S CABIN" (KEYSTON

WALTER MILLER, CORINNE GRIFFITH
IN "A GIRL AT BAY" (VITAGRAPH)

MARIE DORO IN
"THE MYSTERIOUS PRINCESS"

ELLIOTT DEXTER, WANDA HAWLEY IN
"WE CAN'T HAVE EVERYTHING" (PARAMOUNT)

ALEXANDER SALVINI, MARIE DORO
IN "TWELVE TEN" (SELECT)

GARETH HUGHES, SAM SOTHERN, VINCENT SERRANO, RALPH LEWIS,
CLARA KIMBALL YOUNG, PAULINE STARKE, MILTON SILLS,
WILLIAM COURTLEIGH IN "EYES OF YOUTH" (EQUITY)

BETTY BLYTHE, CLARA KIMBALL YOUNG, HERBERT
RAWLINSON, NIGEL BARRIE IN "CHARGE IT" (EQUITY)

NA ASHLING

AS THE DRUG ADDICT

WITH RUDOLPH VALENTINO
CLARA KIMBALL YOUNG IN "EYES OF YOUTH" (EQUITY)

AS THE OPERA SINGER

AS THE SCHOOL TEACHER

1919 Clara Kimball Young made a film of the stage success, "Eyes of Youth." In the cast, playing a bit, was a young Italian named Rudolph Valentino who had been a dancer and played small roles in Universal and Vitagraph pictures.

acDERMOTT, STUART HOLMES, NORMA TALMADGE
IN "THE NEW MOON" (SELECT)

CAROL DEMPSTER
(GRIFFITH)

CLARINE SEYMOUR
(GRIFFITH)

HAZEL DALY
(GOLDWYN)

NORMA TALMADGE, THOMAS MEIGHAN
IN "THE PROBATION WIFE" (SELECT)

EUGENE O'BRIEN
IN "THE PERFECT LOVER" (SELZNICK)

MYRON SELZNICK, ELAINE HAMMERSTEIN AND
DIRECTOR ALAN CROSLAND DISCUSS SCENE

OLIVE THOMAS, ROBERT ELLIS
IN "UPSTAIRS AND DOWN" (SELZNICK)

VIRGINIA PEARSON
(FOX)

ROD LA ROCQUE
(GOLDWYN)

ELAINE HAMMERSTEIN
(SELZNICK)

RICHARD DIX
(GOLDWYN)

SHIRLEY MASON
(PARAMOUNT)

ELLIOTT DEXTER
(PARAMOUNT)

RUSSELL SIMPSON, KAY LAURELL
IN "THE BRAND" (GOLDWYN)

HEDDA HOPPER, NORMA TALMADGE
IN "BY RIGHT OF PURCHASE" (SELECT)

ANTRIM SHORT
(METRO)

CARROLL McCOMAS
(PARAMOUNT)

EDDIE POLO
(UNIVERSAL)

JUANITA HANSEN
(PATHÉ)

ALAN HALE
(SELECT)

CLAIRE A...
(SELEC...)

CULLEN LANDIS, MARY JANE IRVING, WILL ROGERS
IN "ALMOST A HUSBAND" (GOLDWYN)

NICK COGLEY, GEORGE K. KUWA, TOM MOORE, DORIS
PAWN IN "TOBY'S BOW" (GOLDWYN)

MAE MARSH, MARY THURMAN, WALLACE MacDO...
IN "SPOTLIGHT SADIE" (GOLDWYN)

LOU TELLEGEN, GERALDINE FARRAR IN
"THE WORLD AND ITS WOMEN" (GOLDWYN)

GERALDINE FARRAR, LOU TELLEGEN, ALEC B. FRANCIS
IN "FLAME OF THE DESERT" (GOLDWYN)

THOMAS SANTSCHI, GERALDINE FARRAR
IN "SHADOWS" (GOLDWYN)

LE WILLIAMS (VITAGRAPH)   ANITA STEWART (FIRST NATIONAL)   CARLYLE BLACKWELL (WORLD)   LILLIAN WALKER (CREST)   J. WARREN KERRIGAN (PARALTA)   PEARL WHITE (PATHÉ)

GEORGE B. SEITZ, MARGUERITE COURTOT
IN "BOUND AND GAGGED" (PATHÉ)

Triangle Presents
ELLEN TERRY
IN
"Her Greatest Performance"

A triumphant climax to the career of the greatest living actress

A tribute to her artistry, that she should select for screen presentation in the sweetness of her maturity a role portraying the greatest of God's gifts, a mother.

An exquisite production of the greatest of heart-interest themes.

Everybody everywhere knows Ellen Terry. Folks are eagerly awaiting her only screen presentation.

Could the exhibitor have a more profitable offering than the star people are clamoring to see?

A guaranteed success.

Triangle Distributing Corporation
New York

PEARL WHITE, GEORGE B. SEITZ
IN "THE BLACK SECRET" (PATHÉ)

ENTON (RO)   ZASU PITTS (BRENTWOOD)   ROBERT GORDON (PARAMOUNT)

EDYTHE CHAPMAN (GOLDWYN)   HARRISON FORD (PARAMOUNT)   MOLLIE KING (PATHÉ)

1919

First National, with Chaplin, Mary Pickford and brother Jack under contract, went after and signed Anita Stewart and Norma and Constance Talmadge. Anna Case, opera star, made a film for Select, and before they folded, Triangle had released an English-made film starring Ellen Terry. Dustin Farnum and Virginia Pearson were making films for independent companies. W. W. Hodkinson was distributing films starring J. Warren Kerrigan, Louise Glaum and H. B. Warner.

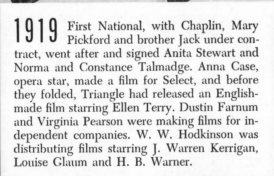

FANNIE WARD, E. W. LAWRENCE
IN "COMMON CLAY" (PATHÉ)

MILDRED DAVIS, HAROLD LLOYD
IN "HIS ROYAL SLYNESS" (PATHÉ)

SHELDON LEWIS, VIRGINIA PEARSON
IN "THE BISHOP'S EMERALDS" (PATHÉ)

TEXAS GUINAN
IN "LITTLE MISS DEPUTY" (TRIANGLE)

NANCE O'NEIL, MASTER BEN GRAUER, ALFRED
HICKMAN IN "THE MAD WOMAN" (UNIVERSAL)

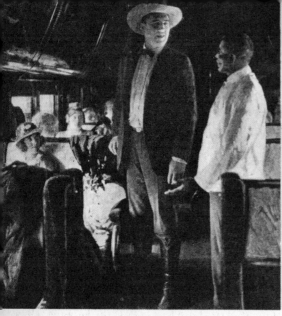

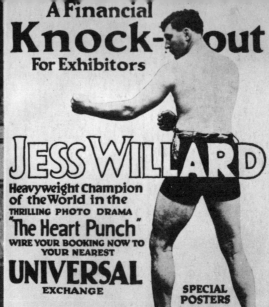

JESS WILLARD
IN "THE CHALLENGE OF CHANCE"

GIBSON GOWLAND, SAM DE GRASSE
IN "BLIND HUSBANDS" (UNIVERSAL)

MARIE WALCAMP, NEAL HART IN QUICKSAND
DURING SCENE FROM UNIVERSAL SERIAL

JAMES J. CORBETT
IN "THE MIDNIGHT MAN"

ELMO LINCOLN
IN "ELMO THE MIGHTY" (UNIVERSAL)

IRENE RICH, LON CHANEY
IN "THE TRAP" (UNIVERSAL)

MAE MURRAY, RUDOLPH VALENTINO
IN "THE DELICIOUS LITTLE DEVIL" (UNIVERSAL)

CULLEN LANDIS, HARRY CAREY, GLORIA HOPE, VICTOR
IN "THE OUTCASTS OF POKER FLAT" (UNIVERSAL

CLAIRE DUBREY, DUSTIN FARNUM
IN "THE MAN IN THE OPEN"
180 (UNITED PICTURES)

WINIFRED KINGSTON, DUSTIN FARNUM
IN "THE CORSICAN BROTHERS" (UNITED PICTURES)

LOUISE GLAUM, THOMAS HOLDING IN
"THE LONE WOLF'S DAUGHTER" (HODKINSON)

BARBARA CARLTON, H. B. WARN
"THE MAN WHO TURNED WHI

MAHLON HAMILTON, MARY PICKFORD
IN "DADDY LONG LEGS"

MARY PICKFORD, WESLEY BARRY
IN "DADDY LONG LEGS"
FIRST NATIONAL FEATURES

MARY PICKFORD, KENNETH HARLAN
IN "THE HOODLUM"

1919 Goldwyn was making films with Geraldine Farrar, Will Rogers, Tom Moore, Mabel Normand and Madge Kennedy. At Universal, James J. Corbett and Jess Willard, world's heavy-weight champion boxers, made films; Erich Von Stroheim wrote and directed his first film," Blind Husbands," and Mae Murray, Harry Carey and Priscilla Dean were their top stars. Nazimova was now Metro's biggest money-making star. May Allison, Edith Storey, Hale Hamilton, Viola Dana, were still Metro stars, but Ethel Barrymore's "The Divorcee" was her last picture on that lot. Grace La Rue, famous musical comedy and vaudeville star, made her one and only silent screen appearance opposite her husband, Hale Hamilton, in "That's Good," but she used the name of Stella Gray and received no billing.

CHARLES CHAPLIN
IN "SUNNYSIDE" (FIRST NATIONAL)

CHARLES CHAPLIN
IN "A DAY'S PLEASURE" (FIRST NATIONAL)

OBBY CONNELLY, WESLEY BARRY, MARY ALDEN,
CHE SWEET IN "THE UNPARDONABLE SIN" (GARSON)

CONWAY TEARLE, HEDDA HOPPER, ANITA STEWART
IN "VIRTUOUS WIVES" (FIRST NATIONAL)

WARREN KERRIGAN IN
WHITE MAN'S CHANCE"
(HODKINSON)

ANITA STEWART IN
"IN OLD KENTUCKY"
(FIRST NATIONAL)

PRISCILLA DEAN
(UNIVERSAL)

BEN TURPIN
(KEYSTONE)

ZASU PITTS, DAVID BUTLER
IN "BETTER TIMES"
(BRENTWOOD)

NAZIMOVA
IN "THE RED LANTERN"

CHARLES BRYANT, NAZIMOVA, BONNIE HILL,
AMY VENESS, IN "THE BRAT"

THE BRAT

NAZIMOVA
IN "OUT OF THE FOG"

NAZIMOVA
IN "THE RED LANTERN"

NAZIMOVA
IN "THE BRAT"

VIRGINIA CALDWELL, GOLDA MADDEN, BERT LYTELL, PATRICIA
HANNAN, JEAN ACKER, ANN MAY IN "LOMBARDI, LTD."

ETHEL BARRYMORE
IN "THE DIVORCEE"

BERT LYTELL
IN "EASY TO MAKE MONEY"

GRACE LA RUE, HALE HAMILTON
IN "THAT'S GOOD"

EDITH STOREY
IN "AS THE SUN WENT DOWN"
METRO FEATURES

ANTRIM SHORT, VIOLA DANA
IN "PLEASE GET MARRIED"

GLORIA SWANSON

CHARLES CHAPLIN, JACKIE COOGAN
IN "THE KID" (FIRST NATIONAL)

JACKIE COOGAN
AS "THE KID"

CHARLES CHAPLIN
IN "THE PAWN SHOP"

CONWAY TEARLE
(SELZNICK)

OLIVE THOMAS
(SELZNICK)

JACK PICKFORD
(GOLDWYN)

THE BIG FOUR OF UNITED ARTISTS
DOUGLAS FAIRBANKS, MARY PICKFORD, CHARLES CHAPLIN, D. W. GRIFFITH

1920 Mary Pickford, Douglas Fairbanks, Charles Chaplin and D. W. Griffith, four of the biggest names in pictures, formed the United Artists Corporation with Hiram Abrams as its president. On March 27, Fairbanks and Miss Pickford were united in marriage. They were the king and queen of filmland, and their home in Beverly Hills, named Pickfair, became the center of the film capital's social activities. Another outstanding event was the discovery by Chaplin of Jackie Coogan. The story goes that Jackie winked at Chaplin in a Los Angeles railway station and was given the role in "The Kid" which skyrocketed little Jackie Coogan to stardom.

MARY PICKFORD
IN "POLLYANNA" (UNITED ARTISTS)

DOUGLAS FAIRBANKS, RUTH RENWICK
IN "THE MOLLYCODDLE" (UNITED ARTISTS)

DOROTHY GISH
(PARAMOUNT)

BUSTER KEATON
(FIRST NATIONAL)

MARY MacLAREN
(UNIVERSAL)

HEDDA HOPPER
(SELECT)

DAVID POWELL
(PARAMOUNT)

CLARINE SEYMOUR
(GRIFFITH)

WALLACE REID

EMIL JANNINGS, POLA NEGRI

POLA NEGRI

POLA NEGRI

SCENES FROM ERNST LUBITSCH'S PRODUCTION "PASSION" (FIRST NATIONAL)

CUNEO
(ENDENT)

FAIRE BINNEY
(PARAMOUNT)

JAMES KIRKWOOD
(FIRST NATIONAL)

1920 Among the pre-eminent attractions were D. W. Griffith's film "Way Down East" and a foreign importation, "Passion," which brought Pola Negri, a Polish actress, and Ernst Lubitsch, a German director, to the attention of the American public. Doris Keane and Otis Skinner filmed their great stage successes, "Romance" and "Kismet" respectively. Florence Lawrence, after an absence of five years, made an unsuccessful return to the screen in "The Enfoldment," an independently produced film.

JEAN PAIGE
(VITAGRAPH)

NOAH BEERY
(PARAMOUNT)

EILEEN PERCY
(FOX)

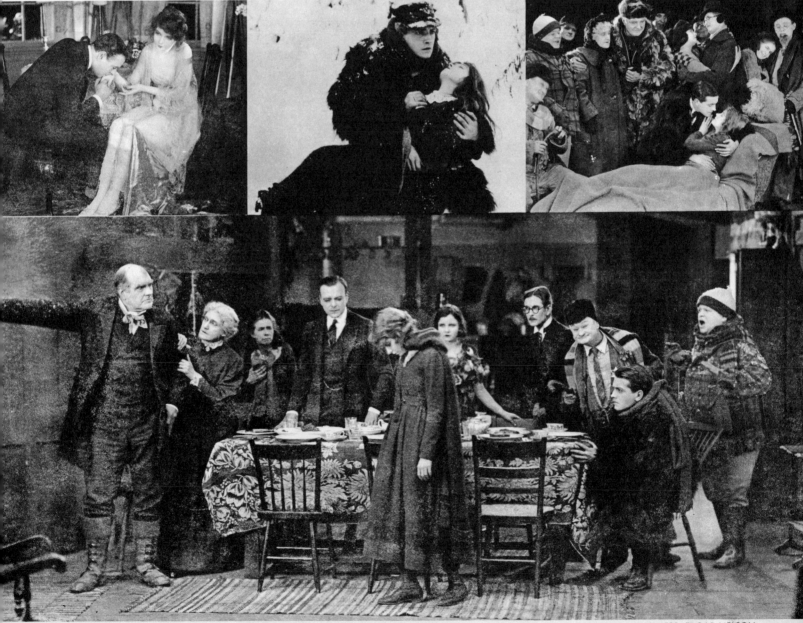

McINTOSH, KATE BRUCE, VIVIA OGDEN, LOWELL SHERMAN, LILLIAN GISH, MARY HAY, CREIGHTON HALE, GEORGE NEVILLE, RICHARD BARTHELMESS, EDGAR NELSON.
VE: (left) LOWELL SHERMAN, LILLIAN GISH; (center) RICHARD BARTHELMESS, LILLIAN GISH; (right) GEORGE NEVILLE, EDGAR NELSON, KATE BRUCE, BURR McINTOSH,
ARD BARTHELMESS, LILLIAN GISH, MARY HAY, CREIGHTON HALE, VIVIA OGDEN, PORTER STRONG
SCENES FROM D. W. GRIFFITH'S "WAY DOWN EAST"

NORMAN TREVOR, DORIS KEANE
IN "ROMANCE" (UNITED ARTISTS)

JAMES KIRKWOOD, DOROTHY PHILLIPS
IN "MAN, WOMAN AND MARRIAGE" (FIRST NATIONAL)

WALTER LONG, ANNETTE KELLERMA
IN "WHAT WOMEN LOVE" (FIRST NAT

NORMAN KERRY
(UNIVERSAL)

MARGUERITE COURTOT
(PATHÉ)

EMORY JOHNSON
(GOLDWYN)

WINIFRED WESTOVER
(PARAMOUNT)

MARSHALL NEILAN
(FIRST NATIONAL)

GLADYS LESLIE
(VITAGRAPH)

RUDOLPH VALENTINO
(EQUITY)

SYLVIA BREAMER
(PARAMOUNT)

WHEELER OA
(UNIVERS

WILLIAM CONKLIN, FLORENCE LAWRENCE
IN "THE ENFOLDMENT" (INDEPENDENT)

LILLIAN GISH, ROBERT HARRON
IN "THE GREATEST QUESTION" (FIRST NATIONAL)

COLLEEN MOORE, KATE PRICE
IN "DINTY" (FIRST NATIONAL)

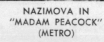

ROSCOE ARBUCKLE IN
"THE ROUND UP"
(PARAMOUNT)

DOROTHY GISH IN
"REMODELING HER HUSBAND"
(PARAMOUNT)

MAE MURRAY IN
"ON WITH THE DANCE"
(PARAMOUNT)

NAZIMOVA IN
"MADAM PEACOCK"
(METRO)

OTIS SKINNER IN
"KISMET"
(ROBERTSON-COLE)

188

ROTHY DE VORE, CHARLES RAY IN "45 MINUTES FROM BROADWAY" (FIRST NATIONAL)

ALBERT ROSCOE, BARBARA BEDFORD, LILLIAN HALL, HARRY LORRAINE IN "THE LAST OF THE MOHICANS" (ASSOCIATE PRODUCERS)

FAIRE BINNEY, GEORGES CARPENTIER IN "THE WONDER MAN" (ROBERTSON-COLE)

N FERGUSON (UNIVERSAL)

FANNIE WARD (PATHÉ)

ALFRED WHITMAN (VITAGRAPH)

EDITH STOREY (METRO)

GEORGE LARKIN (UNIVERSAL)

ANN LITTLE (PARAMOUNT)

LARRY SEMON (VITAGRAPH)

RUTH CLIFFORD (UNIVERSAL)

WILFRED LYTELL (FOX)

BABE RUTH IN "HEADIN' HOME" (INDEPENDENT)

COLLEEN MOORE, EARLE RODNEY IN "A ROMAN SCANDAL" (CHRISTIE)

JACK DEMPSEY IN "DAREDEVIL JACK" (PATHÉ SERIAL)

OMAS MEIGHAN IN D IN QUEST OF HIS YOUTH" (PARAMOUNT)

GENE POLLAR AS TARZAN (GOLDWYN)

WALLACE BEERY IN "THE LAST OF THE MOHICANS" (ASSOCIATE PRODUCERS)

LEWIS STONE IN "HELD BY THE ENEMY" (PARAMOUNT)

MR. AND MRS. CARTER DE HAVEN (FLORA PARKER)
IN "TWIN BEDS" (FIRST NATIONAL)

JACK PERRIN, GLADYS WALTON
IN "PINK TIGHTS" (UNIVERSAL)

H. B. WARNER, ANNA Q. NILSSON IN
"ONE HOUR BEFORE DAWN" (PATHÉ)

LOUISE FAZENDA IN MACK SENNETT'S
"DOWN ON THE FARM" (UNITED ARTISTS)

LEON BARY, OTIS SKINNER
IN "KISMET" (ROBERTSON-COLE)

POLA NEGRI IN
"ONE ARABIAN NIGHT" (FIRST NATIO…

BERT LYTELL IN
"ALIAS JIMMY VALENTINE" (METRO)

1920 Babe Ruth, Jack Dempsey and Georges Carpentier, outstanding sports figures, made their film debuts, but it was obvious that acting was not their medium. Hope Hampton, a pretty young girl without any acting experience, was starred in her first film, "A Modern Salome," under the sponsorship of Jules Brulatour. Juanita Hansen and Ruth Roland were the current serial queens, Pearl White having abdicated in favor of dramas for Fox. Lillian Gish continued to give sincere performances in the tragic pathetic characters she portrayed for Griffith. Tom Mix, Harry Carey, and a newcomer, Buck Jones, were hot on the trail of William S. Hart's monarchal sombrero.

ALICE LAKE, FRANK BROWNLEE IN
"SHORE ACRES" (METRO)

WILLIAM DESMOND, BETTY FRANCISCO IN
"THE MAN FROM MAKE BELIEVE"
(PATHÉ)

INA CLAIRE, CLIFTON WEBB, HARRY BENHAM, RALPH GRAVES
IN "POLLY WITH A PAST" (METRO)

MARGARITA FISHER, MILTON SI…
IN "THE WEEK-END" (PATHÉ)

ARTHUR CAREW, ALLEN SEARS, ROSEMARY THEBY
IN "RIO GRANDE" (PATHÉ)

HOPE HAMPTON IN
"A MODERN SALOME" (METRO)

EMMA DUNN, CLARA KNOTT, LAWRENCE UNDERWOOD
IN "OLD LADY 31" (METRO)

LOUISE GLAUM
IN "SEX" (HODKINSON)

MAE BUSCH, CLYDE FILLMORE, EVELYN GOSNELL, MAUDE GEORGE
IN ERICH VON STROHEIM'S "THE DEVIL'S PASS KEY" (UNIVERSAL)

POLA NEGRI, ERNST LUBITSCH IN
"ONE ARABIAN NIGHT" (FIRST NATIONAL)

POLA NEGRI
(FIRST NATIONAL)

BUCK JONES
(FOX)

ALICE JOYCE
(VITAGRAPH)

WESLEY BARRY
(FIRST NATIONAL)

MARY PICKFORD
(UNITED ARTISTS)

THOMAS MEIGHAN
(PARAMOUNT)

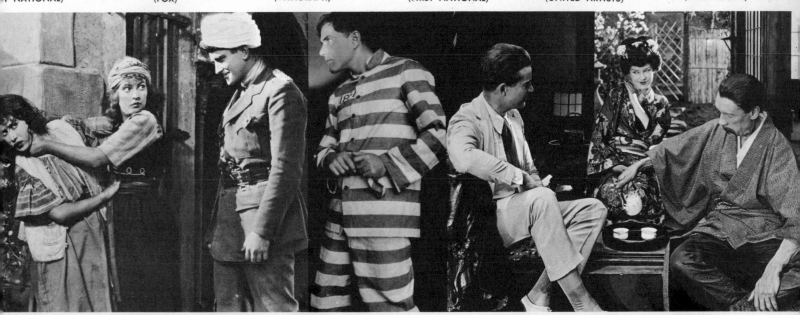

PRISCILLA DEAN (center), WHEELER OAKMAN
IN "THE VIRGIN OF STAMBOUL" (UNIVERSAL)

BERT LYTELL IN
"ALIAS JIMMY VALENTINE"
(METRO)

PELL TRENTON, VIOLA DANA, EDWARD CONNELLY
IN "THE WILLOW TREE" (METRO)

191

DODSON MITCHELL, FRANK THOMAS, CORINNE GRIFFITH IN "DEADLINE AT ELEVEN" (VITAGRAPH)

ALICE JOYCE, PERCY MARMONT IN "THE SPORTING DUCHESS" (VITAGRAPH)

PERCY MARMONT, GUSTAV Von SEYFFERTITZ, CATHERINE IN "DEAD MEN TELL NO TALES" (VITAGRAPH)

GEORGES CARPENTIER

BABE RUTH

JACK DEMPSEY

RENEE ADOREE (GOLDWYN)

MITCHELL LEWIS (METRO)

KATHRYN (PATH

CREIGHTON HALE, CLARINE SEYMOUR (also above), RICHARD BARTHELMESS IN "THE IDOL DANCER" (D. W. GRIFFITH)

CLARINE SEYMOUR IN "THE IDOL DANCER" (D. W. GRIFFITH)

JOHN BARRYMORE (also above) IN "SHERLOCK HOLMES" (INDEPENDENT)

DOROTHY PHILLIPS, RUDOLPH VALENTINO IN "ONCE TO EVERY WOMAN" (UNIVERSAL)

CHARLES MEREDITH, BLANCHE SWEET IN "SIMPLE SOULS" (PATHÉ)

JEAN PAIGE, EARLE WILLIAMS IN "THE FORTUNE HUNTER" (VITAGRAPH)

DIRECTOR DELL HENDERSON WITH GEORGE WALSH
FILMING "THE SHARK" (FOX)

TOM MIX VISITS JACK DEMPSEY
FOR A WORKOUT

BUCK JONES, HELEN FERGUSON IN
"STRAIGHT FROM THE SHOULDER" (FOX)

CORNWALL
(PARAMOUNT)

ROBERT ELLIS
(METRO)

VERA GORDON
(PARAMOUNT)

JAMES CRANE
(PARAMOUNT)

GRETCHEN HARTMANN
(FOX)

JAMES MORRISON
(VITAGRAPH)

WILLIAM FARNUM IN
"IF I WERE KING" (FOX)

WILLIAM FARNUM (also above), BETTY ROSS
CLARKE IN "IF I WERE KING" (FOX)

E TAYLOR, WILLIAM FARNUM IN "THE ADVENTURER"
(OX) Above: WILLIAM FARNUM, JACKIE SAUNDERS IN
"DRAG HARLAN" (FOX)

1920 Will Rogers was a quaint, clumsy actor devoid of every alluring asset save sincerity, but his pictures were received enthusiastically everywhere. Alice Joyce continued to grow in stature as an actress. William Farnum maintained his hold on the public and was outstanding in "If I Were King." Thomas Meighan was thoroughly deserving of his new star billing. Richard Barthelmess, after his fine work in "Broken Blossoms" and "Way Down East," achieved stardom. Constance Talmadge, Mabel Normand and Dorothy Gish continued as the screen's most delightful comediennes. Chaplin and Harold Lloyd were among the leading comedians. A scandal finished Roscoe Arbuckle's acting career. Using the name Will B. Good, he became a director.

ESTELLE TAYLOR, MARC MacDERMOTT
IN "WHILE NEW YORK SLEEPS" (FOX)

PEARL WHITE IN
"THE WHITE MOLL" (FOX)

WILL ROGERS
(GOLDWYN)

CONSTANCE TALMADGE
(FIRST NATIONAL)

OWEN MOORE
(SELZNICK)

ELSIE JANIS, MATT MOORE
IN "EVERYBODY'S SWEETHEART" (SELZNICK)

OLIVE THOMAS
IN "THE FLAPPER" (SELZNICK)

EUGENE PALLETTE, RUTH STONEHOUSE IN
"PARLOR, BEDROOM AND BATH" (METRO)

WILL ROGERS, PEGGY WOOD IN
"ALMOST A HUSBAND" (GOLDWYN)

EDWARD M. KIMBALL, J. FRANK GLENDON, CLARA KIMBALL
YOUNG IN "MID-CHANNEL" (EQUITY)

KATHLYN WILLIAMS, ROY STEWART, LEATRICE JO
IN "JUST A WIFE" (SELZNICK)

LOU TELLEGEN, GERALDINE FARRAR, MACEY HARLAN
IN "THE WOMAN AND THE PUPPET"
(GOLDWYN)

JACK PICKFORD IN
"THE LITTLE SHEPHERD OF KINGDOM COME"
(GOLDWYN)

MYRTLE STEDMAN, CURTIS COOKSEY
IN "THE SILVER HORDE"
(GOLDWYN)

194

BETTY COMPSON
(PARAMOUNT)

EUGENE O'BRIEN
(SELZNICK)

KATHERINE MacDONALD
(FIRST NATIONAL)

IRENE RICH, WILL ROGERS IN
"JES' CALL ME JIM" (GOLDWYN)

PAULINE FREDERICK, CASSON FERGUSON
IN "MADAME X" (GOLDWYN)

CULLEN LANDIS, WILLARD LOUIS
IN "GOING SOME" (GOLDWYN)

NALD BARKER DIRECTS BARBARA CASTLETON AND
ELL SIMPSON IN "THE BRANDING IRON" (GOLDWYN)

1920 Buster Keaton was a comer, while Ben Turpin was starring his way to fame in Sennett's comedies. Bert Lytell was doing notably good work, and so was Wallace Reid. Eugene O'Brien, Owen Moore, Jack Holt; Harrison Ford, Charles Ray, Antonio Moreno, Tom Moore, Herbert Rawlinson—all good actors, enjoyed wide favor. Geraldine Farrar continued to interest but she never touched the heights of popularity she reached in her first picture, "Carmen." Nazimova was suffering from poor stories. Clara Kimball Young, Norma Talmadge, Anita Stewart, Ethel Clayton, Blanche Sweet, held their exalted positions. Gloria Swanson, once only a beautiful woman with strange clothes and coiffures, was learning how to act. Marion Davies, too, was acquiring more than one emotion.

JEANNE CALHOUN, JEROME PATRICK, TOM MOORE
IN "OFFICER 666" (GOLDWYN)

BARBARA CASTLETON, JAMES KIRKWOOD
IN "THE BRANDING IRON" (GOLDWYN)

MABEL NORMAND, TULLY MARSHALL IN
"THE SLIM PRINCESS" (GOLDWYN)

HAZEL DALY, TOM MOORE
IN "STOP THIEF" (GOLDWYN)

WALLACE REID IN
"WHAT'S YOUR HURRY?" (PARAMOUNT)

WALLACE REID, WANDA HAWLEY IN "DOUBLE SPEED"
Above: WALLACE REID, BEBE DANIELS IN "SICK ABED"
(PARAMOUNT)

WALLACE REID IN
"THE DANCIN' FOOL" (PARAMOUNT)

VERA GORDON, BOBBY CONNELLY

ANNA WALLECK, VERA GORDON, ALMA RUBENS, GASTON GLASS
SCENES FROM "HUMORESQUE" (PARAMOUNT-ARTCRAFT)

GASTON GLASS, VERA GORDO

DOROTHY GISH, JAMES RENNIE IN
"REMODELING HER HUSBAND"
(PARAMOUNT)

LEWIS STONE, AGNES AYRES, JACK HOLT
IN "HELD BY THE ENEMY" (PARAMOUNT)

DOUGLAS MacLEAN, DORIS MAY IN
"MARY'S ANKLE" (PARAMOUNT)

THOMAS MEIGHAN, GLORIA SWANSON
bove: BEBE DANIELS, THOMAS MEIGHAN

THEODORE KOSLOFF, GLORIA SWANSON

BEBE DANIELS, GLORIA SWANSON, THOMAS MEIGHAN
Above: THOMAS MEIGHAN, BEBE DANIELS

SCENES FROM CECIL B. DE MILLE'S PRODUCTION "WHY CHANGE YOUR WIFE?" (PARAMOUNT)

'N WILLIAMS, EDWARD SUTHERLAND IN
ONRAD IN QUEST OF HIS YOUTH"
(PARAMOUNT)

THOMAS MEIGHAN, MARTHA MANSFIELD
IN "CIVILIAN CLOTHES" (PARAMOUNT)

MARION DAVIES, CARLYLE BLACKWELL
IN "THE RESTLESS SEX" (PARAMOUNT)

ANNA Q. NILSSON, CONRAD NAGEL, RUTH
HELMS IN "THE FIGHTING CHANCE"
(PARAMOUNT)

THA MANSFIELD,
HN BARRYMORE

JOHN BARRYMORE

JOHN BARRYMORE

JOHN BARRYMORE

MARTHA MANSFIELD,
JOHN BARRYMORE

SCENES FROM "DR. JEKYLL AND MR. HYDE" (PARAMOUNT)

DAVID POWELL, MAE MURRAY IN
"RIGHT TO LOVE" and above in
"IDOLS OF CLAY" (PARAMOUNT-ARTCRAFT)

LIONEL BARRYMORE
IN "THE COPPERHEAD"
(PARAMOUNT-ARTCRAFT)

THEODORE ROBERTS, GLORIA SWANSON, ELLIOTT D
Above: ELLIOTT DEXTER, GLORIA SWANSON
Scenes from "SOMETHING TO THINK ABOUT" (PARAM

HOUDINI IN
"TERROR ISLAND" (PARAMOUNT)

BETTY COMPSON, EMORY JOHNSON
IN "PRISONERS OF LOVE" (GOLDWYN)

WANDA HAWLEY, BRYANT WASHBURN IN
"THE SIX BEST CELLARS" (PARAMOUNT-ARTCRAF

ROSCOE "FATTY" ARBUCKLE, TOM FORMAN
IN "THE ROUND-UP" (PARAMOUNT-ARTCRAFT)

CONSTANCE BINNEY, REGINALD DENNY
IN "39 EAST" (REALART)

ROBERT WARWICK, WALTER HIERS IN
"HUNTING TROUBLE" (PARAMOUNT)

LOIS WILSON
(PARAMOUNT)

CONSTANCE BINNEY
(REALART)

CONRAD NAGEL
(PARAMOUNT)

MR. and MRS. CARTER DE HAVEN
(FLORA PARKER)
(FIRST NATIONAL)

THEODORE ROBERTS
(PARAMOUNT)

ENID BENNETT
(PARAMOUNT)

WANDA HAWL
(PARAMOUNT

SEARS, THEODORE ROBERTS, MARY MILES MINTER,
ZI RIDGEWAY, and above: THEODORE ROBERTS,
ALLAN SEARS, MARY MILES MINTER
IN "JUDY OF ROGUES HARBOR" (REALART)

LON CHANEY, DIRECTOR MAURICE TOURNEUR, SHIRLEY
MASON, and above: A SCENE FROM
"TREASURE ISLAND" (PARAMOUNT)

GEORGE REED AS JIM, LEWIS SARGENT AS HUCK,
GORDON GRIFFITH AS TOM (ABOVE: WITH THELMA
SALTER AS BECKY) IN "HUCKLEBERRY FINN" (PARAMOUNT)

ORMAN, NOAH BEERY, MABEL JULIENNE SCOTT
IN "THE SEA WOLF" (GEORGE MEDFORD)

1920 John Barrymore's performance was acclaimed in "Dr. Jekyll and Mr. Hyde," and a beautiful show girl named Nita Naldi was first noticed in this. Comparative newcomers who were springing into favor included Agnes Ayers, Lois Wilson, Martha Mansfield, Irene Rich, Katherine MacDonald (dubbed the American Beauty), Estelle Taylor, Constance Binney, Mildred Davis, Gareth Hughes, Richard Dix, Edmund Lowe, Conrad Nagel and Reginald Denny. Pauline Frederick had great success with "Madame X" after appearing in a series of inferior pictures. Mary Miles Minter, Alice Brady, Elsie Ferguson, Billie Burke, Marguerite Clark, Corinne Griffith, were all appearing in unworthy vehicles. Theda Bara, Francis X. Bushman, Beverly Bayne and Crane Wilbur were appearing on the stage.

HELEN WARE, MIRIAM COOPER
IN "THE DEEP PURPLE" (REALART)

N MARION
SENNETT)

WILLIAM DESMOND, MARY
THURMAN IN "THE PRINCE
AND BETTY" (PATHÉ)

JACK MULHALL AND MARGUERITE CLARK
FILMING "ALL OF A SUDDEN PEGGY"
(PARAMOUNT)

KARLA SCHRAMM, GENE POLLAR
IN "THE RETURN OF TARZAN"
(GOLDWYN)

MIRIAM BATTISTA
IN "HUMORESQUE"
(PARAMOUNT-ARTCRAFT)

EEN MOORE
(FOX)

MARTHA MANSFIELD
(PARAMOUNT)

DAVID BUTLER
(PREFERRED)

FLORENCE LAWRENCE
(INDEPENDENT)

ANTONIO MORENO
(VITAGRAPH)

ALICE LAKE
(METRO)

IRENE RICH
(GOLDWYN)

BETTY BLYTHE, FRITZ LEIBER
IN "THE QUEEN OF SHEBA".

NELL CRAIG IN   HARRY C. MYERS AND PAULINE STARKE   BUCK JONES
"THE QUEEN OF SHEBA"   IN "A CONNECTICUT YANKEE IN   "THE SQUARE SH
KING ARTHUR'S COURT"

BETTY BLYTHE IN
"THE QUEEN OF SHEBA"

FOX PRODUCTIONS

HARRY C. MYERS, PAULINE STARKE
(Also above) IN "A CONNECTICUT YANKEE
IN KING ARTHUR'S COURT"

PEARL WHITE, WILFRED LYTELL
IN "KNOW YOUR MEN"

DIRECTOR FRED SITTENHAM FILMING A SCENE OF "FINE FEATHERS"
WITH THOMAS W. ROSS, JUNE ELVIDGE, EUGENE PALLETTE,
CLAIRE WHITNEY, WARBURTON GAMBLE (METRO)

21 Rudolph Valentino's meteoric rise stands out as the year's most important personal event. A bit player, he was picked by June Mathis for "The Four Horsemen of The Apocalypse," and the is history. He made "The Conquering Power" and played Armand osite Nazimova's Camille for Metro, then signed a contract with Para- nt where he appeared in the title role of "The Sheik." This film eased his mounting popularity. Prior to this a popularity contest con- ed by a trade journal revealed the top fifteen men at the box office e Wallace Reid, Charles Ray, Thomas Meighan, Eugene O'Brien, glas Fairbanks, William S. Hart, William Farnum, Tom Mix, Tom re, Harrison Ford, Richard Barthelmess, Bryant Washburn, Charles lin, Earle Williams and Harold Lloyd.

RUDOLPH VALENTINO
e: JOSEPH SWICKARD, RUDOLPH
VALENTINO, ALICE TERRY

ALICE TERRY, RUDOLPH VALENTINO

SCENES FROM "THE FOUR HORSEMEN OF THE APOCALYPSE" (METRO)

RUDOLPH VALENTINO

EVA NOVAK
(UNIVERSAL)

HARRY MESTAYER
(PATHÉ)

MARY HAY
(FIRST NATIONAL)

JOE RYAN
(VITAGRAPH)

ANN MAY
(PARAMOUNT)

CHARLES
HUTCHINSON
(PATHÉ)

MOLLY MALONE
(UNIVERSAL)

WARD CRANE
(METRO)

LUCY COTT
(COSMOPOLI

MARY CARR WITH HER TWO DAUGHTERS, ROSEMARY
AND MAYBETH, AND HER SONS, STEPHEN AND THOMAS

MARY CARR

MARY CARR

SCENES FROM "OVER THE HILL" (FOX)

NAZIMOVA, RUDOLPH VALENTINO

NAZIMOVA, RUDOLPH VALENTINO

NAZIMOVA, RUDOLPH VALENTINO

SCENES FROM "CAMILLE" (METRO)

PEARL WHITE IN
"A VIRGIN PARADISE" (FOX)

GARETH HUGHES IN
"THE HUNCH" (METRO)

CARL MILLER, BARBARA BEDFORD, TOM McGUIRE,
BARBARA LA MARR IN "CINDERELLA OF THE HILLS" (FOX)

MAURICE FLYNN IN
"BUCKING THE LINE" (FOX)

HAROLD GOODWIN
"OLIVER TWIST, JR."

JUSTINE
JOHNSTONE
(REALART)

EDWARD HEARN
(PATHÉ)

GLADYS GEORGE
(INCE)

HOLMES HERBERT
(FOX)

MILDRED MANNING
(FOX)

MONTY BANKS
(WARNER)

ELINOR FAIR
(FOX)

ALBERT RAY
(FOX)

MARY McIV
(INCE)

FORMAN
(MOUNT)

ANN FORREST
(PARAMOUNT)

JIMMY AUBREY
(PATHÉ)

GLORIA HOPE
(GOLDWYN)

BERT LYTELL
(METRO)

BARBARA
CASTLETON
(GOLDWYN)

THEODORE KOSLOFF
(PARAMOUNT)

MARIE MOSQUINI
(PATHÉ)

JACK MULHALL
(METRO)

CATHERINE CALVERT, CRANE WILBUR IN
"THE HEART OF MARYLAND" (VITAGRAPH)

GILBERT EMORY, ALICE JOYCE
IN "COUSIN KATE" (VITAGRAPH)

ALICE TERRY, RUDOLPH VALENTINO
IN "THE CONQUERING POWER" (METRO)

JUNE WALKER, ROBERT HARRON
IN "COINCIDENCE" (METRO)

COLLEEN MOORE, JOHN BARRYMORE
IN "THE LOTUS EATER" (FIRST NATIONAL)

TYRONE POWER, TOM DOUGLAS
IN "FOOTFALLS" (FOX)

MacDERMOTT, ESTELLE
OR IN "BLIND WIVES"
(FOX)

MAHLON HAMILTON, LOUISE
GLAUM IN "I AM GUILTY!"
(ASSOCIATED PRODUCERS)

JACK MULHALL, VIOLA DANA, DIRECTOR DALLAS
FITZGERALD FILMING "THE OFFSHORE PIRATE"
(METRO)

HOOT GIBSON
IN "ACTION"
(UNIVERSAL)

KATHRYN McGUIRE, MAURICE
FLYNN IN "BUCKING THE
LINE" (FOX)

A MURPHY
(FOX)

GASTON GLASS
(PARAMOUNT)

KATHRYN PERRY
(SELZNICK)

CHARLES MEREDITH
(PARAMOUNT)

TEXAS GUINAN
(INDEPENDENT)

CLYDE COOK
(FOX)

RUBYE DE REMER
(GOLDWYN)

WALTER HIERS
(PARAMOUNT)

PAULINE CURLEY
(VITAGRAPH)

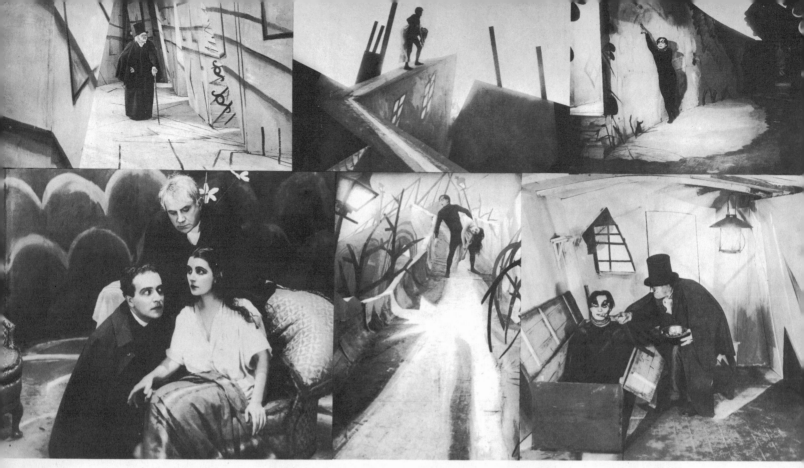

CONRAD VEIDT, LIL DAGOVER, WERNER KRAUSS, FRITZ FEHER IN
SCENES FROM "THE CABINET OF DR. CALIGARI" (GOLDWYN)

POLA NEGRI IN
"GYPSY BLOOD" (FIRST NATIONAL)

ASTA NIELSEN
AS HAMLET (ASTA)

PAUL WEGENER, ALBERT STEINRUCK
IN "THE GOLEM" (UFA)

FERRUCIO BIANCINI, RITA JOLIVET
IN "THEODORA" (GOLDWYN)

On the right, EMIL JANNINGS, HENNY PORTEN
IN "DECEPTION" (PARAMOUNT)

POLA NEGRI IN
"MAD LOVE"
(FIRST NATIONAL)

GEORGE ARLISS
IN "DISRAELI"
(UNITED ARTISTS)

NORMA TALMADGE IN
"THE PASSION FLOWER"
(FIRST NATIONAL)

DOUGLAS FAIRBANKS IN
"THE THREE MUSKETEERS"
(UNITED ARTISTS)

MARY PICKFORD IN
"LITTLE LORD FAUNTLEROY"
(UNITED ARTISTS)

1921 The top fifteen women were Norma Talmadge, Constance Talmadge, Mary Pickford, Anita Stewart, Dorothy Gish, Clara Kimball Young, Gloria Swanson, Mary Miles Minter, Katherine MacDonald, Pearl White, Marguerite Clark, Ethel Clayton, Elsie Ferguson, Elaine Hammerstein and Enid Bennett. Fox produced three pictures, "Over The Hill," "A Connecticut Yankee in King Arthur's Court" and "The Queen of Sheba," which found public favor. George Arliss, a distinguished actor, began his successful film career with "The Devil" and followed it with "Disraeli," both adapted from his stage successes. Pearl White, who had made a series of mediocre features for Fox, retired and went to Europe to live.

T McKIM, DOUGLAS FAIRBANKS, MARGUERITE DE LA
TE IN "THE MARK OF ZORRO" (UNITED ARTISTS)

HARRISON FORD, NORMA TALMADGE, COURTENAY FOOTE
IN "THE PASSION FLOWER" (FIRST NATIONAL)

LES MEREDITH, KATHERINE MacDONALD
IN "THE BEAUTIFUL LIAR"
(FIRST NATIONAL)

EDMUND LOWE, GEORGE ARLISS, SYLVIA BREAMER
IN "THE DEVIL" (PATHÉ)

KENNETH HARLAN, CONSTANCE TALMADGE
IN "LESSONS IN LOVE"
(FIRST NATIONAL)

MARY PICKFORD, CLAUDE GILLINGWATER
IN "LITTLE LORD FAUNTLEROY" (UNITED ARTISTS)

MARY PICKFORD IN "LITTLE
LORD FAUNTLEROY" (UNITED ARTISTS)

FRED THOMSON, MARY PICKFORD
IN "THE LOVE LIGHT" (UNITED ARTISTS)

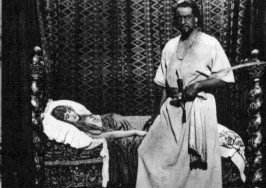

JACKIE COOGAN IN
"PECK'S BAD BOY" (FIRST NATIONAL)

MATHESON LANG IN
"CARNIVAL" (UNITED ARTISTS)

PRISCILLA DEAN IN
"UNDER TWO FLAGS" (UNIVERSAL)

LEON BARRY, DOUGLAS FAIRBANKS, GEORGE
SIEGMANN, MARGUERITE DE LA MOTTE,
EUGENE PALLETTE

EUGENE PALLETTE, DOUGLAS FAIRBANKS, LEON BARRY, GEORGE SIEGMANN

SCENES FROM "THE THREE MUSKETEERS" (UNITED ARTISTS)

DOUGLAS FAIRBANKS,
MARGUERITE DE LA MOTTE

HARRY CAREY, IRENE RICH
IN "DESPERATE TRAILS" (UNIVERSAL)

JAMES KIRKWOOD, HELENE CHADWICK, RICHARD DIX
IN "THE SIN FLOOD" (GOLDWYN)

CORINNE GRIFFITH IN
"THE SINGLE TRACK" (VITAGRAPH)

PHE MENJOU IN
HREE MUSKETEERS"
NITED ARTISTS)

CONSTANCE BINNEY IN
"SUCH A LITTLE QUEEN"
(REALART)

BUSTER KEATON
IN "THE PLAYHOUSE"
(FIRST NATIONAL)

WILLIAM FAVERSHAM IN
"THE SIN THAT WAS HIS"
(SELZNICK)

RICHARD BARTHELMESS
IN "TOL'ABLE DAVID"
(FIRST NATIONAL)

IVOR NOVELLO
IN "CARNIVAL"
(UNITED ARTISTS)

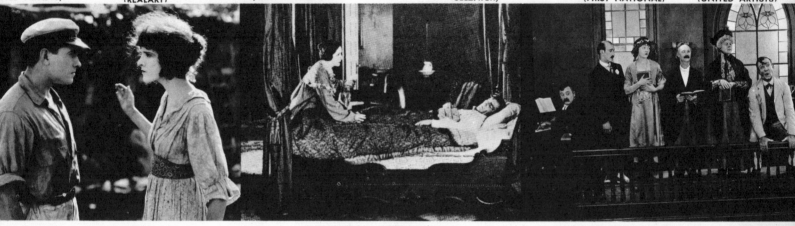

RICHARD BARTHELMESS, CAROL DEMPSTER
IN "THE LOVE FLOWER" (GRIFFITH)

MABEL BALLIN, NORMAN TREVOR
IN "JANE EYRE" (HODKINSON)

PHYLLIS HAVER, BEN TURPIN, CHARLIE MURRAY
IN "A SMALL TOWN IDOL" (SENNETT)

GERALDINE FARRAR IN
THE RIDDLE WOMAN" (PATHÉ)

RICHARD BARTHELMESS, GLADYS HULETTE
IN "TOL'ABLE DAVID" (FIRST NATIONAL)

RAMON NOVARRO, DERELYS PERDUE
IN "A SMALL TOWN IDOL" (SENNETT)

ONSTANCE TALMADGE, HARRISON FORD
N "WEDDING BELLS" (FIRST NATIONAL)

PAULINE FREDERICK, JOHN BOWERS, JANE NOVAK
IN "ROADS OF DESTINY" (GOLDWYN)

LEW CODY, NORMA TALMADGE IN
"THE SIGN ON THE DOOR" (FIRST NATIONAL)

207

RAYMOND HATTON, LEATRICE JOY IN "BUNTY PULLS THE STRINGS" (GOLDWYN)

SYLVIA BREAMER, WILL ROGERS IN "DOUBLING FOR ROMEO" (GOLDWYN)

ANITA STEWART, WALTER McGRAIL IN "PLAYTHINGS OF DESTINY" (FIRST NATIONAL)

LIONEL BARRYMORE IN "THE GREAT ADVENTURE" (FIRST NAT

ROBERT WARWICK (PARAMOUNT)

NAZIMOVA (METRO)

GEORGE ARLISS (UNITED ARTISTS)

VIOLA DANA (METRO)

JOHN BARRYMORE (PARAMOUNT)

MARGUERITE CLAR (FIRST NATIONAL

CONSTANCE BINNEY, GLENN HUNTER IN "THE CASE OF BECKY" (REALART)

1921 Pickford and Fairbanks, in their prime, were making their own films on the United Artists lot. Chaplin was finishing his contract at First National before joining them. First National signed Richard Barthelmess who received considerable acclaim in his first starring picture, "Tol'able David." Norma and Constance Talmadge, Anita Stewart, Buster Keaton and Jackie Coogan, their other contract stars, were all potent moneymakers. Since the importation of "Passion," German films were having a popular vogue. Pola Negri starring vehicles and Ernst Lubitsch directed pictures were in demand. "The Cabinet of Dr. Caligari," "The Golem" and "Deception" which starred Emil Jannings, a Brooklyn-born German star, all found receptive public and critical approval. At the Goldwyn studio, Richard Dix and Leatrice Joy were on the ascent.

SYDNEY CHAPLIN IN "KING, QUEEN, JOKER" (PARAMOUNT)

REGINALD DENNY, ELSIE FERGUSON IN "FOOTLIGHTS" (PARAMOUNT)

MARY MILES MINTER, WILLIAM BOYD IN "MOONLIGHT AND HONEYSUCKLE" (REALART)

LOIS WILSON, CONRAD NAGEL IN "WHAT EVERY WOMAN KNOWS" (PARAMOUNT)

K. LINCOLN, HAZEL DAWN IN
...TION" (ASSOCIATED PRODUCERS)

ALICE CALHOUN, JAMES MORRISON
IN "THE LITTLE MINISTER" (VITAGRAPH)

BETTY COMPSON, GEORGE HACKATHORNE
IN "THE LITTLE MINISTER" (PARAMOUNT)

JOHN BOWERS AND STRONGHEART
IN "THE SILENT CALL" (FIRST NATIONAL)

...A KIMBALL YOUNG
(METRO)

REGINALD DENNY
(REALART)

POLA NEGRI
(PARAMOUNT)

GARETH HUGHES
(PARAMOUNT)

GLORIA SWANSON
(PARAMOUNT)

HARRY CAREY
(UNIVERSAL)

CLAIRE WINDSOR, LOUIS CALHERN
IN "THE BLOT" (F. B. WARREN)

FORREST STANLEY, MARION DAVIES
IN "ENCHANTMENT" (PARAMOUNT)

HAROLD LLOYD, MILDRED DAVIS
IN "AMONG THOSE PRESENT" (PATHÉ)

JUNE CAPRICE, GEORGE B. SEITZ
IN "ROGUES AND ROMANCE" (PATHÉ)

HARRISON FORD, JUSTINE JOHNSTONE
IN "A HEART TO LET" (REALART)

JAMES KIRKWOOD IN HIS DUAL ROLE
IN "THE GREAT IMPERSONATION" (PARAMOUNT)

THEODORE ROBERTS, ETHEL CLAYTON
IN "SHAM" (PARAMOUNT)

RUDOLPH VALENTINO, AGNES AYRES (also above)
IN "THE SHEIK" (PARAMOUNT)

RUDOLPH VALENTINO
IN "THE SHEIK" (PARAMOUNT)

RICHARD BARTHELMESS (ALSO ABOVE WITH NITA
NALDI), MILDRED REARDON, LILYAN TASHMAN,
CHARLES STEVENSON IN "EXPERIENCE" (PARAMOUNT

PAT O'MALLEY
(FIRST NATIONAL)

ESTELLE TAYLOR
(FOX)

JOHNNIE WALKER
(FOX)

ROSCOE ARBUCKLE
(PARAMOUNT)

DORIS MAY
(PARAMOUNT)

WILLIAM DESMOND
(PATHÉ)

LILLIAN RICH
(PATHÉ

GLORIA SWANSON, JULIA FAYE
Above: WALLACE REID
SCENES FROM "THE AFFAIRS OF ANATOL" (PARAMOUNT)

BEBE DANIELS, WALLACE REID
Above: ELLIOTT DEXTER, GLORIA SWANSON, WALLACE
REID, WANDA HAWLEY

CHARLES CHAPLIN (also above), EDNA PURVIANCE
IN "THE IDLE CLASS" (FIRST NATIONAL)

WALLACE REID, GLORIA SWANSON, ELLIOTT DEXTER
DOROTHY CUMMINGS, WALLACE REID, ELLIOTT DEXTER
SCENES FROM "DON'T TELL EVERYTHING" (PARAMOUNT)

GARETH HUGHES IN
"SENTIMENTAL TOMMY" (PARAMOUNT)

GARETH HUGHES, MAY McAVOY, MABEL TALIAFERRO,
KEMPTON GREENE. Above: May McAVOY, GARETH HUGHES
SCENES FROM "SENTIMENTAL TOMMY" (PARAMOUNT)

MARY CARR
(FOX)

LLOYD HUGHES
(INCE)

1921

Both Paramount and Vitagraph filmed a version of James M. Barrie's "The Little Minister." His "Sentimental Tommy" was also made into a delightful film in which Gareth Hughes gave a glowing performance. Gloria Swanson was reigning queen at Paramount while Wallace Reid was undisputed king, with Thomas Meighan runner-up. Corinne Griffith was progressing, and so was "Hoot" Gibson. The top producers were Paramount, First National, Goldwyn and Metro. Fox divided its releases between "big specials" and their regular cheap dramas. Pathé was still making serials and releasing Harold Lloyd's pictures. Selznick curbed its production activities. Universal and Robertson-Cole turned out the usual melodramas. Vitagraph was slowly passing out of the picture.

NATALIE TALMADGE
(FIRST NATIONAL)

JAMES RENNIE
(PARAMOUNT)

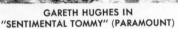
MABEL NORMAND   JACK MULHALL
IN "MOLLY O" (ASSOCIATED PRODUCERS)

CHARLES EMMETT MACK, CAROL DEMPSTER
ALPH GRAVES, CAROL DEMPSTER, CHARLES EMMETT MACK
SCENES FROM D. W. GRIFFITH'S "DREAM STREET"

JOHN DAVIDSON, MILDRED HARRIS, CONRAD NAGEL
IN "FOOL'S PARADISE" (PARAMOUNT)

ELSIE FERGUSON, WALLACE REID
Above: DOLORES CASSINELLI, PAUL McALLISTER, ELLIOTT DEXTER,
BARBARA DEAN, WALLACE REID, ELSIE FERGUSON, CHILDREN:
NELL ROY BUCK, CHARLES EATON IN "FOREVER" (PARAMOUNT)

ROBERT GORDON
(PARAMOUNT)

MILDRED REARDON
(PARAMOUNT)

RICHARD TUCKER
(GOLDWYN)

BETTY ROSS CLARKE
(FOX)

GEORGE FAWCETT
(PARAMOUNT)

ALLENE RAY
(PATHÉ)

HAROLD GOODWIN
(FOX)

LEATRICE JOY
(GOLDWYN)

WILLIAM DU
(VITAGRA

MARGARITA FISHER

DOUGLAS FAIRBANKS, MARY PICKFORD

WALLACE REID AND SON

LOIS WILSON

BESSIE LOVE

MAURICE FLYNN

HOPE HAMPTON

CULLEN LANDIS

VIOLA DANA

RUTH CLIFFOR

MARGARET
LOOMIS
(PARAMOUNT)

CHARLES EMMETT
MACK
(GRIFFITH)

DAGMAR
GODOWSKY
(UNIVERSAL)

BULL
MONTANA
(FIRST NATIONAL

DOROTHY
DE VORE
(CHRISTIE)

CLYDE
FILLMORE
(PARAMOUNT)

MISS
DU PONT

TOM
GALLERY
(GOLDWYN)

DOROT
DICKSO
(PARAMO

212

CONSTANCE AND NORMA TALMADGE

VIOLET MERSEREAU
IN "NERO" (FOX)

BUSTER KEATON IN
"DAY DREAMS" (FIRST NATIONAL)

HELEN FERGUSON IN
"HUNGRY HEARTS" (GOLDWYN)

REGINALD DENNY IN
"THE LEATHER PUSHERS" (UNIVERSAL)

CONSTANCE TALMADG
"EAST IS WEST" (FIRST NAT

LADY DIANA MANNERS, CARLYLE BLACKWELL
IN "THE VIRGIN QUEEN" (J. STUART BLACKTON)

ROBERT FLAHERTY, PRODUCER
OF "NANOOK OF THE NORTH"

"NANOOK OF THE NORTH"
(PATHÉ)

EARLE WILLIAMS IN
"THE MAN FROM DOWNING STREET"
(VITAGRAPH)

MAE MURRAY
IN "FASCINATION"
(METRO)

THOMAS MEIGHAN
IN "MANSLAUGHTER"
(PARAMOUNT)

NAZIMOVA
IN "A DOLL'S HOUSE"
(UNITED ARTISTS)

ART ACORD IN
"THE DAYS OF BUFFALO B
(UNIVERSAL)

CONWAY TEARLE IN
"HE ETERNAL FLAME"
(FIRST NATIONAL)

ELSIE FERGUSON
IN "OUTCAST"
(PARAMOUNT)

CHARLES CHAPLIN
IN "THE PILGRIM"
(FIRST NATIONAL)

GLADYS WALTON IN
"TOP O' THE MORNING"
(UNIVERSAL)

BERT LYTELL IN
"TO HAVE AND TO HOLD"
(PARAMOUNT)

1922 The most important event of the year occurred when the motion picture industry hired Will Hays, a member of President Harding's cabinet, to head the Motion Picture Producers and Distributors of America, Inc. The year's most exciting discovery was when Rex Ingram saw Ramon Samanyagos, a Mexican dancer and extra player, changed his name to Ramon Novarro and gave him a role in "The Prisoner of Zenda." Robert J. Flaherty's "Nanook of The North" was one of the outstanding films and one of the first of the documentary style. Nazimova's own production of "Salome" with sets designed from the drawings of Beardsley was most unusual and exotic. It was an artistic success but a financial failure and cost Nazimova her life's savings. The star system was still all important. Popular stars continued to be box-office attractions regardless of the quality of their pictures.

ON LACKAYE, CONSTANCE BENNETT, MONTAGU LOVE
"WHAT'S WRONG WITH WOMEN?" (INDEPENDENT)

RUSSELL FRANCIS GRIFFIN, BILLIE DOVE, HUNTLY GORDON
IN "BEYOND THE RAINBOW" (ALDINE)

AGMAR GODOWSKY
"THE ALTAR STAIRS"
(UNIVERSAL)

JACKIE COOGAN
IN "OLIVER TWIST"
(FIRST NATIONAL)

GLORIA SWANSON
IN "HER GILDED CAGE"
(PARAMOUNT)

ERICH VON STROHEIM
IN "FOOLISH WIVES"
(UNIVERSAL)

ROSEMARY THEBY
IN "RICH MEN'S WIVES"
(PREFERRED)

MABEL BALLIN
(HODKINSON)

NILES WELSH
(REALART)

MARY ALDEN
(GOLDWYN)

KENNETH HARLAN
(FIRST NATIONAL)

MILDRED DAVIS
(PATHÉ)

MONTE BLUE
(WARNER)

HOPE HAMPTON
(FIRST NATIONAL)

BUCK JON
(FOX)

NAZIMOVA IN SCENES FROM HER OWN PRODUCTION OF
"SALOME"

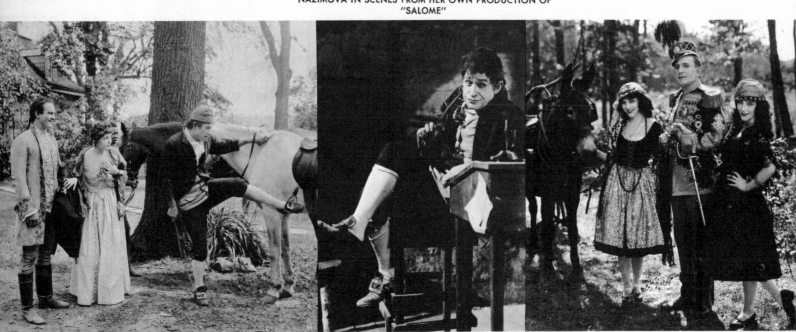

BEN HENDRICKS, JR., LOIS MEREDITH, WILL ROGERS
IN "THE HEADLESS HORSEMAN"
(HODKINSON)

WILL ROGERS IN
"THE HEADLESS HORSEMAN"
(HODKINSON)

RAYMOND HITCHCOCK AND THE FAIRBANKS TWINS
IN "THE BEAUTY SHOP" (PARAMOUNT)

UISE GLAUM
ODKINSON)

GLENN HUNTER
(PARAMOUNT)

AGNES AYRES
(PARAMOUNT)

EDMUND LOWE
(PARAMOUNT)

MADGE BELLAMY
(FIRST NATIONAL)

JACK HOXIE
(UNIVERSAL)

LILYAN TASHMAN
(PARAMOUNT)

HARRY C. MYERS
(FOX)

RUDOLPH VALENTINO IN SCENES FROM
"BLOOD AND SAND" WITH NITA NALDI

RUDOLPH VALENTINO IN SCENES FROM
"THE YOUNG RAJAH" WITH WANDA HAWLEY

RUDOLPH VALENTINO, NITA NALDI
IN "BLOOD AND SAND"

RUDOLPH VALENTINO, WANDA HAWLEY
IN "THE YOUNG RAJAH"

RUDOLPH VALENTINO PARAMOUNT PHOTOPLAYS

217

WALLACE REID, BEBE DANIELS, CONRAD NAGEL
IN "NICE PEOPLE" (PARAMOUNT)

FRANK ELLIOTT, GLORIA SWANSON, CONRAD NAGEL
IN "THE IMPOSSIBLE MRS. BELLEW" (PARAMOUNT)

DOROTHY DALTON, RUDOLPH VALENTINO, WALTER
IN "MORAN OF THE LADY LETTY" (PARAMOUN

GLORIA SWANSON, RUDOLPH VALENTINO

RUDOLPH VALENTINO
SCENES FROM "BEYOND THE ROCKS" (PARAMOUNT)

GLORIA SWANSON, RUDOLPH VALENTINO

GLENN HUNTER, RAYMOND HACKETT, DOROTHY GISH,
ALFRED HACKETT IN "THE COUNTRY FLAPPER" (PARAMOUNT)

CECIL B. DE MILLE AND STAFF
FILMING ON PARAMOUNT LOT

AGNES AYRES, JACK HOLT IN
"BOUGHT AND PAID FOR" (PARAMOUNT)

WARNER BAXTER, ETHEL CLAYTON
IN "IF I WERE QUEEN"
(R. C.)

JAMES KIRKWOOD, ANNA Q. NILSSON
IN "THE MAN FROM HOME"
(PARAMOUNT)

TOP TO BOTTOM: WESLEY
BARRY, SUNSHINE SAMMY
MORRISON, FLORENCE MORRISON,
GORDON GRIFFITH IN "PENROD" (FN)

BETTY COMPSON, THEODORE KOSLOFF
IN "THE GREEN TEMPTATION"
(PARAMOUNT)

T. ROY BARNES, MARION DA
IN "ADAM AND EVA"
(PARAMOUNT)

218

POLA NEGRI IN
"THE LAST PAYMENT" (PARAMOUNT)

MARION DAVIES, WILLIAM POWELL IN
"WHEN KNIGHTHOOD WAS IN FLOWER"

DAGNY SERVAES, HARRY LIEDTKE IN ERNST
LUBITSCH'S "THE LOVES OF PHARAOH" (PARAMOUNT)

ORREST STANLEY, MARION DAVIES, LYNN HARDING

MARION DAVIES, FORREST STANLEY

ERNEST GLENDENNING, RUTH SHEPLEY,
FORREST STANLEY, MARION DAVIES

SCENES FROM "WHEN KNIGHTHOOD WAS IN FLOWER" (COSMOPOLITAN-PARAMOUNT PRODUCTION)

1922 Rudolph Valentino made a series of mediocre films for Paramount which failed to dim his popularity. Gloria Swanson, Wallace Reid and Thomas Meighan were other Paramount stars in this category. Jackie Coogan was another pet of the public. He had success with "Oliver Twist." Paramount elevated Agnes Ayres and Bebe Daniels to stardom. Marion Davies continued to make elaborate costume pictures. Douglas Fairbanks made a hit with "Robin Hood," and Mary Pickford filmed a remake of her earlier success, "Tess of The Storm Country." Lon Chaney and Wallace Beery were forging ahead as character actors. Charles Chaplin and Ben Turpin continued as top comics while Harold Lloyd and Buster Keaton were increasing their fans.

MILTON SILLS, JACQUELINE LOGAN
IN "BURNING SANDS" (PARAMOUNT)

THEODORE KOSLOFF, BETTY COMPSON, BERT LYTELL
IN "TO HAVE AND TO HOLD" (PARAMOUNT)

OHN MILTERN, THOMAS MEIGHAN, LEATRICE JOY

LEATRICE JOY

LEATRICE JOY, THOMAS MEIGHAN

SCENES FROM "MANSLAUGHTER" (PARAMOUNT)

MARY PICKFORD
IN "TESS OF THE STORM COUNTRY" (UNITED ARTISTS)

LLOYD HUGHES, MARY PICKFORD (also above)
IN "TESS OF THE STORM COUNTRY" (UNITED ARTIST

PATSY RUTH MILLER, MAURICE FLYNN
Above: GUY BATES POST, VIRGINIA BROWN FAIRE
SCENES FROM "OMAR THE TENTMAKER" (TULLY)

DOUGLAS FAIRBANKS IN SCENES FROM "ROBIN HOOD" (UNITED ARTISTS)
WITH ENID BENNETT, WALLACE BEERY AND ALAN HALE

BEN TURPIN
(SENNETT)

STRONGHEART
(FIRST NATIONAL)

BEBE DANIELS
(PARAMOUNT)

GUY BATES POST IN DUAL ROLE
IN "THE MASQUERADER" (FIRST NATIONAL)

1922 Guy Bates Post, stage star, filmed two of his stage hits. Glenn Hunter and Joseph Schildkraut also deserted the stage for films. Larry Trimble, who introduced filmdom's first dog star, Jean, was responsible for Strongheart's movie career. At his suggestion, the German police dog who had served in the German Red Cross was bought by Jane Murfin. She wrote a series of pictures in which the famous dog was starred. D. W. Griffith's contribution this year was "Orphans of the Storm," a new version of "The Two Orphans," with Lillian and Dorothy Gish embellishing the cast.

CHARLES CHAPLIN IN
"THE PILGRIM" (FIRST NATIONAL)

AGNES AYRES, WALLACE REID, ADOLPHE MENJOU
Above: KATHLYN WILLIAMS, WALLACE REID, MAY McAVOY
IN SCENES FROM "CLARENCE"

WALLACE REID
IN "RENT FREE"
WALLACE REID — PARAMOUNT PHOTOPLAYS

LILA LEE, WALLACE REID
Above: WALLACE REID, WALTER LONG
IN SCENES FROM "THE DICTATOR"

HOOT GIBSON
(UNIVERSAL)

ELSIE FERGUSON
(PARAMOUNT-ARTCRAFT)

TOM MIX
(FOX)

JACQUELINE LOGAN
IN "EBB TIDE" (PARAMOUNT)

MARY MILES MINTER
IN "THE HEART SPECIALIST" (REALART)

LEATRICE JOY
IN "MANSLAUGHTER" (PARAMOUNT)

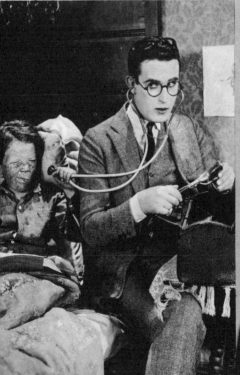

MICKEY DANIELS, HAROLD LLOYD
IN "DOCTOR JACK"

HAROLD LLOYD
IN "A SAILOR MADE MAN"
HAL ROACH PRODUCTIONS

HAROLD LLOYD, ANNA TOWNSEND
IN "GRANDMA'S BOY"

SHELDON LEWIS, LUCILLE LA VERNE, FRANK PUGLIA, DOROTHY GISH
Above: DOROTHY AND LILLIAN GISH

JOSEPH SCHILDKRAUT, LILLIAN GISH
Above: LILLIAN GISH (center)

LILLIAN GISH, JOSEPH SCHILDKRAUT

SCENES FROM D. W. GRIFFITH'S "ORPHANS OF THE STORM" (UNITED ARTISTS)

ANNA Q. NILSSON, FRANK KEENAN, RICHARD TUCKER
IN "HEARTS AFLAME" (METRO)

EDMUND BURNS, GEORGE ARLISS
IN "THE RULING PASSION" (UNITED ARTISTS)

HOWARD RALSTON, AGNES AYRES
IN "A DAUGHTER OF LUXURY" (PARAMOUNT

NAZIMOVA, ALAN HALE
IN "A DOLL'S HOUSE"
(UNITED ARTISTS)

WILLIAM HAINES (right) IN HIS FIRST
PICTURE "BROTHERS UNDER THE
SKIN" WITH NORMAN KERRY
(GOLDWYN)

MAY ALLISON, ROBERT ELLIS
IN "THE WOMAN WHO FOOLED HERSELF"
(ASSOCIATED EXHIBITORS)

LAURA LA PLANTE, WILLIAM DESM
IN "PERILS OF THE YUKON"
(UNIVERSAL)

LILLIAN AND DOROTHY GISH
IN "ORPHANS OF THE STORM"

RAMON NOVARRO   ALICE TERRY   BARBARA LA MARR, RAMON NOVARRO   BARBARA LA MARR   LEWIS STONE

Above: MALCOLM McGREGOR, LEWIS STONE, RAMON NOVARRO   Above: LEWIS STONE, ALICE TERRY, STUART HOLMES   Above: LEWIS STONE, ALICE TERRY, STUART HOL[M]

SCENES AND PLAYERS FROM "THE PRISONER OF ZENDA" (METRO)

| ALICE CALHOUN (VITAGRAPH) | T. ROY BARNES (COSMOPOLITAN) | MARGUERITE DE LA MOTTE (UNITED ARTISTS) | THEODORE VON ELTZ (PARAMOUNT) | FRANK CURRIER (METRO) | BARBARA BEDFORD (GOLDWYN) | TOM DOUGLAS (FOX) | LOTTIE PICKFORD (INDEPENDENT) | LIL DAGO (GOLDW |

EUGENE O'BRIEN, NORMA TALMADGE
IN "THE VOICE FROM THE MINARET"
(FIRST NATIONAL)

Standing: ELMO LINCOLN, EDWARD CONNELLY, VICTOR POTEL, ANDREW ARBUCKLE
Seated: CLAIRE McDOWELL, BARBARA LA MARR, LON CHANEY, BLANCHE SWEET, JOHN BOWERS
On floor: BILLY FRANEY, LOUISE FAZENDA, GALE HENRY, HANK MANN
CAST OF "QUINCY ADAMS SAWYER" (METRO)

WILLIAM COLLIER, JR., BETTY CA[R]
IN "CARDIGAN" (AMERICAN)

TALMADGE, IRVING CUMMINGS. Above: NORMA
GE, CONWAY TEARLE, ROSEMARY THEBY, KATE LESTER
SCENES FROM "THE ETERNAL FLAME"

NORMA TALMADGE, HARRISON FORD
Above: WYNDHAM STANDING, NORMA TALMADGE,
ALEC B. FRANCIS   SCENES FROM "SMILIN' THROUGH"
FIRST NATIONAL RELEASES

CONSTANCE TALMADGE, NIGEL BARRIE
Above: EDWARD BURNS, CONSTANCE TALMADGE,
WARNER OLAND   SCENES FROM "EAST IS WEST"

NUB
LLARD
ROACH)

GLADYS
HULETTE
(FIRST NATIONAL)

EDMUND
BURNS
(UNITED ARTISTS)

SHANNON
DAY
(PARAMOUNT)

ARTHUR
RANKIN
(METRO)

VIRGINIA
BROWN FAIRE
(FIRST NATIONAL)

AGNES
VERNON
(UNIVERSAL)

HARRY
LIEDTKE
(PARAMOUNT)

LOUISE
HUFF
(FIRST NATIONAL)

"THE BLACKSMITH"   "DAY DREAMS"   "THE ELECTRIC HOUSE"   "THE BOAT"

BUSTER KEATON FEATURES (FIRST NATIONAL)

BRYANT WASHBURN
(SELZNICK)

MARION DAVIES
(COSMOPOLITAN)

DOUGLAS MacLEAN
(PARAMOUNT)

PRISCILLA DEAN
(UNIVERSAL)

WILLIAM S. HART
(PARAMOUNT)

DOROTHY DALTON
(PARAMOUNT)

LIONEL BELMORE, AGGIE HERRING, JACKIE COOGAN, JOSEPH HAZELTON, ESTHER RALSTON. Above: EDOUARD TREBAOL, JACKIE COOGAN, LON CHANEY, TAYLOR GRAVES IN "OLIVER TWIST" (FIRST NATIONAL)

ADVERTISEMENT FOR "OLIVER TWIST"

JOHN GILBERT, ESTELLE TAYLOR
Above: JOHN GILBERT
SCENES FROM "MONTE CRISTO" (FOX)

RUSH HUGHES, TOM GALLERY, DANA TODD, GERTRUDE ASTOR, RICHARD DIX, COLLEEN MOORE IN "THE WALL FLOWER" (GOLDWYN)

CYRIL CHADWICK, NORMAN KERRY (right)
IN "THREE LIVE GHOSTS" (PARAMOUNT)

DOUGLAS MacLEAN IN
"THE HOTTENTOT" (FIRST NATIONAL)

DOROTHY WOODS, ART ACORD IN
"IN THE DAYS OF BUFFALO BILL" (UNIVERSAL)

HOOT GIBSON (right)
IN "THE BEARCAT" (UNIVERSAL)

FRANK MAYO
IN "AFRAID TO FIGHT" (UNIVERSAL)

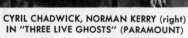

228

CLYN ARBUCKLE IN
PRODIGAL JUDGE"
(VITAGRAPH)

MABEL NORMAND
IN "SUZANNA"
(SENNETT)

WILLIAM FAIRBANKS
(INDEPENDENT)

COLLEEN MOORE
IN "THE WALL FLOWER"
(GOLDWYN)

NITA NALDI
(PARAMOUNT)

GUY BATES POST IN
"OMAR THE TENTMAKER"
(FIRST NATIONAL)

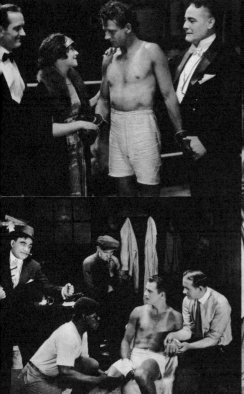

AM RYAN, REGINALD DENNY, HAYDEN STEVENSON
Above: REGINALD DENNY
CENES FROM "THE LEATHER PUSHERS" (UNIVERSAL)

MAUDE GEORGE, ERICH VON STROHEIM,
MISS DU PONT (MARGUERITE ARMSTRONG)
IN "FOOLISH WIVES" (UNIVERSAL)

MISS DU PONT, ERICH VON STROHEIM
SCENES FROM "FOOLISH WIVES"
(UNIVERSAL)

STRONGHEART, IRENE RICH IN
"BRAWN OF THE NORTH" (FIRST NATIONAL)

1922 Erich Von Stroheim followed his first directorial assignment, "Blind Wives," with "Foolish Wives." It was well received and was a "prestige" picture for Universal. Tom Mix's and Buck Jones' western pictures were top money-makers for Fox. William Farnum was slipping with the fans, and John Gilbert was winning new ones. He appeared in a new film version of "The Count of Monte Cristo." Clara Kimball Young, after a series of Metro pictures unworthy of her talents, embarked on a very responsive "personal appearance" tour. Pauline Frederick and Eugene O'Brien returned to the stage. Norma and Constance Talmadge were still First National's top draws. Newcomers included Constance Bennett, Billie Dove and William Haines.

HARRY C. MYERS, KENNETH HARLAN, MARIE PREVOST
IN "THE BEAUTIFUL AND THE DAMNED" (WARNER)

N MOORE, MALCOLM McGREGOR, ERNEST TORRENCE
IN "BROKEN CHAINS" (GOLDWYN)

VIRGINIA VALLI, HOUSE PETERS
IN "THE STORM"
(UNIVERSAL)

DOROTHY PHILLIPS, WALLACE BEERY
IN "HURRICANE'S GAL"
(FIRST NATIONAL)

CLARA KIMBALL YOUNG, ELLIOTT DEXTER,
LOUISE DRESSER (right) IN "ENTER MADAME"
(METRO)

JACQUELINE LOGAN (PARAMOUNT)

BEN LYON (FIRST NATIONAL)

MARY MILES MINTER (PARAMOUNT)

LEWIS STONE (METRO)

LAURA LA PLANTE (UNIVERSAL)

ALFRED LUNT (GOLDWYN)

GERTRUDE OLMSTEAD (UNIVERSAL)

GEORGE HACKATHORNE (UNIVERSAL)

PATSY R MILLE (UNIVERS

JOSEPH DOWLING, BERYL MERCER, MAHLON HAMILTON, RICHARD DIX, MAE BUSCH, GARETH HUGHES

MAE BUSCH, RICHARD DIX
SCENES FROM "THE CHRISTIAN" (GOLDWYN)

BERYL MERCER, MAE BUSCH, RICHARD DIX

BESSIE LOVE, CARMEL MYERS, GEORGE WALSH IN "SLAVE OF DESIRE" (GOLDWYN)

NEAL BURNS, BOBBY VERNON, JIMMIE HARRISON, JIMMIE ADAMS, EARL RODNEY (CHRISTIE COMEDIANS)

BARNEY BERNARD, ALEXANDER CARR, DE SACIA MO IN "POTASH AND PERLMUTTER" (GOLDWYN

CONSTANCE TALMADGE IN "THE DANGEROUS MAID" (FIRST NATIONAL)

CHARLES RAY IN "THE COURTSHIP OF MILES STANDISH" (ASSOCIATED EXHIBITORS)

ALMA RUBENS IN "UNDER THE RED ROBE" (COSMOPOLITAN)

RICHARD DIX IN "THE CHRISTIAN" (GOLDWYN)

CORINNE GRIFFITH IN "BLACK OXEN" (FIRST NATIONAL)

230

ZASU
PITTS
(UNIVERSAL)

EARLE
FOXE
(GOLDWYN)

MARY
PHILBIN
(UNIVERSAL)

BEN
ALEXANDER
(FIRST NATIONAL)

MAUDE
GEORGE
(UNIVERSAL)

NOAH
BEERY
(GOLDWYN)

EDNA MAY
OLIVER
(PARAMOUNT)

NEIL
HAMILTON
(GRIFFITH)

BERYL
MERCER
(GOLDWYN)

MABEL BALLIN, GEORGE WALSH

GEORGE WALSH, HARRISON FORD, EARLE FOXE, MRS. CRAUFURD KENT,
MABEL BALLIN, ADELE ROWLAND, ELEANOR BOARDMAN
SCENES FROM "VANITY FAIR" (GOLDWYN)

WILLARD LOUIS, ELEANOR BOARDMAN,
MABEL BALLIN

LON CHANEY, RAYMOND McKEE
IN "A BLIND BARGAIN" (GOLDWYN)

1923 "The Covered Wagon" was the first of the large-scale epic films. A great success, it was directed by James Cruze, former actor with the old Thanhauser company. Cecil B. De Mille's large-scale contribution was "The Ten Commandments." Erich Von Stroheim left "Merry-Go-Round" in the middle of production at Universal and Rupert Julian finished the film. Metro and Goldwyn consolidated as Metro-Goldwyn and Von Stroheim signed with them and made "Greed," considered by many his best. Charles Ray put his own money into an elaborate historical picture, "The Courtship of Miles Standish," which was a failure and forced him into bankruptcy.

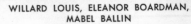

BARBARA LA MARR, ELEANOR BOARDMAN, ERNST LUBITSCH,
RICHARD DIX, FRANK MAYO, MAE BUSCH IN
"SOULS FOR SALE" (GOLDWYN)

HARRISON FORD IN
"LITTLE OLD NEW YORK"
(GOLDWYN)

JEAN ARTHUR
IN "CAMEO KIRBY"
(FOX)

JOHN GILBERT
IN "CAMEO KIRBY"
(FOX)

BLANCHE SWEET IN
"IN THE PALACE OF THE KING"
(GOLDWYN)

EDMUND LOWE IN
"IN THE PALACE OF THE KING"
(GOLDWYN)

RICHARD DIX, ROD LA ROCQUE, LEATRICE JOY
Top: CHARLES DE ROCHE (center)
Center: CHARLES DE ROCHE, THEODORE ROBERTS,
ESTELLE TAYLOR

ROD LA ROCQUE, RICHARD DIX, EDYTHE CHAPMAN
Top: ESTELLE TAYLOR (left)
Center: THEODORE ROBERTS, CHARLES DE ROCHE, PAT MOORE
SCENES FROM CECIL B. DE MILLE'S "THE TEN COMMANDMENTS"

LEATRICE JOY, ROD LA ROCQUE
Top: THEODORE ROBERTS AS MOSES
Center: CHARLES DE ROCHE, ROD LA ROCQUE, NITA

MIMI PALMERI, ALFRED LUNT
IN "THE RAGGED EDGE"
(GOLDWYN)

BILLY SULLIVAN
IN "THE LEATHER PUSHERS"
(UNIVERSAL)

PAULINE STARKE, EDMUND LOWE
IN "IN THE PALACE OF THE KING"
(GOLDWYN)

LOIS WILSON, J. WARREN KERRIGAN   TULLY MARSHALL, LOIS WILSON   J. WARREN KERRIGAN, LOIS WILSON

p: CHARLES OGLE, LOIS WILSON, ALAN HALE, J. WARREN KERRIGAN, ETHEL WALES

SCENES FROM "THE COVERED WAGON" (PARAMOUNT)

ANTONIO MORENO, BEBE DANIELS
IN "THE EXCITERS"
(PARAMOUNT)

ANTONIO MORENO, MARY MILES MINTER, ERNEST TORRENCE
IN "THE TRAIL OF THE LONESOME PINE"
(PARAMOUNT)

GLORIA SWANSON, HUNTLEY GORDON
IN "BLUEBEARD'S EIGHTH WIFE"
(PARAMOUNT)

POLA NEGRI

NIO MORENO, GARETH HUGHES, ADOLPHE MENJOU   ADOLPHE MENJOU, POLA NEGRI   POLA NEGRI   POLA NEGRI, WALLACE BEERY

SCENES FROM "THE SPANISH DANCER" (PARAMOUNT)

POLA NEGRI, JACK HOLT, CHARLES DE ROCHE   ANTONIO MORENO   KATHLYN WILLIAMS   POLA NEGRI, CHARLES DE ROCHE
IN "THE CHEAT" (PARAMOUNT)   IN "THE CHEAT" (PARAMOUNT)

IN "THE SPANISH DANCER" (PARAMOUNT)

1923 Pola Negri, Polish actress whose German films had great popularity in America, was signed by Paramount. Her first American-made film was "Bella Donna." She became the only real rival of Gloria Swanson on the Paramount lot. Warner Brothers, headed by Harry Warner who had begun in the exchange business and made several earlier independent films, were coming into their own as top-ranking producers. Barbara La Marr was heading for stardom. A young Brooklyn girl, Clara Bow, won a beauty contest and appeared in "Down To The Sea In Ships." Jean Arthur, with little acting experience, was John Gilbert's leading lady at Fox. Ronald Colman, young English actor, made his bow on the American screen in "The White Sister."

POLA NEGRI   POLA NEGRI   POLA NEGRI   POLA NEGRI

MACEY HARLAM, CONRAD NAGEL, POLA NEGRI   POLA NEGRI, CONWAY TEARLE   MACEY HARLAM, CONRAD NAGEL, POLA NEGRI

SCENES FROM "BELLA DONNA" (PARAMOUNT)

RAYMOND GRIFFITH, PRISCILLA DEAN, MATT MOORE, WALLACE BEERY IN "THE WHITE TIGER" (UNIVERSAL-JEWEL)

THOMAS MEIGHAN, LAURANCE WHEAT, GERTRUDE ASTOR IN "THE NE'ER-DO-WELL" (PARAMOUNT)

LOUISE DRESSER, EDWARD EVERETT HORTON, ERN??? TORRENCE, WILLIAM AUSTIN IN "RUGGLES OF RED ??? (PARAMOUNT)

WARNER BAXTER (PARAMOUNT)

JEAN ARTHUR (FOX)

MATT MOORE (METRO)

NORMA SHEARER (METRO)

ADOLPHE MENJOU (PARAMOUNT)

BESSIE LOVE (GOLDWYN)

DAVID POWELL, NITA NALDI, BEBE DANIELS IN "THE GLIMPSES OF THE MOON" (PARAMOUNT)

CHARLES DE ROCHE IN "THE MARRIAGE MAKER" (PARAMOUNT)

CHARLES DE ROCHE IN "THE MARRIAGE MAKER" (PARAMOUNT)

JEAN HERSHOLT (UNITED ARTISTS)

MARY MacLAREN (METRO)

MALCOLM McGREGOR (METRO)

JULANNE JOHNSTON (UNITED ARTISTS)

WILLIAM HAINES (GOLDWYN)

DERLYS PERDUE (F.B.O.)

CULLEN LANDIS (UNIVERSAL)

BETTY BLYTHE (FOX)

LOWEL? SHERMA? (FIRST NATIO???

MAURICE FLYNN, JACQUELINE LOGAN, GEORGE FAWCETT IN "SALOMY JANE" (PARAMOUNT)

DOUGLAS FAIRBANKS, JR. (left) IN HIS FIRST FILM "STEPHEN STEPS OUT," HARRY C. MYERS (right) (PARAMOUNT)

CASSON FERGUSON, THEODORE ROBERTS, CHARLES ??? IN "GRUMPY" (PARAMOUNT)

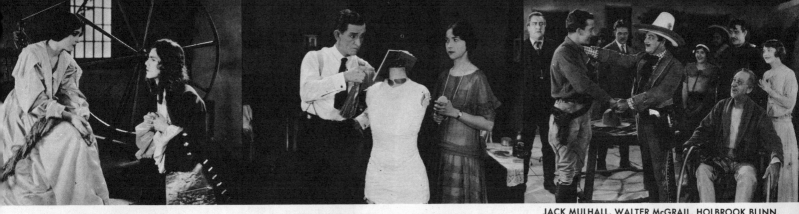

MARY ASTOR, GLENN HUNTER
IN "THE SCARECROW"

EDWARD EVERETT HORTON, HELEN JEROME EDDY
IN "TO THE LADIES" (PARAMOUNT)

JACK MULHALL, WALTER McGRAIL, HOLBROOK BLINN,
HARRY C. MYERS, ENID BENNETT IN "THE BAD MAN"
(FIRST NATIONAL)

ALICE TERRY
(METRO)

EMIL JANNINGS
(PARAMOUNT)

LEATRICE JOY
(PARAMOUNT)

JAMES CRUZE
(PARAMOUNT)

MAE MURRAY
(METRO)

MILTON SILLS
(FIRST NATIONAL)

CARMEL MYERS, MALCOLM McGREGOR
IN "THE DANCER OF THE NILE" (EARLE)

ANDREE LAFAYETTE, ARTHUR EDMUND CAREW,
CREIGHTON HALE IN "TRILBY" (FIRST NATIONAL)

FRANK EVANS, ALFRED LUNT
IN "BACKBONE" (DISTINCTIVE)

JOHN
DAVIDSON
(UNIVERSAL)

PAULINE
STARKE
(GOLDWYN)

GEORGE
O'HARA
(F. B. O.)

MARTHA
MANSFIELD
(FIRST NATIONAL)

WILLIAM
DESMOND
(UNIVERSAL)

PHYLLIS
HAVER
(UNIVERSAL)

ROBERT
AGNEW
(METRO)

VIRGINIA
VALLI
(UNIVERSAL)

HUNTLEY
GORDON
(SELZNICK)

JOHNNY ARTHUR, DOROTHY PHILLIPS, HENRY B.
WALTHALL IN "THE UNKNOWN PURPLE" (CARLOS)

JACK MOWER, EILEEN SEDGWICK
IN "THE DAYS OF DANIEL BOONE"
(UNIVERSAL)

SYDNEY CHAPLIN, OWEN MOORE
IN "HER TEMPORARY HUSBAND"
(FIRST NATIONAL)

KENNETH HARLAN, FLORENCE VIDOR
IN "THE VIRGINIAN"
(PREFERRED)

237

ALMA RUBENS (left), LIONEL BARRYMORE
IN "ENEMIES OF WOMEN" (PARAMOUNT)

GERTRUDE OLMSTEAD, JOHN GILBERT
IN "CAMEO KIRBY" (FOX)

VIOLET MERSEREAU, GUIDO TRENTO, NERIO BERNA
IN "THE SHEPHERD KING" (FOX)

1923 Douglas Fairbanks, Jr., at fifteen, starred in his first film, "Stephen Steps Out," for Paramount. An up and coming stage actor, Alfred Lunt, made two films but he preferred the stage and other film appearances were rare. Laurette Taylor filmed her great success, "Peg O' My Heart." Paramount made a version of it with Wanda Hawley in 1919 but they could not clear the rights so it was never released. Blanche Sweet appeared to advantage in the first filming of Eugene O'Neill's "Anna Christie." Richard Barthelmess, Corinne Griffith, Thomas Meighan, Richard Dix, Leatrice Joy, Ramon Novarro, Colleen Moore, Rod La Rocque, Pola Negri and Milton Sills were building into big box office favorites.

RAMON NOVARRO, ALICE TERRY
IN "WHERE THE PAVEMENT ENDS" (METRO)

BETTY COMPSON, EDMUND LOWE
IN "THE WHITE FLOWER" (PARAMOUNT)

MATT MOORE (center), BARBARA LA MARR
IN "STRANGERS OF THE NIGHT" (METRO)

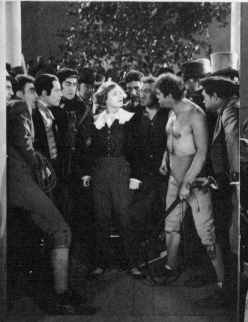

HARRISON FORD, MARION DAVIES,
LOUIS WOLHEIM

GEORGE BARRAUD, NORVAL KEEDWELL, MAHLON HAMILTON, HARRISON FORD, MARION DAVIES

HARRISON FORD, MARION D

SCENES FROM "LITTLE OLD NEW YORK" (COSMOPOLITAN)

ON SILLS, PAULINE GARON, THEODORE KOSLOFF   THEODORE KOSLOFF, ANNA Q. NILSSON, MILTON SILLS   MILTON SILLS, ELLIOTT DEXTER
SCENES FROM CECIL B. DE MILLE'S "ADAM'S RIB" (PARAMOUNT)

GARETH HUGHES, MAY McAVOY,   MARIE PREVOST   MAE MARSH, IVOR NOVELLO
Above: BETTY COMPSON, BERT LYTELL, WALTER LONG   (WARNER BROS.)   Above: NEIL HAMILTON, CAROL DEMPSTER
SCENES FROM "KICK IN" (PARAMOUNT)   SCENES FROM D. W. GRIFFITH'S "THE WHITE ROSE"

NE HAMMERSTEIN, BERT LYTELL   IRVING CUMMINGS, BRYANT WASHBURN, BERT LYTELL, ELAINE HAMMERSTEIN, CLAIRE WINDSOR   BERT LYTELL, LEW CODY
SCENES FROM "RUPERT OF HENTZAU" (SELZNICK)

NORMA TALMADGE, WALLACE BEERY   ANDRÉ DE BERANGER, CONWAY
Above: NORMA TALMADGE, WALLACE BEERY,   BETTY FRANCISCO
CONWAY TEARLE   SCENES FROM "ASHES OF VENGEANCE" (FIRST NATION

NORMA TALMADGE, JOSEPH SCHILDKRAUT
IN "DUST OF DESIRE" (FIRST NATIONAL)

CHARLES RAY IN
"THE GIRL I LOVE"
(UNITED ARTISTS)

ENID BENNETT, CHARLES RAY IN
"THE COURTSHIP OF MILES STANDISH"
(ASSOCIATED EXHIBITORS)

ETHEL GRANDIN, CHARLES RA
IN "A TAILOR MADE MAN"
(FIRST NATIONAL)

NCHE SWEET, GEORGE MARION   BLANCHE SWEET
Above: BLANCHE SWEET, WILLIAM RUSSELL
SCENES FROM "ANNA CHRISTIE" (INCE)

HARD BARTHELMESS, WILLIAM POWELL   DOROTHY GISH
RICHARD BARTHELMESS, DOROTHY GISH
SCENES FROM "THE BRIGHT SHAWL" (FIRST NATIONAL)

BLANCHE SWEET AS ANNA CHRISTIE

BARBARA LA MARR, LIONEL BARRYMORE, BERT LYTELL Center: BERT LYTELL, BARBARA LA MARR, LIONEL BARRYMORE ·LIONEL BARRYMORE, BARBARA LA MARR

SCENES FROM "THE ETERNAL CITY" (FIRST NATIONAL)

EDNA PURVIANCE (UNITED ARTISTS)   RONALD COLMAN (INSPIRATION)   MAY McAVOY (PARAMOUNT)   JOHN GILBERT (FOX)   ELAINE HAMMERSTEIN (SELZNICK)   RICARDO CORTE (PARAMOUNT)

LILLIAN GISH, RONALD COLMAN   LILLIAN GISH, RONALD COLMAN   LILLIAN GISH, RONALD COLMAN

SCENES FROM "THE WHITE SISTER" (INSPIRATION)

"DADDY"   WITH PEACHES JACKSON IN "CIRCUS DAYS"   "DADDY"   "CIRCUS DAYS"   "THE YOUNG KING"   "DADDY"

242   SCENES FROM JACKIE COOGAN FILMS (FIRST NATIONAL)

NORMA TALMADGE, LEW CODY
IN "WITHIN THE LAW" (FIRST NATIONAL)

J. WARREN KERRIGAN, RUSSELL SIMPSON (right)
IN "THE GIRL OF THE GOLDEN WEST" (FIRST NATIONAL)

CLAUDE GILLINGWATER, CONSTANCE TALMADGE,
JOHNNY HARRON IN "DULCY" (FIRST NATIONAL)

SHIRLEY MASON
(FOX)

RAMON NOVARRO
(METRO)

1923 "Siegfried," a German import, was favorably received, and its beautiful photography caused much comment. Harold Lloyd became his own producer with a Paramount releasing outlet. Norma Shearer, former model, and Billie Dove, Ziegfeld beauty, were beginning to be noticed, and so were William Haines and Richard Arlen, then using his own name, Van Mattimore. Chaplin directed a serious picture, "A Woman of Paris," which the critics liked. Among the top directors were Cecil B. and William De Mille, James Cruze, Rex Ingram, Frank Lloyd, Henry King, Fred Niblo, Erich Von Stroheim and Ernst Lubitsch.

DOUGLAS FAIRBANKS, JR.
(PARAMOUNT)

NORMAN KERRY
(UNIVERSAL)

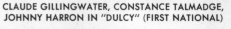

EDWARD EVERETT
HORTON
(PARAMOUNT)

PAUL
RICHTER
(UFA)

LOUIS
WOLHEIM
(COSMOPOLITAN)

CONWAY TEARLE, CONSTANCE TALMADGE
IN "THE DANGEROUS MAID" (FIRST NATIONAL)

PAUL RICHTER
IN "SIEGFRIED" (UFA)

PAUL RICHTER
IN "SIEGFRIED" (UFA)

RICHARD BARTHELMESS, DOROTHY GISH
IN "FURY" (INSPIRATION)

CORINNE GRIFFITH
IN "BLACK OXEN" (FIRST NATIONAL)

DOROTHY MACKAILL, RICHARD BARTHELMESS
IN "THE FIGHTING BLADE"
(FIRST NATIONAL)

243

ALICE JOYCE IN "THE GREEN GODDESS" (GOLDWYN)

J. WARREN KERRIGAN IN "THE COVERED WAGON" (PARAMOUNT)

Top row: LILLIAN RICH, LOIS WILSON, VOLA VALE; GLORIA HOPE, HELEN FERGUSON, CLAIRE ADAMS; VIRGINIA FOX, HAROLD LLOYD, PATSY RUTH MILLER; EDNA MURPHY, MILDRFD DAVIS, MAY McAVOY

IRVING CUMMINGS IN "RUPERT OF HENTZAU" (SELZNICK)

PHYLLIS HAVER IN "THE TEMPLE OF VEN (FOX)

H. B. WARNER, GLORIA SWANSON (also above) FERDINAND GOTTSCHALK, LUCILLE LAVERNE IN "ZAZA" (PARAMOUNT)

CARLYLE BLACKWELL, EVELYN GREELY IN "BULLDOG DRUMMOND" (HODKINSON)

GLADYS COOPER, IVOR NOVELLO Above: GLADYS COOPER, ELLEN TERRY SCENES FROM "THE BOHEMIAN GIRL" (KNOLES)

NORMAN KERRY IN "THE HUNCHBACK OF NOTRE DAME" (UNIVERSAL)

PATSY RUTH MILLER IN "THE HUNCHBACK OF NOTRE DAME" (UNIVERSAL)

LLOYD HUGHES IN "SCARS OF JEALOUSY" (INCE)

SYDNEY CHAPLIN IN "THE RENDEZVOUS" (GOLDWYN)

VIRGINIA VALLI IN "A LADY OF QUALITY" (UNIVERSAL)

MILTON SILLS IN "A LADY OF QUALITY" (UNIVERSAL)

TONIO MORENO IN
Y AMERICAN WIFE''
(PARAMOUNT)

HOPE HAMPTON
IN ''DOES IT PAY?''
(FOX)

GEORGE O'HARA (right)
IN ''FIGHTING BLOOD''
(F. B. O.)

ANNA Q. NILSSON
IN ''PONJOLA''
(FIRST NATIONAL)

JOSEPH SCHILDKRAUT
IN ''SONG OF LOVE''
(FIRST NATIONAL)

DOROTHY DAVENPORT (MRS. WALLACE REID),
BESSIE LOVE IN ''HUMAN WRECKAGE'' (INCE)

LEATRICE JOY, ALBERT ROSCOE
IN ''JAVA HEAD'' (PARAMOUNT)

MYRTLE STEDMAN, JOHN PATRICK, COLLEEN MOORE
IN ''FLAMING YOUTH'' (FIRST NATIONAL)

EO, BEN ALEXANDER, JOE BUTTERWORTH, BUDDY
NGER IN ''PENROD AND SAM'' (FIRST NATIONAL)

ON LOCATION FOR ''WINTER HAS CAME'' (CHRISTIE COMEDY)
In group: BABE LONDON, WILLIAM IRVING, DOROTHY DEVORE, EARL
RODNEY, LYDIA YEAMANS TITUS, WILLIAM CHAPMAN, VICTOR RODMAN

FLORENCE VIDOR, CLAUDE GILLINGWATER,
MARGARET McWADE, HAROLD GOODWIN
IN ''ALICE ADAMS'' (ASSOCIATED EXHIBITORS)

WARREN KERRIGAN (left), PAT O'MALLEY (center)
IN ''THE MAN FROM BRODNEY'S'' (VITAGRAPH)

GLENN HUNTER
IN ''THE SCARECROW''
(PARAMOUNT)

STAN LAUREL
IN ''WHEN KNIGHTS
WERE COLD'' (METRO)

WILLIAM HAINES, ALEC B. FRANCIS, WILLIAM H. CRANE,
CLAUDE GILLINGWATER, ELEANOR BOARDMAN IN
''THREE WISE FOOLS'' (METRO-GOLDWYN)

NITA NALDI IN
"THE GLIMPSES OF THE MOON"
(PARAMOUNT)

BERTRAM GRASSBY, GEORGE FAWCETT, MARY MILES MINTER,
MAURICE FLYNN. Above: MAURICE FLYNN, NOBLE JOHNSON
SCENES FROM "THE DRUMS OF FATE" (PARAMOUNT)

BULL MONTANA IN "ROB 'EM GOOD" (METRO)
Above: BULL MONTANA IN "THE TWO TWINS" (METRO)

GASTON GLASS I
"DAUGHTERS OF THE
(PREFERRED)

1923 In Sweden, a girl named Greta Gustafsson appeared in a film, "The Atonement of Gösta Berling." Later, as Greta Garbo, she became one of the greatest figures in film history. Lon Chaney increased his reputation as an actor of weird make-ups in "The Hunchback of Notre Dame."

VIRGINIA BROWN FAIRE, VAN MATTIMORE (RICHARD
ARLEN), RALPH LEWIS IN "VENGEANCE OF THE DEEP"
(AMERICAN)

ETHEL GREY
TERRY
(METRO)

IVOR
NOVELLO
(GRIFFITH)

LENORE
ULRIC
(WARNER)

MONTE BLUE, ALAN HALE, LOUISE FAZENDA,
FLORENCE VIDOR IN "MAIN STREET" (WARNER)

PHYLLIS HAVER, DAVID BUTLER (right)
Above: DAVID BUTLER, MARY PHILBIN
SCENES FROM "THE TEMPLE OF VENUS"

DAVID POWELL, HARRY MOREY, ALICE JOYCE, GEORGE ARLISS
IN "THE GREEN GODDESS" (GOLDWYN)

BILLIE DOVE
(FOX)

GRETA GARBO IN
"THE ATONEMENT OF GÖSTA BERLING"

GRETA GARBO IN
"THE ATONEMENT OF GOSTA BERLING"

NORMA SHEARER
(METRO)

PERCY MARMONT, ANN FORREST
IN "IF WINTER COMES" (FOX)

PERCY MARMONT IN
"IF WINTER COMES"
(FOX)

ALMA RUBENS, JOHN CHARLES THOMAS
IN "UNDER THE RED ROBE"
(COSMOPOLITAN)

ROBERT B. MANTELL, GENEVIEVE HAMPER, ROSE COGHLAN,
IAN MacLAREN, MARY McLAREN, WILLIAM POWELL
IN "UNDER THE RED ROBE" (COSMOPOLITAN)

MARY PICKFORD, HOLBROOK BLINN, GEORGE WALSH

HOLBROOK BLINN, MARY PICKFORD
Above: GEORGE WALSH, MARY PICKFORD

SCENES FROM ERNST LUBITSCH'S "ROSITA" (UNITED ARTISTS)

247

CHARLES EMMETT MACK, ELINOR FAIR, EMILY FITZROY
IN "DRIVEN" (UNIVERSAL)

MARGUERITE DE LA MOTTE, HUNTLEY GORDON, MYRTLE STEDMAN,
CULLEN LANDIS IN "THE FAMOUS MRS. FAIR" (METRO)

MR. GALLAGHER AND MR. SHEAN (RAY AND A
IN "AROUND THE TOWN" (FOX)

BARBARA LA MARR
(METRO)

THOMAS MEIGHAN
(PARAMOUNT)

MONTE BLUE, MARIE PREVOST
IN "BRASS"
(WARNER)

ANTONIO MORENO, GLORIA SWANSON
IN "MY AMERICAN WIFE"
(PARAMOUNT)

ANNA MAY WONG, KENNETH
HARLAN IN "THE TOLL OF
THE SEA" (METRO)

CORINNE GRIFFITH, CONWAY TEARLE
IN "THE COMMON LAW"
(FIRST NATIONAL)

GASTON GLASS IN "THE HERO"
(PREFERRED)

WALTER LONG, EDWIN J. BRADY, RICHARD TUCKER, MIRIAM
COOPER, KENNETH HARLAN, MISS DU PONT IN
"THE BROKEN WING" (PREFERRED)

CLARA KIMBALL YOUNG, JOHN BOWERS
IN "THE WOMAN OF BRONZE" (METRO)

ANNA Q. NILSSON
(FIRST NATIONAL)

LIONEL BARRYMORE
(FIRST NATIONAL)

CHARLES "BUCK" JONES, PEGGY SHAW
IN "SKID PROOF"
(FOX)

RALPH GRAVES, DOROTHY GISH
IN "OUT OF LUCK"
(PARAMOUNT)

EVELYN BRENT, HOUSE PETERS
IN "HELD TO ANSWER"
(METRO)

AGNES AYRES, MAHLON HAMILTON
IN "THE HEART RAIDER"
(PARAMOUNT)

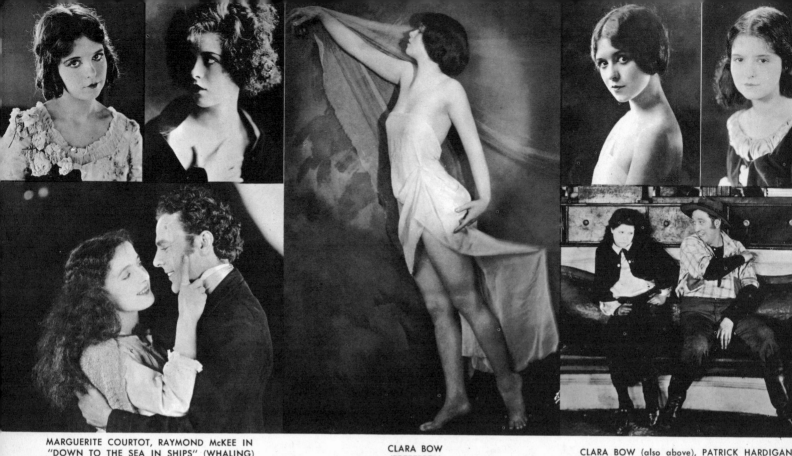

MARGUERITE COURTOT, RAYMOND McKEE IN
"DOWN TO THE SEA IN SHIPS" (WHALING)
Above: CLARA BOW

CLARA BOW
(PREFERRED)

CLARA BOW (also above), PATRICK HARDIGAN
IN "DOWN TO THE SEA IN SHIPS"

"THE BALLOONATIC"
(FIRST NATIONAL)

WITH WALLACE BEERY, OLIVER HARDY
IN "THE THREE AGES" (METRO)
BUSTER KEATON COMEDIES

"THE THREE AGES"
(METRO)

ELINOR FAIR, VINCENT COLEMAN, MARY ALDEN,
CHARLES RICHMAN. Above: HEDDA HOPPER
SCENES FROM "HAS THE WORLD GONE MAD!" (GOODMAN)

EDNA PURVIANCE, ADOLPHE MENJOU IN
"A WOMAN OF PARIS" DIRECTED BY CHARLES CHAPLIN
(UNITED ARTISTS)

THEODORE VON ELTZ, LENORE ULRIC (also above)
FORREST STANLEY IN "TIGER ROSE"
(WARNER BROS.)

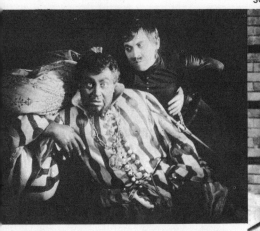

RAMON NOVARRO (also above), ALICE TERRY

RAMON NOVARRO

SCENES FROM REX INGRAM'S "SCARAMOUCHE" (METRO)

RAMON NOVARRO, JULIA SWAYNE GORDON, LEWIS STONE, ALICE TERRY. Above: STONE, NOVARRO

L JANNINGS AND WERNER KRAUSS AS OTHELLO AND IAGO IN "OTHELLO" (EXPORT-IMPORT)

NIGEL BARRIE, ETHEL GREY TERRY, LAURETTE TAYLOR IN "PEG O' MY HEART" (METRO)

ICA LENKEFFY, EMIL JANNINGS IN "OTHELLO" (EXPORT-IMPORT)

JOBYNA RALSTON, HAROLD LLOYD, JOHN AASEN IN "WHY WORRY." Above: HAROLD LLOYD IN "SAFETY LAST" (PATHÉ)

LAURETTE TAYLOR IN "PEG O' MY HEART" (METRO)

251

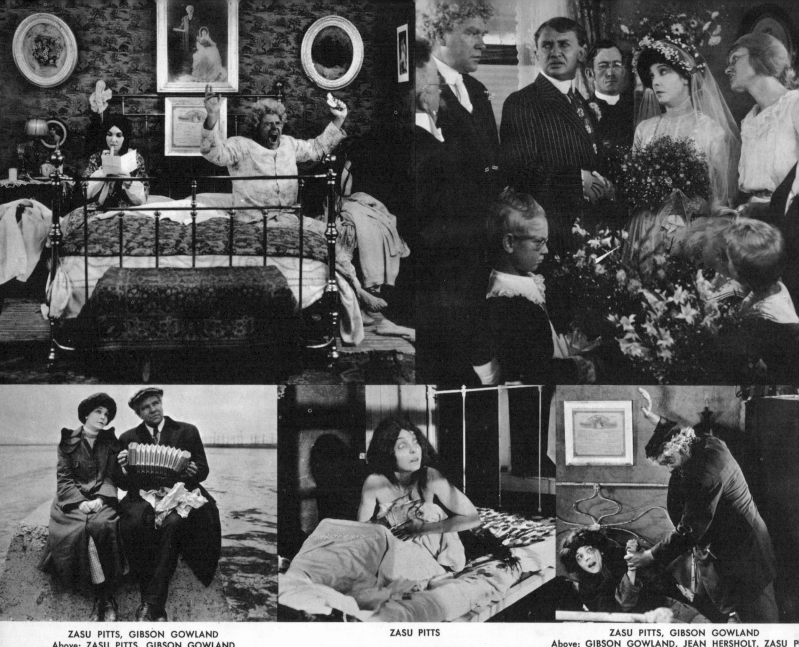

ZASU PITTS, GIBSON GOWLAND
Above: ZASU PITTS, GIBSON GOWLAND

ZASU PITTS

SCENES FROM "GREED" (METRO-GOLDWYN)

ZASU PITTS, GIBSON GOWLAND
Above: GIBSON GOWLAND, JEAN HERSHOLT, ZASU P
JOAN STANDING

CESARE GRAVINA, EDITH YORKE, GEORGE HACKATHORNE
Above: NORMAN KERRY, AL EDMUNDSON

GEORGE
HACKATHORNE

MARY PHILBIN
Above: MARY PHILBIN, NORMAN KERRY

NORMAN KERRY

DOROTHY WALLACE, NORMAN KERRY, MARY PHIL
Above: GEORGE SEIGMANN

SCENES AND PLAYERS IN ERICH VON STROHEIM'S "MERRY-GO-ROUND" (UNIVERSAL)

KATE LESTER, NORMAN KERRY, WINIFRED BRYSON

LON CHANEY IN SCENES FROM "THE HUNCHBACK OF NOTRE DAME" (UNIVERSAL)

D MEEK, RALPH SLIPPERY, THOMAS MITCHELL, ERNEST
. FLORENCE ELDRIDGE. Above: FLORENCE ELDRIDGE,
RNEST TRUEX IN "SIX CYLINDER LOVE" (FOX)

REGINALD DENNY
IN "THE ABYSMAL BRUTE"
(UNIVERSAL)

ANNA Q. NILSSON, ROBERT EDESON, MILTON SILLS
Above: NOAH BEERY, MILTON SILLS
SCENES FROM "THE SPOILERS" (FIRST NATIONAL) 253

HAROLD LLOYD

1924 The motion picture industry was approaching a climax. By public demand everyone was going in for bigger pictures. Among the large-scale efforts were "Romola," filmed in Italy and starring the Gish sisters; Douglas Fairbanks' "The Thief of Bagdad"; Mary Pickford's "Dorothy Vernon of Haddon Hall"; Paramount's version of "Monsieur Beaucaire" starring Valentino; two Marion Davies elaborate costume pictures, "Yolanda" and "Janice Meredith"; Fox's productions "The Iron Horse" and "Dante's Inferno"; D. W. Griffith's "America," and First National's "The Sea Hawk." It was a case of the survival of the "biggest." Producers were again inveighing against the high salaries of the players but they had only themselves to blame. With few exceptions, they were afraid to take a chance on a newcomer. They engaged players by their fame —a fame that in many instances was fictional.

MARY PICKFORD IN
"DOROTHY VERNON OF HADDON HALL"
(UNITED ARTISTS)

MAE MURRAY
IN "CIRCE" (METRO)

DOUGLAS FAIRBANKS
IN "THE THIEF OF BAGDAD"
(UNITED ARTISTS)

RUDOLPH VALENTINO
IN "MONSIEUR BEAUCAIRE"
(PARAMOUNT)

JOHN BARRYMORE
IN "BEAU BRUMMEL"
(WARNER BROS.)

JOHN BARRYMORE (left)
Above: JOHN BARRYMORE, MARY ASTOR
SCENES FROM "BEAU BRUMMEL" (WARNER BROTHERS)

JOHN BARRYMORE (left), CARMEL MYERS, WILLARD LOUIS
Above: CARMEL MYERS, JOHN BARRYMORE

RUDOLPH VALENTINO (also above), NITA N
IN "A SAINTED DEVIL" (PARAMOUNT)

RUDOLPH VALENTINO, LOIS WILSON, BEBE DANIELS
Above: RUDOLPH VALENTINO, DORIS KENYON

ANDRE DAVEN, RUDOLPH VALENTINO
Above: DORIS KENYON, LOIS WILSON

RUDOLPH VALENTINO (right)
Above: RUDOLPH VALENTINO, PAULETTE DU V

SCENES FROM "MONSIEUR BEAUCAIRE" (PARAMOUNT)

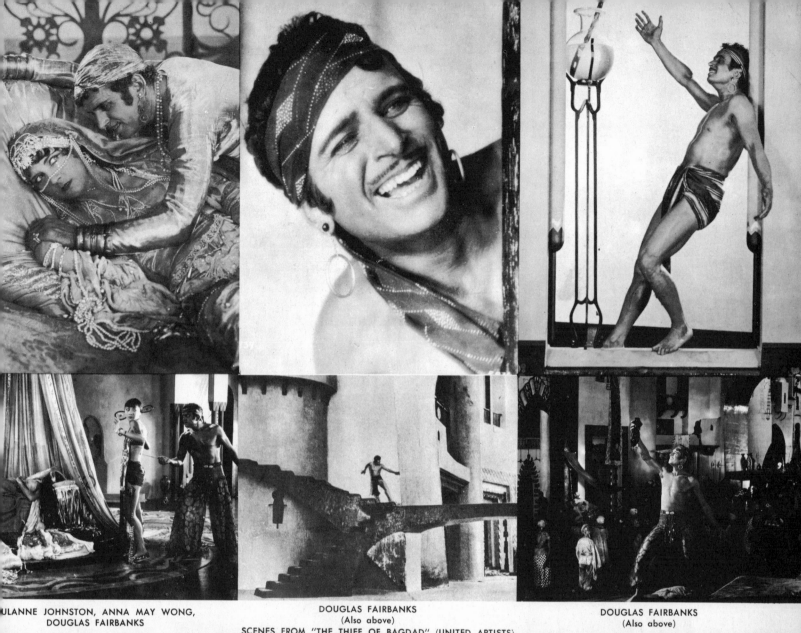

ULANNE JOHNSTON, ANNA MAY WONG,
DOUGLAS FAIRBANKS

DOUGLAS FAIRBANKS
(Also above)
SCENES FROM "THE THIEF OF BAGDAD" (UNITED ARTISTS)

DOUGLAS FAIRBANKS
(Also above)

NEIL HAMILTON, CAROL DEMPSTER IN
SCENES FROM "ISN'T LIFE WONDERFUL"
(D. W. GRIFFITH)

NORMA SHEARER, JOHN GILBERT
IN "HE WHO GETS SLAPPED"
(METRO)

NORMA SHEARER, JOHN GILBERT, TULLY MARSHALL
Above: NORMA SHEARER, JOHN GILBERT, LON CHANEY
SCENES FROM "HE WHO GETS SLAPPED" (METRO)

GEORGE
DURYEA
(FIRST NATIONAL)

PAULINE
FREDERICK
(VITAGRAPH)

JOHN
ROCHE
(FIRST NATIONAL)

ANNA MAY
WONG
(PARAMOUNT)

JOHN
PATRICK
(WARNER BROS.)

BILLIE
DOVE
(FOX)

GEORGE
WALSH
(GOLDWYN)

MAE
BUSCH
(METRO)

DAVID
TORREN
(PARAMO

CYRIL RING, BETTY BLYTHE, GEORGE SIDNEY, ALEXANDER
CARR IN "IN HOLLYWOOD WITH POTASH AND PERLMUTTER"

FLORENCE VIDOR, IAN KEITH IN
"CHRISTINE OF THE HUNGRY HEART"
FIRST NATIONAL PRODUCTIONS

CONSTANCE BENNETT, NORMAN KERRY,
LEWIS STONE IN "CYTHEREA"

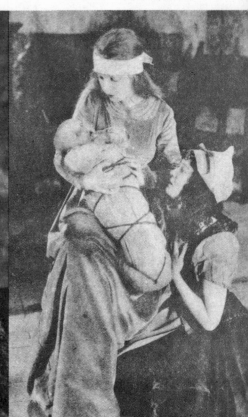

RONALD COLMAN, LILLIAN GISH

LILLIAN GISH

LILLIAN AND DOROTHY GISH

SCENES FROM HENRY KING'S "ROMOLA" (METRO-GOLDWYN)

HOLMES HERBERT, MAY McAVOY, RICHARD BARTHELMESS
IN "THE ENCHANTED COTTAGE"

RICHARD BARTHELMESS IN
"THE ENCHANTED COTTAGE"

MADGE EVANS, RICHARD
BARTHELMESS IN "CLASSMATES"

NAZIMOVA, MILTON SILLS
IN "MADONNA OF THE STREETS"

FIRST NATIONAL PRODUCTIONS

LALLAM
DOOLEY
(FIRST NATIONAL)

DALE
FULLER
(UNIVERSAL)

JOHNNY
HINES
(FIRST NATIONAL)

MARY
ASTOR
(FIRST NATIONAL)

CHARLES
DE ROCHE
(PARAMOUNT)

CARMELITA
GERAGHTY
(SELZNICK)

FRANK
MAYO
(UNIVERSAL)

DOROTHY
DWAN
(FOX)

RICHARD
TALMADGE
(F.B.O.)

LOU TELLEGEN, CORINNE GRIFFITH, MILTON SILLS
IN "SINGLE WIVES" (FIRST NATIONAL)

HENRY B. WALTHALL, KATHLYN
WILLIAMS IN "SINGLE WIVES"
(FIRST NATIONAL)

BARBARA LA MARR, CONWAY
TEARLE IN "THE WHITE MOTH"
(FIRST NATIONAL)

BARBARA LA MARR, BEN LYON
IN "THE WHITE MOTH" (FIRST NATIONAL)

WILLIAM CONKLIN, JEAN HERSHOLT, JACK MULHALL,
CONSTANCE TALMADGE IN "THE GOLDFISH." Above: RONALD
COLMAN, CONSTANCE TALMADGE IN "HEART TROUBLE"

NORMA TALMADGE
IN "SECRETS"
(FIRST NATIONAL)

NORMA TALMADGE, EUGENE O'BRIEN
IN SCENES FROM "SECRETS"
(FIRST NATIONAL)

THE SLAVE GALLEY

MILTON SILLS

ENID BENNETT, MILTON SILLS

ENID BENNETT, MILTON SILLS, LLOYD HUGHES

SCENES FROM "THE SEA HAWK" (FIRST NATIONAL)

259

LOIS WILSON, RICHARD DIX (center)
IN "ICEBOUND" (PARAMOUNT)

BEBE DANIELS, RICHARD DIX
IN "SINNERS IN HEAVEN" (PARAMOUNT)

ERNEST TORRENCE, ANNA Q. NILSSON, NEIL
HAMILTON IN "SIDE SHOW OF LIFE" (PARAMOUNT

1924 Louis B. Mayer joined Metro-Goldwyn and the combined Metro-Goldwyn-Mayer became one of the most powerful companies in the business. Warner Brothers continued to grow in prestige. They signed Ernst Lubitsch who directed "The Marriage Circle," one of the year's most delightful comedies, and persuaded John Barrymore, fresh from his stage triumph in "Hamlet," to return to the screen. Also, they acquired Rin-Tin-Tin who became the most famous of all dog stars. Among the producers, Joseph Schenck, who made the pictures of Norma and Constance Talmadge and Buster Keaton, averaged high with good pictures.

HENRY B. WALTHALL   CORINNE GRIFFITH

ANITA STEWART   GLENN HUNTER

ROD LA ROCQUE, JULIA FAYE, RICARDO CORTEZ, WILLIAM
BOYD. Above: VERA REYNOLDS, ROBERT EDESON,
ROD LA ROCQUE, RICARDO CORTEZ, JULIA FAYE IN "FEET OF CLAY"

ROD LA ROCQUE, LEATRICE JOY
IN "TRIUMPH" (PARAMOUNT)

MAURICE FLYNN (also above), VIOLA DANA
IN "OPEN ALL NIGHT" (PARAMOUNT)

WALLACE BEERY
(PARAMOUNT)

AILEEN PRINGLE
(METRO)

BERT LYTELL
(PARAMOUNT)

DORIS KENYON
(FIRST NATIONAL)

WILLIAM BOYD
(PARAMOUNT)

ALMA RUBENS
(COSMOPOLITAN

JACK HOLT, NORMA SHEARER
IN "EMPTY HANDS" (PARAMOUNT)

ANTONIO MORENO, AGNES AYRES, JACK BOHN
IN "THE STORY WITHOUT A NAME" (PARAMOUNT)

GENE DUMONT, BEBE DANIELS, WILLIAM POWELL
IN "DANGEROUS MONEY" (PARAMOUNT)

LLIAM S. HART   NORMA TALMADGE

THOMAS MEIGHAN, ESTELLE TAYLOR
IN "THE ALASKAN" (PARAMOUNT)

MAURICE FLYNN   CONSTANCE BENNETT

GLENN HUNTER (also above)
IN "MERTON OF THE MOVIES" (PARAMOUNT)

MAY McAVOY, GEORGE FAWCETT, GLENN HUNTER, ERNEST
TORRENCE, ANN SCHAEFFER. Above: GLADYS FELDMAN,
GLENN HUNTER, IN "WEST OF THE WATER TOWER"

CARMEL MYERS
(METRO)

ROD LA ROCQUE
(PARAMOUNT)

THOMAS MEIGHAN
IN "THE ALASKAN"
(PARAMOUNT)

RALPH GRAVES
(GRIFFITH)

AGNES AYRES
(PARAMOUNT)

261

WITH BEN LYON
IN "LILY OF THE DUST"

WITH ROD LA ROCQUE, PAULINE STARKE IN "FORBIDDEN PARADISE." Above: WITH ROBERT FRAZER IN "MEN"

POLA NEGRI PARAMOUNT FILMS

"FORBIDDEN PARADISE"

"SHADOWS OF PARIS"

HARRY C. MYERS, NOBLE JOHNSON·
IN "ROBINSON CRUSOE" (UNIVERSAL)

JOHNNY WALKER IN
"CAPTAIN FLY-BY-NIGHT" (F.B.O.)

JACK HOLT, BILLIE DOVE IN
"WANDERER OF THE WASTELAND" (PARAMOUNT)

HERBERT RAWLINSON, EDDIE GR
IN "THE VICTOR" (UNIVERSA

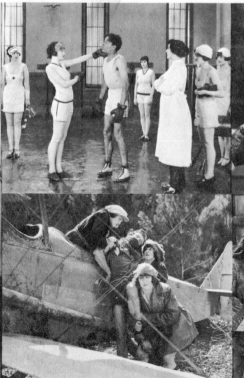

TOM BROWN
IN "THE HOOSIER SCHOOLMASTER"
(PRODUCERS DISTRIBUTING CORP.)

EARLE FOXE, DERLYS PERDUE, GRACE CUNARD
Above: EARLE FOXE, DERLYS PERDUE
SCENES FROM "THE LAST MAN ON EARTH" (FOX)

ALLAN FORREST, J. WARREN KERRIGAN,
JAMES MORRISON. Above: J. WARREN
KERRIGAN, JEAN PAIGE IN "CAPTAIN BLOOD"
(VITAGRAPH)

J. WARREN KERRIGAN
IN "CAPTAIN BLOOD"
(VITAGRAPH)

WITH IAN KEITH IN SCENES FROM "MANHANDLED"

"THE HUMMING BIRD"

WITH ROD LA ROCQUE IN "A SOCIETY SCANDAL"

GLORIA SWANSON PARAMOUNT FILMS

WITH ALAN SIMPSON IN "A SOCIETY SCANDAL"
Above: WITH NORMAN TREVOR (center), BEN LYON (right) IN "THE WAGES OF VIRTUE"

GEORGE O'BRIEN IN "THE ROUGHNECK" (FOX)

VICTOR SCHERTZINGER DIRECTING EVA AND JANE NOVAK IN "THE MAN LIFE PASSED BY" (METRO)

BERT LYTELL, FRANK MORGAN, DORIS KENYON, J. BARNEY SHERRY, CULLEN LANDIS, CLAIRE WINDSOR IN "BORN RICH" (NATIONAL FILMS)

ANTONIO MORENO "THE BORDER LEGION" (PARAMOUNT)

HARRY CAREY IN "THE FOX" (UNIVERSAL)

JACK DEMPSEY, GEORGE OVEY IN "FIGHT AND WIN"

HOOT GIBSON IN "SURE FIRE" (UNIVERSAL)

JACK HOLT IN "WANDERER OF THE WASTELAND" (PARAMOUNT)

SCENES FROM "DANTE'S INFERNO" (FOX)
WITH PAULINE STARKE, RALPH LEWIS, JOSEPH SWICKARD, WILL SCOTT, GLORIA GREY,
LAWSON BUTT, HAROLD GAYE

BLANCHE MEHAFFEY, GLENN
TRYON IN "THE WHITE SHEEP"
(HAL ROACH)

WARNER BAXTER, GRACE
DARMOND IN "ALIMONY"
(F.B.O.)

DOROTHY MACKAILL, GEORGE O'BRIEN
IN "THE MAN WHO CAME BACK"
(FOX)

HAL COOLEY, MADGE BELLAMY
IN "THE WHITE SIN"
(F.B.O.)

RICHARD TALMADGE, GE
WARDE IN "AMERICAN MA
(F.B.O.)

BUCK JONES, PEGGY SHAW, EDDIE HEARN
IN "WINNER TAKE ALL"
(FOX)

WILLIAM RUSSELL, VICTOR McLAGLEN
IN "THE BELOVED BRUTE"
(VITAGRAPH)

BOB TRENT, FRED THOMSON
IN "THE DANGEROUS COWARD"
(F.B.O.)

SCENES FROM JOHN FORD'S "THE IRON HORSE" (FOX)
WITH GEORGE O'BRIEN, MADGE BELLAMY, JACK O'BRIEN, J. FARRELL MacDONALD

1924 In a popularity contest conducted by *Photoplay* magazine, the ranking stars were Thomas Meighan, Norma Talmadge, Harold Lloyd, Tom Mix, Mary Pickford, Douglas Fairbanks, Gloria Swanson, Pola Negri, Jackie Coogan and Rudolph Valentino. The top directors polled were Cecil B. De Mille, D. W. Griffith, Rex Ingram, Allan Dwan, Marshall Neilan, William De Mille, James Cruze and George Fitzmaurice. Among the important continuity writers, strangely enough, women outranked the men. Frances Marion was probably greatest at this time. Jeanie Macpherson was Cecil B. De Mille's assistant and wrote "The Ten Commandments" script. June Mathis, Clara Beranger and Ouida Bergere were other top writers.

ET LANDIS, JACK HOXIE
E WESTERN WALLOP"
(UNIVERSAL)

KENNETH HARLAN, LAURA LA
PLANTE, NORMAN KERRY IN
"BUTTERFLY" (UNIVERSAL)

FLORENCE VIDOR, EDMUND LOWE
IN "BARBARA FRIETCHIE"
(HODKINSON)

HENRY HULL, IRMA HARRISON
IN "FOR WOMAN'S FAVOR"
(LEE-BRADFORD)

MUND LOWE, BRENDA BOND, RAY BLOOMER
IN "THE FOOL"
(FOX)

ALBERT WILLIAMS, BABY PEGGY, JACK EARLE
IN "JACK AND THE BEANSTALK"
(UNIVERSAL)

ALMA BENNETT, TEMPE PIGGOTT, JACQUELINE LOGAN,
DAVID TORRENCE, OTTO MATTIESEN IN "THE DAWN OF
TOMORROW" (PARAMOUNT)

CLAUDE GILLINGWATER, HARRY C. MYERS, MAE MARSH
IN "DADDIES" (WARNER BROS.)

FLORENCE VIDOR, CREIGHTON HALE
IN ERNST LUBITSCH'S "THE MARRIAGE CIRCLE"
(WARNER BROS.)

EDITH ROBERTS, BEVERLY BAYNE, ELLIOTT DEXT
IN "AGE OF INNOCENCE" (WARNER BROS.)

| MONTE BLUE (WARNER BROS.) | FLORENCE VIDOR (WARNER BROS.) | VINCENT COLEMAN (PARAMOUNT) | JANE NOVAK (METRO) | HOUSE PETERS (UNIVERSAL) | SEENA OWEN (PARAMOUNT) | CONRAD NAGEL (METRO) | HELENE CHADWICK (FIRST NATIONAL) | JAC HOL (PARAMO |

MARY PICKFORD, MARC MacDERMOTT, ANDERS RANDOLF, ALLAN FORREST   ALLAN FORREST, MARY PICKFORD   COURTENAY FOOTE, CLARE EAMES, MARY PICKFO

SCENES FROM "DOROTHY VERNON OF HADDON HALL" (UNITED ARTISTS)

| IAN KEITH (PARAMOUNT) | MADGE EVANS (FIRST NATIONAL) | ROBERT FRAZER (UNIVERSAL) | ELEANOR BOARDMAN (METRO) | FRANK MORGAN (VITAGRAPH) | CLAIRE WINDSOR (FIRST NATIONAL) | HERBERT RAWLINSON (UNIVERSAL) | CLARA KIMBALL YOUNG (METRO) | GEOR SIDN (UNIVE |

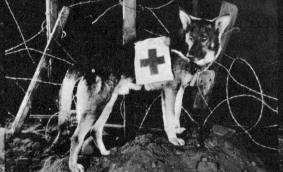

AILEEN PRINGLE, CONRAD NAGEL
IN "THREE WEEKS"
(METRO-GOLDWYN)

RIN-TIN-TIN
IN "FIND YOUR MAN"
(WARNER BROS.)

RAMON NOVARRO, ALICE TERRY
IN "THE ARAB"
(METRO-GOLDWYN)

MONTE BLUE, VIOLA DANA
IN "REVELATION"

JACKIE COOGAN
IN "A BOY OF FLANDERS"
METRO-GOLDWYN PRODUCTIONS

CHARLES GERRARD, MAE MURRAY, WILLIAM HAINES
IN "CIRCE"

GALE
HENRY
(UNIVERSAL)

TOM
TYLER
(F.B.O.)

HELEN
FERGUSON
(UNIVERSAL)

JOSEPH
SCHILDKRAUT
(PARAMOUNT)

BABY
PEGGY
(LESSER)

REX
INGRAM
(METRO)

EVELYN
BRENT
(METRO)

J. WARREN
KERRIGAN
(VITAGRAPH)

LOUISE
DRESSER
(UNIVERSAL)

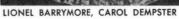

LOUIS WOLHEIM   CHARLES EMMETT MACK, CAROL DEMPSTER, ERVILLE ALDERSON   LIONEL BARRYMORE, CAROL DEMPSTER   NEIL HAMILTON

SCENES FROM D. W. GRIFFITH'S "AMERICA"

ERVILLE
CALDWELL
(INDEPENDENT)

BETTY
COMPSON
(PARAMOUNT)

LOU
TELLEGEN
(VITAGRAPH)

OLIVE
HASBROUCK
(UNIVERSAL)

FRED
THOMSON
(F.B.O.)

ESTHER
RALSTON
(PARAMOUNT)

JIMMY
HARRISON
(CHRISTIE)

DOROTHY
DAVENPORT
(MRS. WALLACE REID)

JAMES
KIRKWOOD
(PARAMOUNT)

JOHN GILBERT, NORMA SHEARER, CONRAD NAGEL
IN "THE SNOB"
METRO-GOLDWYN PRODUCTIONS

WARNER OLAND, TOM MOORE, LAURETTE TAYLOR, WILLIAM
HUMPHREY, MISS DU PONT IN "ONE NIGHT IN ROME"

FRANK CURRIER, ENID BENNETT, RAMON NOVARRO
IN "THE RED LILY"

267

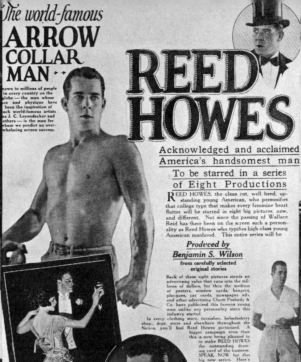

BUSTER KEATON IN "THE NAVIGATOR"
Above: BUSTER KEATON IN "SHERLOCK, JR."
(METRO)

REED HOWES ADVERTISEMENT

JOBYNA RALSTON, HAROLD LLOYD (also abov
IN "GIRL SHY" (PATHÉ)

MAY VOKES, MARION DAVIES, MACLYN
ARBUCKLE, HATTIE DELARO

HARRISON FORD, HOLBROOK BLINN,
MARION DAVIES, GEORGE NASH
SCENES FROM "JANICE MEREDITH" (COSMOPOLITAN PRODUCTION)

MARION DAVIES, W. C. FIELDS

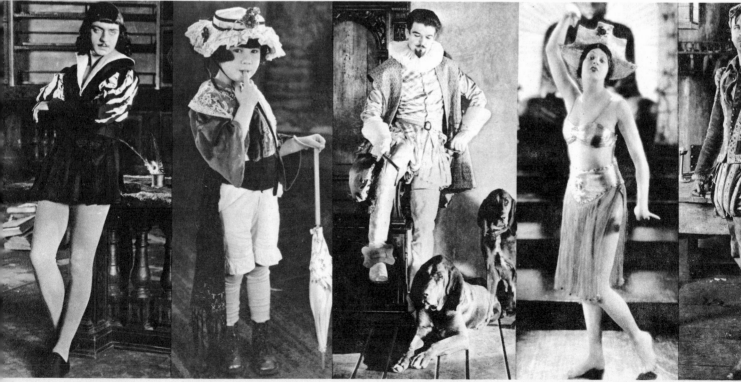

WILLIAM POWELL
IN "ROMOLA"
(M-G)

BABY PEGGY
IN "CAPTAIN JANUARY"

WALLACE MacDONALD
IN "THE SEA HAWK"
(FIRST NATIONAL)

BARBARA LA MARR IN
"THE SHOOTING OF DAN McGREW"
(M-G)

MILTON SILLS
IN "THE SEA HAWK"
(FIRST NATIONAL)

LINCOLN STEDMAN, HOBART BOSWORTH, BABY PEGGY
IN "CAPTAIN JANUARY"

OSCAR SHAW, ANITA STEWART
Above: TOM WISE, OSCAR SHAW
ES FROM "THE GREAT WHITE WAY" (COSMOPOLITAN)

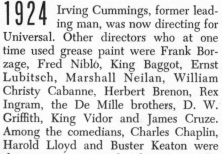

BENNY LEONARD, DIANA ALLEN
IN "FLYING FISTS"

RALPH GRAVES, MARION DAVIES (also above)
SCENES FROM "YOLANDA" (COSMOPOLITAN)

1924 Irving Cummings, former leading man, was now directing for Universal. Other directors who at one time used grease paint were Frank Borzage, Fred Niblo, King Baggot, Ernst Lubitsch, Marshall Neilan, William Christy Cabanne, Herbert Brenon, Rex Ingram, the De Mille brothers, D. W. Griffith, King Vidor and James Cruze. Among the comedians, Charles Chaplin, Harold Lloyd and Buster Keaton were the most consistent laugh getters. The newcomers catching the public fancy included Norma Shearer, George O'Brien, Baby Peggy, Dorothy Mackaill, Mary Astor, and William Boyd who later became famous as Hopalong Cassidy.

RGE O'BRIEN   EVELYN BRENT IN   BEN LYON IN
 IRON HORSE"   "SILK STOCKING   "LILY OF THE DUST"
(FOX)   SAL" (F.B.O.)   (PARAMOUNT)

ALLAN FORREST IN   KATHLYN WILLIAMS MONTE BLUE IN "TH
"DOROTHY VERNON OF IN "THE CITY THAT LOVER OF CAMILLE"
HADDON HALL" (UA) NEVER SLEEPS" (PARA) (WARNER BROS.)

HEDDA HOPPER
IN "FREE LOVE"
(M-G-M)

ROD LA ROCQUE
IN "TRIUMPH"
(PARAMOUNT)

HOPE HAMPTON
IN "PRICE OF A PARTY"
(ASSOCIATED EXHIBITORS)

RICHARD DIX
IN "MANHATTAN"
(PARAMOUNT)

LOIS WILSON
IN "NORTH OF 36"
(PARAMOUNT)

LOUISE DRESSER, RUDOLPH VALENTINO (also above) IN "THE EAGLE" (UNITED ARTISTS)

CHARLES CHAPLIN IN SCENES FROM "THE GOLD RUSH" (UNITED ARTISTS) WITH GEORGIA HALE (center right)

MARY PICKFORD (center)
IN "LITTLE ANNIE ROONEY" (UNITED ARTISTS)

OTTO MATTIESEN, GEORGIA HALE, GEORGE ARTHUR IN
OSEF VON STERNBERG'S "THE SALVATION HUNTERS" (UNITED ARTISTS)

25 The industry was in the doldrums. Theatre owners were worrying about their box-office receipts, which showed an alarming drop. Radio, now an important part of American life, was blamed s. That Hollywood was turning out comparatively few worthwhile pic- t this time was seldom mentioned. Films making money for the exhibi- cluded "The Big Parade," a memorable war picture; "The Phantom of pera" with Lon Chaney continuing his series of weird characteriza- Charles Chaplin's "The Gold Rush"; "Stella Dallas," a real tear-jerker had the critics cheering Belle Bennett's performance; the first filming es Barrie's immortal "Peter Pan," and "The Sea Beast" starring John ore. A German importation, Ufa's production of "The Last Laugh" mil Jannings and directed by F. W. Murnau, was considered by many the most perfect pictures ever made. It was unique in that it told y without subtitles.

JAMES PAGE, ETHEL SHANNON, DAVID JAMES, EULALIE JENSEN, JIMMY
HARRISON AND SYDNEY CHAPLIN AS "CHARLEY'S AUNT" (CHRISTIE)

MARY ASTOR, DOUGLAS FAIRBANKS (also above), DONALD CRISP
IN "DON Q, SON OF ZORRO" (UNITED ARTISTS)

NORMA SHEARER IN "LADY OF THE NIGHT"
Above: NORMA SHEARER, LEW CODY IN
"HIS SECRETARY" (METRO-GOLDWYN)

EMIL JANNINGS (also above) IN SCENES
FROM "THE LAST LAUGH" (UFA)

RICHARD DIX (also above WITH LO
WILSON) IN "THE VANISHING AMERIC
(PARAMOUNT)

HARRISON FORD
(FIRST NATIONAL)

BELLE BENNETT
(FIRST NATIONAL)

FRANCIS X. BUSHMAN
(M-G-M)

KATHLYN WILLIAMS
(PARAMOUNT)

WILLIAM POWELL
(PARAMOUNT)

IRENE RICH
(WARNER BROS

LOUISE DRESSER, JACK PICKFORD
IN "THE GOOSE WOMAN"
(UNIVERSAL)

BETTY MORRISSEY, REGINALD DENNY, ARTHUR LAKE
IN "SKINNER'S DRESS SUIT" (UNIVERSAL)

REGINALD DENNY, OTIS HARLAN
IN "WHAT HAPPENED TO JONES"
(UNIVERSAL)

ALICE JOYCE, BELLE BENNETT
e: BELLE BENNETT, LOIS MORAN

DOUGLAS FAIRBANKS, JR., LOIS MORAN, ALICE JOYCE, BELLE BENNETT
Above: RONALD COLMAN, LOIS MORAN, ALICE JOYCE

BELLE BENNETT, JEAN HERSHOLT
Above: BELLE BENNETT, RONALD COLMAN

SCENES FROM SAMUEL GOLDWYN'S PRODUCTION "STELLA DALLAS" (UNITED ARTISTS) DIRECTED BY HENRY KING

VON STROHEIM
(UNIVERSAL)

MARIE PREVOST
(WARNER BROS.)

TOM MOORE
(PARAMOUNT)

BLANCHE SWEET
(FIRST NATIONAL)

CLIVE BROOK
(UNIVERSAL)

LOIS WILSON
(PARAMOUNT)

NOMO, LOUISE LORRAINE
GREAT CIRCUS MYSTERY"
(UNIVERSAL)

MALCOLM McGREGOR, VIRGINIA LEE CORBIN
IN "HEADLINES"
(ASSOCIATED EXHIBITORS)

LAURA LA PLANTE, EUGENE O'BRIEN
IN "DANGEROUS INNOCENCE"
(UNIVERSAL)

HOUSE PETERS, FREEMAN WOOD
IN "RAFFLES"
(UNIVERSAL)

273

RUDOLPH VALENTINO
IN "COBRA"
(PARAMOUNT)

ANNA Q. NILSSON
IN "THE SPLENDID ROAD"
(FIRST NATIONAL)

JOHNNY HINES
IN "THE CRACKERJACK"
(EAST COAST)

ANITA STEWART
IN "BAREE, SON OF KAZAN"
(VITAGRAPH)

RICARDO CORTEZ
IN "THE SPANIARD"
(PARAMOUNT)

RENEE ADO
IN "THE BIG P
(METRO-GOLDW

TOM RICKETTS, EMILY FITZROY, KENNETH HARLAN, JOHN
ROCHE, MARIE PREVOST, REED HOWES IN "BOBBED HAIR"
(WARNER BROS.)

CHARLIE MURRAY, JACK PICKFORD, NAZIMOVA,
IAN KEITH IN "MY SON"
(FIRST NATIONAL)

PAULINE GARON, RAYMOND McKEE, IRENE R
CLIVE BROOK IN "COMPROMISE"
(WARNER BROS.)

JUNE MARLOWE, RIN-TIN-TIN, CHARLES FARRELL
IN "THE CLASH OF THE WOLVES"
(WARNER BROS.)

GILBERT ROLAND, DONALD KEITH, CLARA BOW
IN "THE PLASTIC AGE"
(SCHULBERG)

MONTE BLUE, MARIE PREVOST
IN ERNST LUBITSCH'S "KISS ME AGAIN"
(WARNER BROS.)

BOB CUSTER IN
"THE TEXAS BEARCAT"
(F.B.O.)

CLAIRE WINDSOR
IN "SOULS FOR SABLES"
(TIFFANY)

RICHARD BARTHELMESS
IN "SHORE LEAVE"
(FIRST NATIONAL)

BARBARA LA MARR
IN "HEART OF A SIREN"
(FIRST NATIONAL)

DOUGLAS MacLEAN
IN "INTRODUCE ME"
(ASSOCIATED EXHIBITORS)

HOUSE PETE
IN "HEAD WI
(UNIVERSAL

...MOND HATTON IN "THUNDERING HERD" (PARAMOUNT)

MARY ASTOR IN "DON Q, SON OF ZORRO" (UNITED ARTISTS)

HANK MANN (FOX)

POLA NEGRI IN "THE CHARMER" (PARAMOUNT)

LEON ERROL IN "CLOTHES MAKE THE PIRATE" (FIRST NATIONAL)

JETTA GOUDAL IN "THE COMING OF AMOS" (PRODUCERS DISTR. CO.)

...ES PADDOCK (center), OTIS HARLAN (right center) IN "9 3/5 SECONDS" (STERN)

LARRY SEMON, DOROTHY DWAN, OLIVER HARDY IN "THE WIZARD OF OZ" (CHADWICK)

ELLIOTT NUGENT, HARRY MOREY, VIRGINIA LEE CORBIN, ALICE JOYCE, MALCOLM McGREGOR IN "HEADLINES" (ASSOCIATED EXHIBITORS)

...MILLER, OTIS HARLAN, LOU TELLEGEN, NAZIMOVA IN "THE REDEEMING SIN" (VITAGRAPH)

STANHOPE WHEATCROFT, JULIAN ELTINGE, ANN PENNINGTON IN "MADAME BEHAVE" (PRODUCERS DISTRIBUTING CORP.)

W. C. FIELDS, CAROL DEMPSTER IN "SALLY OF THE SAWDUST" (D. W. GRIFFITH)

MONTE BANKS "KEEP SMILING" ...CIATED EXHIBITORS)

CORINNE GRIFFITH IN "DÉCLASSÉE" (FIRST NATIONAL)

EDMUND LOWE IN "EAST LYNNE" (FOX)

SYDNEY CHAPLIN IN "CHARLEY'S AUNT" (PDC)

CHARLES DE ROCHE IN "MADAME SANS GENE" (PARAMOUNT)

COLLEEN MOORE IN "SO BIG" (FIRST NATIONAL)

275

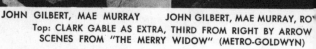

JOHN GILBERT, MAE MURRAY   JOHN GILBERT, MAE MURRAY, RO
Top: CLARK GABLE AS EXTRA, THIRD FROM RIGHT BY ARROW
SCENES FROM "THE MERRY WIDOW" (METRO-GOLDWYN)

1925 Fairbanks, Pickford, Chaplin, Valentino, Lloyd and
son were still the big names in filmdom, and so we
Negri, the Talmadge sisters and the Gish girls. John Barry
popularity was increasing and his leading lady, Dolores C
daughter of Maurice Costello, early film idol, was headed fo
dom. Colleen Moore, Corinne Griffith and Richard Barthelme
reached the top. Approaching it were Richard Dix, John C
Norma Shearer, Reginald Denny, Rod La Rocque, and Vilma
and Ronald Colman as a team. Nita Naldi was now the most
vamp in films. Vitagraph, last of the old guard film companie
out to Warner Brothers. Cecil B. De Mille severed his twelv
connection with Paramount to make his pictures independentl
a Producers Distributing Corporation release.

MAE MURRAY
IN "THE MERRY WIDOW" (METRO-GOLDWYN)
(ERICH VON STROHEIM'S PRODUCTION)

BLANCHE SWEET, RONALD COLMAN
IN "THE SPORTING VENUS"
(METRO-GOLDWYN)

CONSTANCE BENNETT, JOAN CRAWFORD, SALLY O'NEIL
IN "SALLY, IRENE AND MARY"
(METRO-GOLDWYN)

VILMA BANKY, RONALD COLMAN IN GEORGE
FITZMAURICE'S "THE DARK ANGEL"
(GOLDWYN)

JOHN GILBERT, RÉNEE ADORÉE (also center pictures)
Top: JOHN GILBERT, KARL DANE

JOHN GILBERT

SCENES FROM "THE BIG PARADE" (M-G-M) DIRECTED BY KING VIDOR

NORMA SHEARER, LEW CODY
: NORMA SHEARER, LON CHANEY, IAN KEITH
ENES FROM "THE TOWER OF LIES" (M-G-M)

BUSTER KEATON
IN "GO WEST"
(M-G-M)

BESSIE LOVE, LEWIS STONE, WALLACE BEERY,
LLOYD HUGHES, ARTHUR HOYT
SCENES FROM "THE LOST WORLD"
(FIRST NATIONAL)

KATHRYN HILL, WILLIAM COLLIER, JR., GEORGE RIGOS
Above: WILLIAM COLLIER, JR., GRETA NISSEN

WILLIAM COLLIER, JR.
SCENES FROM RAOUL WALSH'S "THE WANDERER" (PARAMOUNT)

GRETA NISSEN, WALLACE BEERY
Above: WILLIAM COLLIER, JR., GRETA NISSEN

VIRGINIA LEE CORBIN (UNIVERSAL)   PHILO McCULLOUGH (FOX)   YOLA D'ARVIL (M-G-M)   EDWARD PHILLIPS (UNIVERSAL)   JETTA GOUDAL (PARAMOUNT)   KARL DANE (M-G-M)   DOROTHY DUNBAR (FIRST NATIONAL)   OTIS HARLAN (UNIVERSAL)   SIGRI HOLMQU (PARAMO

JOSEPH DEPEW, RICARDO CORTEZ, GEORGE WALCOTT, FRANCES HOWARD IN "THE SWAN" (PARAMOUNT)

RUDOLPH VALENTINO (also above WITH NITA NALDI) IN "COBRA" (PARAMOUNT)

GLORIA SWANSON (also above), WARWICK WARD IN "MADAME SANS GENE" (PARAMOUNT)

IVAN LINOW, LON CHANEY Above: LON CHANEY, LILA LEE IN "THE UNHOLY THREE" (METRO-GOL

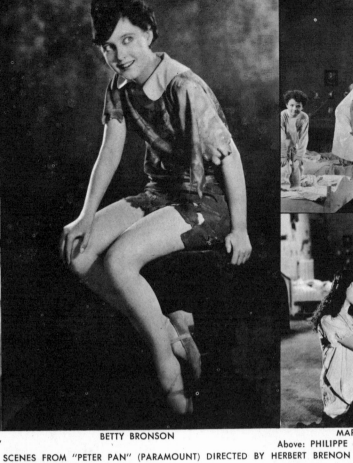

E de LACY, GEORGE ALI. Above: RICHARD FRAZIER,
Y BARBAT, PHILIPPE de LACY, ERNEST TORRENCE

BETTY BRONSON

MARY BRIAN, BETTY BRONSON
Above: PHILIPPE de LACY, MARY BRIAN, BETTY BRONSON

SCENES FROM "PETER PAN" (PARAMOUNT) DIRECTED BY HERBERT BRENON

NITZ
VARDS
IATIONAL)

JANE
WINTON
(PARAMOUNT)

FRANKIE
DARRO
(FIRST NATIONAL)

HEDDA
HOPPER
(M-G-M)

REED
HOWES
(WARNER BROS.)

PAULINE
GARON
(PARAMOUNT)

CHARLES "BUDDY"
ROGERS
(PARAMOUNT)

DOROTHY
SEBASTIAN
(M-G-M)

DOUGLAS
FAIRBANKS, JR.
(UNITED ARTISTS)

EVELYN BRENT, SHELDON LEWIS, PIERRE
GENDRON IN "THE DANGEROUS FLIRT" (F.B.O.)

MARGARET LIVINGSTON, MADGE BELLAMY,
GEORGE O'BRIEN IN "HAVOC" (FOX)

JOAN CRAWFORD
IN "PRETTY LADIES"
(M-G-M)

GEORGE WALSH, WANDA HAWLEY
IN "AMERICAN PLUCK"
(CHADWICK)

EDWARD HEARN, PAULINE
STARKE IN "THE MAN
WITHOUT A COUNTRY" (FOX)

GEORGE LEWIS, RUDOLPH
SCHILDKRAUT IN "PROUD HEART"

TOM MOORE IN
"THE SONG AND DANCE MAN"
(PARAMOUNT)

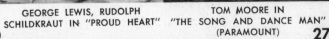

RICHARD BARTHELMESS
(FIRST NATIONAL)

RICHARD BARTHELMESS, CARLOTTA MONTEREY IN "SOUL-FIRE
Top: BESSIE LOVE, RICHARD BARTHELMESS IN "SOUL-FIRE"
Center: RICHARD BARTHELMESS, DOROTHY MACKAILL IN "SHORE L

BARBARA LA MARR, CLIFTON WEBB
IN "THE HEART OF A SIREN"
(FIRST NATIONAL)

WALLACE MacDONALD, NORMA TALMADGE
IN "THE LADY"
(FIRST NATIONAL)

ELEANOR BOARDMAN, CONRAD NAGEL
IN "THE ONLY THING"
(METRO-GOLDWYN-MAYER)

MARION DAVIES, JACKIE HUFF, HOLB
BLINN IN "ZANDER THE GREAT
(COSMOPOLITAN)

COLLEEN MOORE IN "WE MODERNS"
er: WALLACE BEERY, COLLEEN MOORE (also at top)
IN "SO BIG" (FIRST NATIONAL)

COLLEEN MOORE
(FIRST NATIONAL)

1925 Actors whose names were to become household words were beginning their Hollywood struggles. Gary Cooper was playing bits in western pictures. A Middle-West housewife won $500 from *Movie Weekly*'s contest when she gave the name of Joan Crawford to Lucille Le Sueur, a former Shubert chorus girl, then a promising youngster on the Metro lot. Clark Gable was an extra in "The Merry Widow" and "Déclassée." Charles Farrell was supporting Rin-Tin-Tin. Carole Lombard appeared briefly in a Buck Jones Western, "Hearts and Spurs." On the Fox lot, Janet Gaynor was playing small parts. B. P. Schulberg, well-known independent producer, gave a Mexican youth, Luis Alonso, a break in "The Plastic Age" under the name of Gilbert Roland. Paramount opened an acting school which developed Charles "Buddy" Rogers and Thelma Todd.

NWAY TEARLE, ALICE TERRY, WALLACE BEERY
IN "THE GREAT DIVIDE"
(METRO-GOLDWYN-MAYER)

LLOYD HUGHES, LILYAN TASHMAN, CORINNE GRIFFITH
IN "DECLASSEE" (FIRST NATIONAL)

JOHN BARRYMORE
(WARNER BROS.)

ELENA DI SANCRO, EMIL JANNINGS IN
"QUO VADIS" (FIRST NATIONAL)

CORINNE GRIFFITH
(FIRST NATIONAL)

TULLY MARSHALL, DOROTHY GISH, LEON ERROL, EDNA
MURPHY, NITA NALDI IN "CLOTHES MAKE THE PIRATE"
(FIRST NATIONAL)

BRYANT WASHBURN, PAULINE
GARON IN "PASSIONATE
YOUTH" (TRUART)

DOROTHY MACKAILL, JOHN
BOWERS IN "CHICKIE"
(FIRST NATIONAL)

PHILO McCULLOUGH, KATHLEEN MYERS, TOM M
IN "DICK TURPIN" (FOX)

RICHARD ARLEN
(PARAMOUNT)

CONSTANCE BENNETT
(UNIVERSAL)

REGINALD DENNY
(UNIVERSAL)

RÉNÉE ADORÉE
(METRO-GOLDWYN)

WILLIAM COLLIER, JR.
(PARAMOUNT)

GRETA NISSEN
(PARAMOUNT)

MAY ALLISON, ANNA Q. NILSSON, CONWAY TEARLE
IN "THE VIENNESE MEDLEY"
(FIRST NATIONAL)

JACKIE COOGAN, JOAN CRAWFORD
IN "OLD CLOTHES"
(METRO-GOLDWYN-MAYER)

FREDERIC NORTON, BETTY BLYTHE
IN "CHU-CHIN-CHOW"
(METRO-GOLDWYN-MAYER)

NITA NALDI
(PARAMOUNT)

CECIL B. DE MILLE AND ERNST LUBITSCH
TWO TOP DIRECTORS

ANTONIO MORENO
(PARAMOUNT)

NOAH BEERY, ROD LA ROCQUE, JETTA GOUDAL
IN "THE COMING OF AMOS" (P.D.C.)

FLORENCE VIDOR, ADOLPHE MENJOU
IN "THE GRAND DUCHESS AND THE WAITER"
(PARAMOUNT)

LAWRENCE GREY, RICHARD ARLEN, GLORIA SWANSON
IN "COAST OF FOLLY" (PARAMOUNT)

GEORGE O'BRIEN
(FOX)

MARY BRIAN
(PARAMOUNT)

BILLIE DOVE
(FOX)

GILBERT ROLAND
(PARAMOUNT)

EDITH CHAPMAN, JAY HUNT, OTIS HARLAN
IN "LIGHTNIN'" (FOX)

HAROLD LLOYD AND JOBYNA RALSTON (above)
IN "THE FRESHMAN" (PATHÉ)

LEW FIELDS, VIRGINIA BROWN FAIRE, JACK MULHALL,
JOE WEBER IN "FRIENDLY ENEMIES" (P.D.C.)

PHILIPPE
DE LACY
(PARAMOUNT)

ARLETTE
MARCHAL
(M-G-M)

ROY
D'ARCY
(M-G-M)

MADELINE
HURLOCK
(PARAMOUNT)

WILLIAM
AUSTIN
(PARAMOUNT)

MILDRED
HARRIS
(PARAMOUNT)

KING
VIDOR
(M-G-M)

LUCILLE
RICKSEN
(M-G-M)

JACK
COOG
(M-G-

JOHN BARRYMORE, DOLORES COSTELLO
Top and center: JOHN BARRYMORE
SCENES FROM "THE SEA BEAST"
(WARNER BROS.)

LON CHANEY, MARY PHILBIN
Top and center: NORMAN KERRY, MARY PHILBIN
SCENES FROM "THE PHANTOM OF THE OPERA"
(UNIVERSAL)

JOSEPH SCHILDKRAUT, VERA REYNOLDS, WILLIAM
Top and center: WILLIAM BOYD
SCENES FROM CECIL B. DE MILLE'S "THE ROA
TO YESTERDAY" (P.D.C.)

DOROTHY
MACKAILL
(FIRST NATIONAL)

VICTOR
VARCONI
(PARAMOUNT)

FRANCES
HOWARD
(PARAMOUNT)

JACK
DAUGHERTY
(UNIVERSAL)

MARY
McALISTER
(UNIVERSAL)

GEORGE K.
ARTHUR
(UNITED ARTISTS)

GEORGIA
HALE
(UNITED ARTISTS)

LEE
MORGAN
(UNIVERSAL)

ALBER
VAUG
(F.B.C

RUDOLPH VALENTINO

COLLEEN MOORE, GEORGE K. ARTHUR
IN "IRENE" (FIRST NATIONAL)

DOROTHY DUNBAR, RICHARD
BARTHELMESS IN "THE AMATEUR
GENTLEMAN" (FIRST NATIONAL)

GILBERT ROLAND, ANN RORK
IN "THE BLONDE SAINT" (FIRST NATIONAL)

JOHN BARRYMORE
IN "DON JUAN"
(WARNER BROS.)

PATSY RUTH MILLER IN
"WHY GIRLS GO BACK HOME"
(WARNER BROS.)

RALPH FORBES
IN "BEAU GESTE"
(PARAMOUNT)

LILLIAN GISH
IN "THE SCARLET LETTER"
(M-G-M)

JOHN GILBERT
IN "LA BOHEME"
(M-G-M)

RUTH ROLAND
"THE MASKED WO
(FIRST NATIONA

PERCY
MARMONT
(PARAMOUNT)

KATHLEEN
KEY
(M-G-M)

WALTER
MILLER
(PATHÉ)

JANET
GAYNOR
(FOX)

OWEN
MOORE
(M-G-M)

1926 With the motion picture industry reaching a clir is interesting to note some statistical figures as re in the film trade paper, *The Motion Picture News* 400 feature pictures were produced in the United States duri year, and one hundred and twenty million dollars was spent i ing them. There were 14,673 picture theatres in this count this number, 7,178 were in towns and cities of over 5,000 p tion, and 7,495 in towns and villages under 5,000. New York led in motion picture houses, having a total of 1,194. Pennsy

HARRY LANGDON, JOAN CRAWFORD
IN "TRAMP, TRAMP, TRAMP"
(FIRST NATIONAL)

WALTER PIDGEON, ANNA Q. NILSSON
IN "MISS NOBODY"
(FIRST NATIONAL)

DOROTHY MACKAILL, JACK MULHALL
IN "LADY BE GOOD"
(FIRST NATIONAL)

AILEEN PRINGLE, BASIL RATH
IN "THE GREAT DECEPTIO
(FIRST NATIONAL)

BETTY BRONSON, MILTON SILLS
IN "PARADISE" (FIRST NATIONAL)

BEN LYON, BLANCHE SWEET
IN "BLUEBEARD'S SEVEN WIVES"
(FIRST NATIONAL)

CHESTER CONKLIN, TULLIO CARMINATI, CONSTANCE TALMADGE
IN "SYBIL" (FIRST NATIONAL)

DDIE CANTOR
"KID BOOTS"
(PARAMOUNT)

NORMA TALMADGE
IN "KIKI"
(FIRST NATIONAL)

RICHARD BARTHELMESS IN
"THE AMATEUR GENTLEMAN"
(FIRST NATIONAL)

DOLORES DEL RIO
IN "WHAT PRICE GLORY"
(FOX)

NEIL HAMILTON
IN "BEAU GESTE"
(PARAMOUNT)

DOROTHY MACKAILL
IN "THE DANCER OF PARIS"
(FIRST NATIONAL)

econd with 1,032 and Illinois was a close third with 1,008.
a was at the bottom of the list of states with 23. Pictures
olaying an important part, not only in the American people's
ainment and recreation, but also in our thinking and manners
shions. The stars were the idols of the young and old alike.
ino's death, on August 23rd, illustrated how beloved these
and goddesses were. All the way from New York to Los
es, throngs assembled for a glimpse of his funeral train and
their last tribute to his memory.

DONALD
KEITH
(PARAMOUNT)

ALICE
DAY
(M-G-M)

VICTOR
McLAGLEN
(FOX)

MARCELINE
DAY
(M-G-M)

GEORGE
LEWIS
(UNIVERSAL)

A ROCQUE, MILDRED HARRIS
E CRUISE OF THE JASPER B"
(DE MILLE)

LAWRENCE GRAY, LOUISE BROOKS
IN "LOVE 'EM AND LEAVE 'EM"
(PARAMOUNT)

PATSY RUTH MILLER, RICHARD BARTHELMESS, WILLIAM H.
TOOKER IN "THE WHITE BLACK SHEEP"
(FIRST NATIONAL)

RONALD COLMAN, NORMA TALMADGE
IN "KIKI"
(FIRST NATIONAL)

MARY PICKFORD IN
"SPARROWS" (UNITED ARTISTS)

MERNA KENNEDY, CHARLES CHAPLIN
IN "THE CIRCUS" (UNITED ARTISTS)

DOUGLAS FAIRBANKS IN
"THE BLACK PIRATE" (UNITED ARTISTS)

MARY PICKFORD IN
"SPARROWS" (UNITED ARTISTS)

CHARLES CHAPLIN IN
"THE CIRCUS" (UNITED ARTISTS)

BILLIE DOVE, DOUGLAS FAIRBANKS
IN "THE BLACK PIRATE" (UNITED ARTISTS)

JANE WINTON, CLIVE BROOK,
IN "WHY GIRLS GO BACK HOME"
(WARNER BROS.)

JEAN ARTHUR, FRANKIE DARRO, TOM TYLER
IN "THE COWBOY COP"

OWEN MOORE, PEGGY HOPKINS JOYCE, EARLE
WILLIAMS IN "THE SKYROCKET"
(ASSOCIATED EXHIBITORS)

WILLY FRITSCH, XENIA D
IN "THE WALTZ DREAM
(UFA)

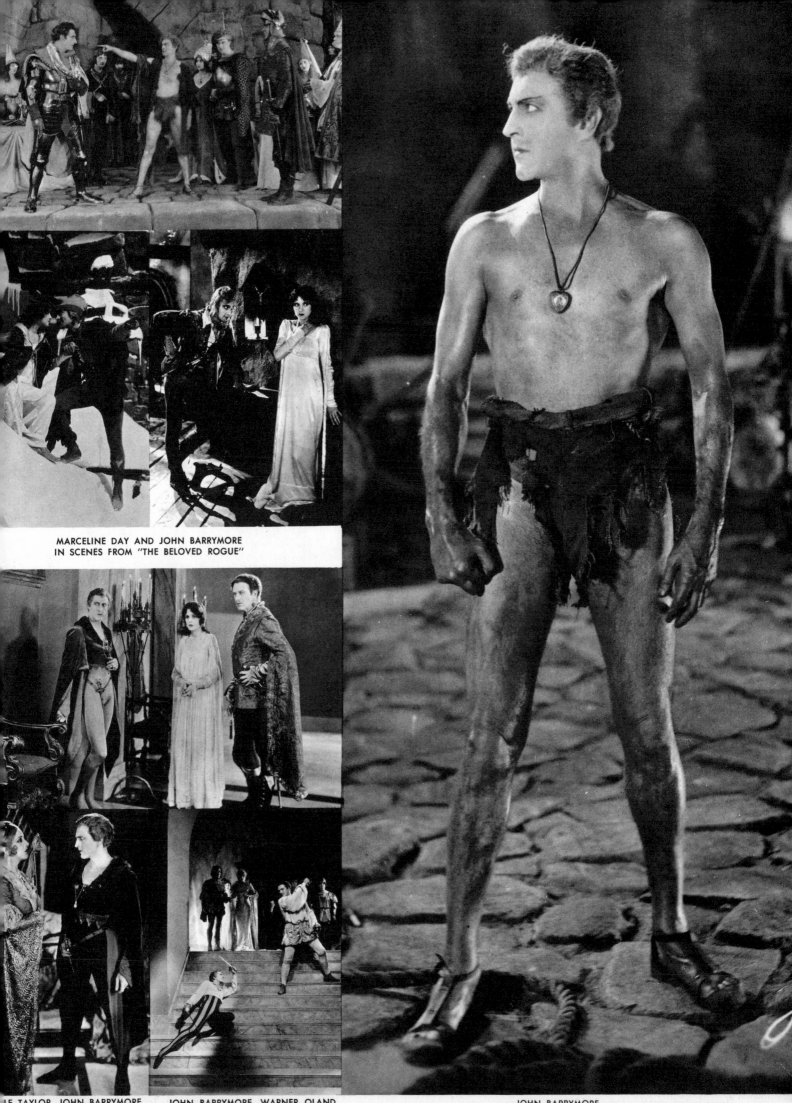

MARCELINE DAY AND JOHN BARRYMORE
IN SCENES FROM "THE BELOVED ROGUE"

LE TAYLOR, JOHN BARRYMORE
OHN BARRYMORE, MARY ASTOR,
MONTAGU LOVE
SCENES FROM "DON JUAN" (WARNER BROS.)

JOHN BARRYMORE, WARNER OLAND,
ESTELLE TAYLOR, MONTAGU LOVE

JOHN BARRYMORE
IN "THE BELOVED ROGUE"
(UNITED ARTISTS)

MARION DAVIES, OWEN MOORE
IN "THE RED MILL" (M-G-M)

FRED THOMSON (left)
IN "A REGULAR SCOUT" (F.B.O.)

WALLY WALES IN
"TWISTED TRIGGERS"
(ASSOCIATED EXHIBITORS)

JUDY KING, BUFFALO BILL, JR.
IN "THE BONANZA BUCKAROO"
(ASSOCIATED EXHIBITORS)

GLORIA SWANSON
(PARAMOUNT)

JOHN GILBERT
(M-G-M)

DOROTHY GISH
(PARAMOUNT)

LAWRENCE GRAY
(PARAMOUNT)

POLA NEGRI
(PARAMOUNT)

MILTON SILL
(FIRST NATION

CLIVE BROOK, ROBERT AMES, JETTA GOUDAL
IN "THREE FACES EAST" (PDC)

HELENE AND DOLORES COSTELLO
(WARNER BROS.)

RED GRANGE, MARY McALLISTER
IN "ONE MINUTE TO PLAY" (F.B.O.)

JOAN CRAWFORD
(M-G-M)

BUSTER KEATON
(UNITED ARTISTS)

MYRNA LOY
(WARNER BROS.)

W. C. FIELDS
(PARAMOUNT)

VILMA BANKY
(UNITED ARTISTS)

HARRY LANGDO
(FIRST NATIONA

ARNOLD GRAY, SEENA OWEN
IN "THE FLAME OF THE YUKON"
(PDC)

TOM TYLER
IN "RED HOT HOOFS"
(F.B.O.)

ALICE TERRY, ANTONIO MORENO
IN "MARE NOSTRUM"
(M-G-M)

SAM HARDY, NATACHA RAMBOV
IN "WHEN LOVE GROWS COLD
(INDEPENDENT)

290

PETER THE GREAT IN
"WILD JUSTICE"
(UNITED ARTISTS)

CONSTANCE BENNETT, GLENN HUNTER
IN "THE PINCH HITTER"
(ASSOCIATED EXHIBITORS)

EDWARD PHILLIPS, LIONEL BARRYMORE
IN "THE BELLS"
(CHADWICK)

TRIXIE FRIGANZA, EDWARD EVERETT HORTON,
OTIS HARLAN IN "THE WHOLE TOWN'S
TALKING" (UNIVERSAL)

LILA LEE
(PARAMOUNT)

WARNER BAXTER
(PARAMOUNT)

BEBE DANIELS
(PARAMOUNT)

BUCK JONES
(FOX)

LILLIAN GISH
(M-G-M)

BEN LYON
(FIRST NATIONAL)

VILMA BANKY, GARY COOPER IN
"THE WINNING OF BARBARA WORTH"
(UNITED ARTISTS)

1926 The advent of the "talkies" was in the offing. Warner Brothers had purchased a device for reproducing sound on a wax recording that was synchronized with the film projector. It was called Vitaphone, and it was the beginning of the end of the silent films. In December, Warners released their first experiment with Vitaphone. It was "Don Juan" starring John Barrymore in a silent film with a synchronized musical score. It was an instantaneous success. The following year came Warners' "The Jazz Singer" with Al Jolson singing songs, and Fox launched its own sound process called Movietone. In 1928 Warners released the first all-talking film and by the end of 1929 silent films were a rarity.

MAUD TRUAX, PAUL NICHOLSON, HARRISON FORD,
MARIE PREVOST IN "UP IN MABEL'S ROOM" (PDC)

RALPH FORBES
(PARAMOUNT)

MAY ALLISON
(FIRST NATIONAL)

JAMES HALL
(PARAMOUNT)

MARY PICKFORD
(UNITED ARTISTS)

WALTER PIDGEON
(FIRST NATIONAL)

ETHEL CLAYTON
(PREFERRED)

LIONEL BARRYMORE, MARCELINE DAY,
H. B. WALTHALL IN "THE BARRIER"
(M-G-M)

DOLORES COSTELLO, TYRONE POWER
IN "BRIDE OF THE STORM"
(WARNER BROS.)

HOLBROOK BLINN, NITA NALDI, WALTER
MILLER IN "THE UNFAIR SEX"
(ASSOCIATED EXHIBITORS)

CLAIRE ADAMS, RALPH INCE, THEODORE
VON ELTZ IN "THE SEA WOLF"
(PDC)

LOUISE FAZENDA, EMILY FITZROY, JACK PICKFORD, HARRY
GRIBBON, JEWEL CARMEN IN "THE BAT"
(UNITED ARTISTS)

VILMA BANKY, RUDOLPH VALENTINO
IN "SON OF THE SHEIK"
(UNITED ARTISTS)

ALEC B. FRANCIS, RICHARD WALLING, JANET GA
JOHN ROCHE IN "THE RETURN OF PETER GRIM
(FOX)

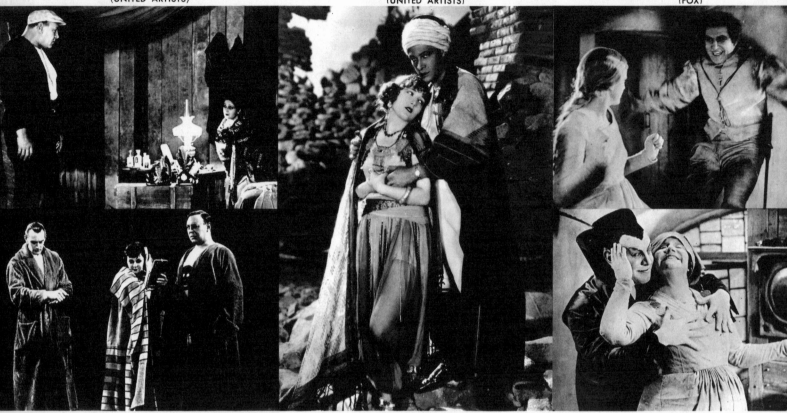

WARWICK WARD, LYA DE PUTTI, EMIL JANNINGS
Above: EMIL JANNINGS, LYA DE PUTTI
SCENES FROM "VARIETY" (PARAMOUNT)

VILMA BANKY, RUDOLPH VALENTINO
IN "SON OF THE SHEIK"
(UNITED ARTISTS)

EMIL JANNINGS, YVETTE GUILBERT
Above: CAMILLA HORN, GÖSTA EKMAN
SCENES FROM "FAUST" (UFA)

WALLACE
MacDONALD
(UNIVERSAL)

JOBYNA
RALSTON
(PARAMOUNT)

JERRY
MILEY
(FOX)

VERA
REYNOLDS
(PARAMOUNT)

LESLIE
FENTON
(FOX)

GILDA
GRAY
(PARAMOUNT)

GOSTA
EKMAN
(UFA)

MERNA
KENNEDY
(UNITED ARTISTS)

CORNE
KEEF
(UNIVEF

RICARDO CORTEZ (center)
IN "THE EAGLE OF THE SEA"
(PARAMOUNT)

WALLACE BEERY, RAYMOND
HATTON IN "WE'RE IN THE
NAVY NOW" (PARAMOUNT)

WILLIAM BOYD, LEATRICE JOY
IN "EVE'S LEAVES"
(PDC)

JACK LUDEN, IRVING HARTLEY, IRIS GREY, CHA
"BUDDY" ROGERS, ROLAND DREW IN "FASCINATING
(PARAMOUNT)

BETTY BLYTHE
IN "QUEEN OF SHEBA"
(FOX)

LOIS WILSON, WARNER BAXTER, HALE HAMILTON,
NEIL HAMILTON IN "THE GREAT GATSBY"
(PARAMOUNT)

VERA HASBROUCK, BOBBY GORDON, VERA GORDON, GEORGE
SIDNEY, CHARLIE MURRAY, KATE PRICE, MICKEY BENNET,
JASON ROBARDS IN "THE COHENS AND THE KELLYS" (UNIV.)

BETTY BRONSON AND TOM MOORE IN
SCENES FROM "A KISS FOR CINDERELLA"
(PARAMOUNT)

GILDA GRAY, WARNER BAXTER
IN "ALOMA OF THE SOUTH SEAS"
(PARAMOUNT)

ELINOR FAIRE, WILLIAM BOYD. Above: WILLIAM BOYD,
JULIA FAYE IN SCENES FROM CECIL B. DE MILLE'S
"THE VOLGA BOATMAN" (PDC)

LLIO
MINATI
ATIONAL)

LOUISE
BROOKS
(PARAMOUNT)

CHARLES
DELANEY
(TIFFANY)

BARBARA
LA MARR
(FIRST NATIONAL)

JOHN
BOWERS
(FIRST NATIONAL)

MARGARET
LIVINGSTON
(FOX)

RAYMOND
KEANE
(UNIVERSAL)

LYA
DE PUTTI
(PARAMOUNT)

ERNEST
TORRENCE
(PARAMOUNT)

EDDIE CANTOR, CLARA BOW
IN "KID BOOTS"
(PARAMOUNT)

MARION NIXON, PAT
O'MALLEY IN "SPANGLES"
(UNIVERSAL)

RICARDO CORTEZ, LYA DE
PUTTI IN "THE SORROWS OF
SATAN" (PARAMOUNT)

ALYCE MILLS, RICHARD DIX
IN "SAY IT AGAIN"
(PARAMOUNT)

PARAMOUNT'S 1926 H...

Our Exceptional Releases from January 1st, to Decem...
Final Scoring of the Years Releases Announced...
HERE ARE THE PICTURES RELEASED AND THE...

No.	Title	Studio	In Charge of Production	Director	Writers	Star	Cast		Assistant Director
1	"Behind the Front"	West Coast	Garnett Weston	Edward Sutherland	Hugh Wiley, Ethel Doherty, Monty Brice	Wallace Beery, Raymond Hatton	Mary Brian, Frances Raymond		Richard Johnston
2	"We're in the Navy Now"	West Coast	Joe Jackson	Edward Sutherland	Monty Brice, John McDermott	Wallace Beery, Raymond Hatton	Lorraine Eason, Tom Kennedy, Chester Conklin	Donald Keith, Max Asher	Paul Jones
3	"The Grand Duchess and the Waiter"	West Coast	John Lynch	Malcolm St. Clair	Alfred Savoir, John Lynch, Pierre Collings	Adolphe Menjou, Florence Vidor	Andre de Beranger, Lawrence Grant, Dot Farley	Barbara Pierce, Kalla Pasha	Art Camp
4	"Let's Get Married"	East Coast	Townsend Martin	Gregory La Cava	H.A. Du Souchet, Joy Clarkson Miller	Richard Dix	Lois Wilson, Edna May Oliver, Joseph Kilgour	"Gunboat Smith", Thomas Findley	David Todd
5	"The Vanishing American"	West Coast	Lucien Hubbard	George B. Seitz	Zane Grey, Lucien Hubbard, Ethel Doherty	Richard Dix			Bert Gilroy
6	"Mantrap"	West Coast	Hector Turnbull	Victor Fleming	Sinclair Lewis, Adelaide Heilbron, Ethel Doherty	Clara Bow	Ernest Torrence, Eugene Pallette, William Orlamond	Kalla Pasha, Tom Kennedy	Henry Hathaway
7	"The Quarterback"	East Coast	Ralph Block	Fred Newmeyer	W.O. McGeehan, William Slavens McNutt, Ray Harris	Richard Dix	Esther Ralston, David Butler, Harry Beresford	Bob Craig, Helen Broderick	Frank Walsh
8	"The Campus Flirt"	West Coast	B.P. Schulberg	Clarence Badger	Louise Long, Lloyd Corrigan	Bebe Daniels	James Hall, Josephine Dunn	Gilbert Roland, Irma Kornelia, Joseph Lee	Paul Jones
9	"Padlocked"	West Coast	B.P. Schulberg	Allan Dwan	Rex Beach, Becky Gardiner, James Hamilton	Lois Moran, Louise Dresser, Noah Beery	Helen Jerome Eddy, Charlie Lane, Douglas Fairbanks Jr., Florence Turner	Richard Arlen, Charles Brry, Allan Simpson	Gordon Cooper
10	"The Blind Goddess"	West Coast	B.P. Schulberg	Victor Fleming	Arthur Train, Hope Loring, Louis Lighton, Gertrude Orr	Esther Ralston, Jack Holt	Ernest Torrence, Louise Dresser, Ward Crane	Richard Tucker, Lewis Payne, Charles Lane, Edwin Connelly	Art Camp

Honorable Mention "Dancing Mothers" "Aloma of the South Seas"

Pictures Which Have Either Appeared On the Honor Roll or Received Honorable Mention: "Mannequin" "Say It Again" "The American Venus" "Hands Up" "The Enchanted Hill" "Desert Gold" "Sea Horses"

Pictures Still To Be Released During 1926: "The Popular Sin" "Stranded in Paris" "Love 'Em and Leave 'Em" "The Canadian" "The Man of the Forest"

Runners-Up for... "Kid Boots" "So's Your O..." "You'd Be Su..." "The Eagle o..."

JOHN WATERS (DIRECTOR), DOUGLAS GILMORE, EDDIE CANTOR, BEBE DANIELS, JIMMY SPEAK (ASSISTANT DIRECTOR), CHESTER CONKLIN, GEORGE BANCROFT, WARNER BAXTER, WILLIAM POWELL, HENRI MENJOU, LAWRENCE GRAY, MAURITZ STILLER, DORIS HILL, JAMES HALL, FLORENCE VIDOR, NOAH BEERY, JOBYNA RALSTON, CLARENCE BADGER (DIRECTOR), EL BRENDEL, BETTY BRONSON, CLIVE BROOK, LOTUS THOMPSON, VICTOR FLEMING (DIRECTOR)

VICTOR McLAGLEN, EDMUND LOWE
Above: EDMUND LOWE, DOLORES DEL RIO,
VICTOR McLAGLEN IN "WHAT PRICE GLORY"
(FOX)

BEATRICE LILLIE (also above), HARRY C. MYER IN "EXIT SMILING"
(M-G-M)

W. C. FIELDS (also above), ALICE JOYCE IN "SO'S YOUR OLD MAN"
(PARAMOUNT)

FAY WRAY, ERICH VON STROHEIM
SCENES FROM "WEDDING MARCH"
(PARAMOUNT)

Top: RALPH FORBES, ALICE JOYCE, NEIL HAMILTON, RONALD COLMAN
Center: NOAH BEERY, RONALD COLMAN; WILLIAM POWELL; RONALD COLMAN, NEIL HAMILTON IN SCENES FROM "BEAU GESTE" (PARAMOUNT)

RALPH FORBES, RONALD COLMAN, NEIL HAMILTON
IN "BEAU GESTE" (PARAMOUNT)

VAN HASSEL, GENO CORRADO, RENEE ADOREE, EDWARD EVERETT HORTON, JOHN GILBERT, LILLIAN GISH
Above: LILLIAN GISH, JOHN GILBERT
SCENES FROM "LA BOHEME" (M-G-M)

LILLIAN GISH
IN "THE SCARLET LETTER"
(M-G-M)

LARS HANSEN, LILLIAN GISH IN SCENES
FROM "THE SCARLET LETTER"
(M-G-M)

IBANEZ'
TORRENT

Ibanez' Torrent! Rushing flood of mighty emotion
Sweeping us on—ever on—breathless...
Ricardo Cortez—dashing—gallant—torrid...
Greta Garbo—Perfection!
Discovered by Metro-Goldwyn-Mayer in stark Sweden—
She is setting the heart of America aflame!
Monta Bell is the director.
You positively musn't miss Ibanez' Torrent!

A Cosmopolitan Production
Scenario by Dorothy Farnum, from the novel by Vicente Blasco Ibanez. Titles by Katherine Hilliker and H. H. Caldwell.

Metro-Goldwyn-Mayer

GRETA GARBO IN SCENES FROM
"TORRENT" WITH RICARDO CORTEZ

GRETA GARBO IN "TORRENT" HER
FIRST AMERICAN FILM

MYRNA LOY IN
"WHY GIRLS GO BACK HOME"
(WARNER BROS.)

RICARDO CORTEZ
IN "TORRENT"
(COSMOPOLITAN)

GRETA GARBO ON HER
ARRIVAL IN AMERICA

ERICH VON STROHEIM
IN "WEDDING MARCH"
(PARAMOUNT)

DOROTHY GISH
IN "NELL GWYNN"
(PARAMOUNT)

N GILBERT, LIONEL BELMORE, GEORGE K. ARTHUR, EMILY
TZROY, ELEANOR BOARDMAN. Above: JOHN GILBERT,
ANOR BOARDMAN IN "BARDELYS THE MAGNIFICENT"

RIN-TIN-TIN

WILLIAM HAINES (also above), MARY BRIAN, JACK
PICKFORD IN "BROWN OF HARVARD"
(M-G-M)

1926

Among the outstanding events was the filming of Douglas Fairbanks' "The Black Pirate" in a new color process called technicolor. It was far from perfect, but it was better than any of its predecessors. "Ben Hur" was hailed as the outstanding picture of the year. "Variety," a German import with Emil Jannings and Lya de Putti, was also acclaimed. Jannings finally was lured to America by Paramount. "Red" Grange, a football hero, was paid $300,000 for making a film. Paramount had had success with James Barrie's "Sentimental Tommy" and "Peter Pan," and scored again with his "A Kiss For Cinderella." Valentino's last film was "The Son of The Sheik." From the stage came Eddie Cantor, Beatrice Lillie, W. C. Fields and Gilda Gray to make films.

HAROLD LLOYD, JOBYNA RALSTON
IN "FOR HEAVEN'S SAKE" (PARAMOUNT)

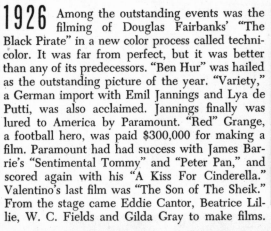

NORMAN TREVOR, CLARA BOW
IN "DANCING MOTHERS" (PARAMOUNT)

EGGY HOPKINS JOYCE
IN "THE SKYROCKET"
SSOCIATED EXHIBITORS)

ROD LA ROCQUE
IN "GIGOLO"
(PDC)

ROD LA ROCQUE IN
"THE CRUISE OF THE JASPER B"
(PDC)

ROD LA ROCQUE
IN "BRAVEHEART"
(PDC)

VILMA BANKY IN
"SON OF THE SHEIK"
(UNITED ARTISTS) **297**

"OUR GANG"

Hal Roach, who had great success with Harold Lloyd comedies, struck another gold mine when late in 1922 he produced the first of his "Our Gang" comedies. In his original gang were Mickey Daniels, Jackie Condon and Sunshine Sammy. This threesome was soon joined by Fat Joe Cobb, Farina, Mary Kornman, "Pete" (a dog), and Jackie Davis. From year to year, "Our Gang" comedies became more popular, and as the kids outgrew their roles, others joined the gang. Among the famous alumni are Johnny Downs, "Stymie," Jean Darling and Jackie Cooper.

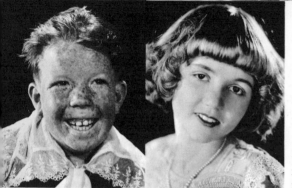

MICKEY DANIELS · MARY KORNMAN

"PETE" · "FARINA"

JEAN DARLING · JOHNNY DOWNS · JOE COBB · "STYMIE"

DOROTHY GULLIVER, GEORGE LEWIS, CHURCHILL ROSS
Above: GEORGE LEWIS, EDWARD PHILLIPS
SCENES FROM "THE COLLEGIANS" SERIES (UNIVERSAL)

BETTY BLYTHE, CARLYLE BLACKWELL
IN "SHE" (ARTLEE)

FRANCIS X. BUSHMAN AS MESSALA
IN "BEN HUR" (M-G-M)

SCENES FROM "BEN HUR" (M-G-M) WITH RAMON NOVARRO AS BEN HUR, FRANCIS X. BUSHMAN AS MESSALA, MAY McAVOY AS ESTHER, CLAIRE McDOWELL AS HUR'S MOTHER, CARMEL MYERS AS IRAS, KATHLEEN KEY AS TIRZAH, FRANK CURRIER AS ARRIUS, NIGEL de BRULIER AS SIMONIDES, MITCHELL LEWIS AS ILDERIM

LARS HANSON
(M-G-M)

CONSTANCE TALMADGE
(FIRST NATIONAL)

PAUL KELLY
(PARAMOUNT)

ALICE JOYCE
(PARAMOUNT)

RICARDO CORTEZ
(PARAMOUNT)

DOLORES DEL R
(FOX)

CHARLES FARRELL, ESTHER RALSTON

CHARLES FARRELL

"OLD IRONSIDES"

WALLACE BEERY

JOHNNIE WALKER

SCENES AND PLAYERS OF "OLD IRONSIDES" (PARAMOUNT)

CHARLES FARRELL, MADGE BELLAMY
IN "SANDY" (FOX)

ELLIOTT DEXTER, MARY PHILBIN
IN "STELLA MARIS" (UNIVERSAL)

VICTOR McLAGLEN IN
"WHAT PRICE GLORY" (FOX)

GREGORY KELLY, LOUISE BROOKS, CLAIRE
McDOWELL IN "THE SHOW-OFF" (PARAMOUNT)

GEORGE O'BRIEN, OLIVE BORDEN
IN "FIG LEAVES" (FOX)

TIM McCOY IN
"WAR PAINT" (M-G-M

H. B. WARNER
(M-G-M)

LEILA
HYAMS
(FIRST NATIONAL)

CHURCHILL
ROSS
(UNIVERSAL)

FLORA
FINCH
(FIRST NATIONAL)

JIMMIE
ADAMS
(EDUCATIONAL)

FAY
WRAY
(UNIVERSAL)

ARTHUR
LAKE
(UNIVERSAL)

ROBERT
AMES
(PDC.)

LEW
CODY
(M-G-M

A LA PLANTE
(NIVERSAL)

GEORGE BANCROFT
(PARAMOUNT)

CLAIRE WINDSOR
(M-G-M)

GARY COOPER
(UNITED ARTISTS)

MARION DAVIES
(M-G-M)

CLARK GABLE
(F.B.O.)

BUSTER KEATON
IN "BATTLING BUTLER" (M-G-M)

1926 Among the newcomers were Greta Garbo, Gary Cooper, Janet Gaynor, Charles "Buddy" Rogers, Dolores Del Rio, Walter Pidgeon, Myrna Loy, James Hall, Vilma Banky, Fay Wray, Ralph Forbes and Basil Rathbone. Garbo scored a great personal success in her first American film, "Torrent." Gary Cooper attracted attention in "The Winning of Barbara Worth." Janet Gaynor's initial break was in "The Johnstown Flood," and Dolores Del Rio's was in "What Price Glory." Ralph Forbes first scored in "Beau Geste."

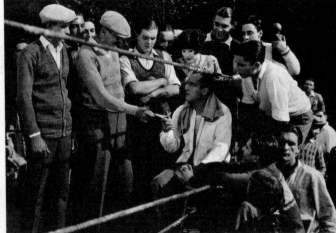

SCENE FROM "FIGHTING BLOOD" SERIES (F.B.O.)
WITH ALBERTA VAUGHN AND GEORGE O'HARA
(ARROW POINTS TO CLARK GABLE AS AN EXTRA)

BETTY COMPSON

PATSY RUTH MILLER

RICHARD DIX

CONSTANCE TALMADGE

Above: NEIL HAMILTON; MARGARET MORRIS, REGINALD DENNY; MALCOLM McGREGOR

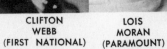

SIE
ERALD
ERSAL)

CLIFTON
WEBB
(FIRST NATIONAL)

LOIS
MORAN
(PARAMOUNT)

JAMES
FORD
(FIRST NATIONAL)

WILLY
FRISCH
(UFA)

JOHNNY
ARTHUR
(WARNER BROS.)

LITA
GREY
(CHAPLIN)

BASIL
RATHBONE
(PDC.)

OLIVE
BORDEN
(FOX)

CLARA BOW

RICHARD DIX
(PARAMOUNT)

GRETA GARBO
(M-G-M)

LON CHANEY
(UNIVERSAL)

COLLEEN MOORE
IN "TWINKLETOES"
(FIRST NATIONAL)

LARRY SEMON
IN "SPUDS"
(PATHÉ)

1927 Clara Bow, dubbed the "It" girl by Elinor Glyn, made a film called "It," and "It" became synonymous with sex appeal. Along with Charles "Buddy" Rogers and Richard Arlen she made a big hit in "Wings," an aviation war film directed by William A. Wellman. It was one of the outstanding films of a year that included "The King of Kings," "Sunrise" and "Seventh Heaven." Greta Garbo was teamed with John Gilbert and they caused a sensation in "Flesh and The Devil," while Janet Gaynor and Charles Farrell also started a profitable professional alliance in "Seventh Heaven." Norma Talmadge, with Gilbert Roland as her leading man, filmed "The Dove" and a modern version of "Camille." Ed Wynn filmed "Rubber Heels" for Paramount while George Jessel made "Sailor Izzy Murphy" for Warner Brothers, but neither of these stage comics scored the success of Eddie Cantor the year before in "Kid Boots."

RAMON NOVARRO
IN "THE STUDENT PRINCE"
(M-G-M)

ANNA MAY WONG
IN "THE CHINESE PARROT"
(UNIVERSAL)

NORMA SHEARER
THE STUDENT PRINCE"
(M-G-M)

RICHARD ARLEN
IN "ROLLED STOCKINGS"
(PARAMOUNT)

BILLIE DOVE IN
"AN AFFAIR OF THE FOLLIES"
(FIRST NATIONAL)

BUSTER KEATON
IN "THE GENERAL"
(UNITED ARTISTS)

JOAN CRAWFORD
IN "THE TAXI DANCER"
(M-G-M)

GRANT
WITHERS
(F.B.O)

JUNE
COLLYER
(FOX)

CHARLES
MORTON
(FOX)

SALLY
BLANE
(PARAMOUNT)

DON
ALVARADO
(UNITED ARTISTS)

BETTY
BRONSON
(PARAMOUNT)

NICK
STUART
(FOX)

MARGARITA
FISHER
(UNIVERSAL)

T
McC
(M-G

DAVID ROLLINS, JOHN DARROW, CHARLES PADDOCK,
SALLY PHIPPS, NICK STUART IN "THE HIGH
SCHOOL HERO" (FOX)

ANNA Q. NILSSON, BABE RUTH
IN "BABE COMES HOME"
(FIRST NATIONAL)

LEILA HYAMS, MONTE BLUE, JAMES J. JEFF
(Ex-Heavyweight Champion) IN "ONE ROUND H
(WARNER BROS.)

EMIL JANNINGS (also above)
IN "THE WAY OF ALL FLESH"
(PARAMOUNT)

CONRAD NAGEL, MARION DAVIES, FLORA FINCH
Above: CONRAD NAGEL, HELEN JEROME EDDY, MARION
DAVIES. SCENES FROM "QUALITY STREET" (M-G-M)

GEORGE BANCROFT, CLIVE BROOK, EVELYN B
SCENES FROM "UNDERWORLD" (PARAMOUN

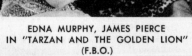

MARIE DRESSLER IN
"BREAKFAST AT SUNRISE"
(FIRST NATIONAL)

TOM GALLERY, RIN-TIN-TIN
IN "A DOG OF THE REGIMENT"
(WARNER BROS.)

EDNA MURPHY, JAMES PIERCE
IN "TARZAN AND THE GOLDEN LION"
(F.B.O.)

ED WYNN
IN "RUBBER HEELS"
(PARAMOUNT

| IVAN OSKINE (UNIVERSAL) | LINA BASQUETTE (UNIVERSAL) | LANE CHANDLER (PARAMOUNT) | THELMA TODD (PARAMOUNT) | BARRY NORTON (FOX) | ALICE WHITE (FIRST NATIONAL) | CHARLEY CHASE (ROACH) | JOSEPHINE DUNN (PARAMOUNT) | ROLAND DREW (PARAMOUNT) |

HUGH ALLEN BESSIE LOVE, WILLIAM BOYD IN "DRESS PARADE" (PATHÉ)

HARRISON FORD, MAY ROBSON IN "THE REJUVENATION OF AUNT MARY" (PDC)

DOUGLAS FAIRBANKS, JR., GEORGE O'BRIEN, EDMUND LOWE IN "IS ZAT SO?" (FOX)

MONA RAY, VIRGINIA GREY
above: MARGARITA FISHER, GEORGE SEIGMANN
Scenes FROM "UNCLE TOM'S CABIN" (UNIVERSAL)

DOLORES COSTELLO AND JOHN BARRYMORE IN SCENES FROM "WHEN A MAN LOVES" (WARNER BROS.)

JANET GAYNOR AND GEORGE O'BRIEN IN SCENES FROM "SUNRISE" (FOX)

ROSETTA AND VIVIAN DUNCAN, NILS ASTHER, MYRTLE FERGUSON IN "TOPSY AND EVA" (UNITED ARTISTS)

DOLORES COSTELLO IN "THE HEART OF MARYLAND" (WARNER BROS.)

CLARA BOW, ANTONIO MORENO IN "IT" (PARAMOUNT)

ROD LA ROCQUE (right) IN "THE FIGHTING EAGLE" (WARNER BROS.)

305

CLIVE BROOK
(PARAMOUNT)

SUE CAROL
(FOX)

STAN LAUREL
(M-G-M)

OLIVER HARDY
(CHADWICK)

LORETTA YOUNG
(M-G-M)

JOHNNY MACK
(M-G-M)

GLORIA SWANSON, JOHN BOLES
IN "LOVE OF SUNYA"
(UNITED ARTISTS)

JACQUES LERNER, OLIVE BORDEN
IN "THE MONKEY TALKS"
(FOX)

RICHARD ARLEN, JACQUELINE LOGAN,
HOBART BOSWORTH IN "THE BLOOD SHI
(COLUMBIA)

GRETA NISSEN IN
"THE POPULAR SIN"
(PARAMOUNT)

SUE CAROL
IN "SOFT CUSHIONS"
(PARAMOUNT)

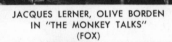

OLIVE BORDEN
IN "THE MONKEY TALKS"
(FOX)

POLA NEGRI
IN "HOTEL IMPERIA
(PARAMOUNT)

GEORGE O'BRIEN
IN "IS ZAT SO?"
(FOX)

SHARON LYNN, REX LEASE
IN "CLANCY'S KOSHER WEDDING"
(F.B.O.)

JUNE COLLYER, WALTER PIDGEON
IN "WOMAN WISE"
(FOX)

JAMES
MURRAY
(M-G-M)

DOROTHY
MACKAILL
(FIRST NATIONAL)

MARCELINE DAY, LARS HANSON
IN "CAPTAIN SALVATION"
(M-G-M)

AL ST. JOHN, RALPH
IN "CASEY JON
(RAYART)

LUPE VELEZ
(UNITED ARTISTS)

JACK OAKIE
(PARAMOUNT)

CAROLE LOMBARD
(FOX)

ADOLPHE MENJOU
(PARAMOUNT)

JEAN ARTHUR
(PARAMOUNT)

KEN MAYNARD
(FIRST NATIONAL)

ANK MARION, VIRGINIA BRADFORD, JANE KECKLEY,
DOLPH SCHILDKRAUT IN "THE COUNTRY DOCTOR"
(FOX)

OLIVE BORDEN, JERRY MILEY
IN "THE JOY GIRL"

CREIGHTON HALE, GERTRUDE ASTOR, FORREST STANLEY,
LAURA LA PLANTE, FLORA FINCH IN "THE CAT AND
THE CANARY" (UNIVERSAL)

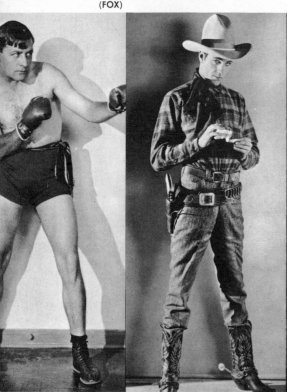

KENNETH HARLAN
IN "TWINKLETOES"
(FIRST NATIONAL)

GARY COOPER
IN "NEVADA"
(PARAMOUNT)

JOHN BARRYMORE IN
"WHEN A MAN LOVES"
(WARNER BROS.)

NICK STUART IN
"THE HIGH SCHOOL HERO"
(FOX)

GRETA GARBO
IN "LOVE"
(M-G-M)

FORBES, LILLIAN GISH
IN "THE ENEMY"
(M-G-M)

DOLORES DEL RIO, DON
ALVARADO IN "LOVES OF
CARMEN" (FOX)

DONALD
REED
(FIRST NATIONAL)

ELEANOR
BOARDMAN
(M-G-M)

NATALIE JOYCE, TOM MIX
IN "THE CIRCUS ACE"

ETHEL WALES, LOUISE FAZENDA,
NICK STUART, DOROTHY PHILLIPS
IN "CRADLE SNATCHERS"

JANET GAYNOR, ALBERT GRAN, GEORGE STONE, CHARLES FARRELL
Above: JANET GAYNOR, CHARLES FARRELL

CHARLES FARRELL, JANET GAYNOR,
GLADYS BROCKWELL

CHARLES FARRELL,
JANET GAYNOR

JANET GAYNOR, CHARLES FA

SCENES FROM "SEVENTH HEAVEN" (FOX)

GEORGE BANCROFT, NOAH BEERY, FRANK HOOPER
Above: MARY ASTOR, CHARLES FARRELL
[SC]ENES FROM "THE ROUGH RIDERS" (PARAMOUNT)

RICARDO CORTEZ, MARIA CORDA
IN "THE PRIVATE LIFE OF HELEN OF TROY"
(FIRST NATIONAL)

NORMA TALMADGE, MAURICE COSTELLO
Above: GILBERT ROLAND, NORMA TALMADGE
SCENES FROM "CAMILLE" (FIRST NATIONAL)

[GI]LBERT
[C]ONTI
[WARN]ER BROS.)

MOLLY
O'DAY
(FIRST NATIONAL)

LE ROY
MASON
(PDC.)

SALLY
O'NEIL
(M-G-M)

EL
BRENDEL
(FOX)

MARJORIE
DAW
(FOX)

LARRY
KENT
(FOX)

FLORENCE
TURNER
(TIFFANY)

FRANK
MARION
(FOX)

1927 The Academy of Motion Picture Arts and Sciences was launched in Hollywood by the leading producers, writers, actors and directors. The first Academy awards went to: Janet Gaynor as the best actress for her performances in "Seventh Heaven," "Sunrise" and "Street Angel"; Emil Jannings as the best actor for "The Way of All Flesh," his first American-made film, and "The Last Command"; to Frank Borzage for directing "Seventh Heaven" and Lewis Milestone for his direction of "Two Arabian Knights," and to "Wings" (Paramount) and "Sunrise" (Fox) as outstanding productions. Charles Rosher and Karl Struss received awards for their photography in "Sunrise," and William Cameron Menzies was cited for his art direction in "Temptation" and "The Dove."

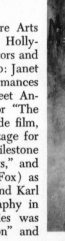

B. WARNER IN
[FAR]RELL AND SON"
[U]NITED ARTISTS)

CORINNE GRIFFITH
IN "THE GARDEN OF EDEN"
(UNITED ARTISTS)

OLGA BACLANOVA
IN "THE STREET OF SIN"
(PARAMOUNT)

MONTE BLUE
IN "ONE ROUND HOGAN"
(WARNER BROS.)

JACK MULHALL, BRUCE GORDON
IN "THE POOR NUT"
(FIRST NATIONAL)

GILBERT ROLAND, MARY ASTOR
IN "ROSE OF THE GOLDEN
WEST" (FIRST NATIONAL)

LLOYD HUGHES, BILLIE DOVE
IN "AMERICAN BEAUTY"
(FIRST NATIONAL)

MOLLY O'DAY, RICHARD BARTHELMESS
IN "THE PATENT LEATHER KID"
(FIRST NATIONAL)

GARY COOPER
(PARAMOUNT)

CLAUDETTE COLBERT, BEN
LYON IN "FOR THE LOVE OF
MIKE" (FIRST NATIONAL)

CHARLES "BUDDY" ROGERS, MARY PICKFORD
IN "MY BEST GIRL" (UNITED ARTISTS)

NORMA TALMADGE
(FIRST NATIONAL)

GLORIA SWANSON
IN "LOVE OF SUNYA"
(UNITED ARTISTS)

ANTONIO MORENO
IN "VENUS OF VENICE"
(FIRST NATIONAL)

CONSTANCE TALMADGE
IN "VENUS OF VENICE"
(FIRST NATIONAL)

GEORGE BANCR
IN "THE ROUGH R
(PARAMOUNT

RICHARD ARLEN
(PARAMOUNT)

DOUGLAS FAIRBANKS, LUPE VELEZ
IN "THE GAUCHO"
(UNITED ARTISTS)

CLARA BOW
(PARAMOUNT)

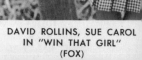

DAVID ROLLINS, SUE CAROL
IN "WIN THAT GIRL"
(FOX)

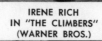

NORMAN KERRY, LILLIAN GISH, CREIGHTON HALE
IN "ANNIE LAURIE" (M-G-M)

IRENE RICH
IN "THE CLIMBERS"
(WARNER BROS.)

NORMA SHEARER
(M-G-M)

MARIA CORDA IN
PRIVATE LIFE OF HELEN
ROY" (FIRST NATIONAL)

GILBERT ROLAND IN
"ROSE OF THE GOLDEN WEST"
(FIRST NATIONAL)

ALICE WHITE
IN "THE SEA TIGER"
(FIRST NATIONAL)

WILLIAM HAINES
IN "SPRING FEVER"
(M-G-M)

RONALD COLMAN
(UNITED ARTISTS)

ON DAVIES, JOHNNY MACK BROWN
IN "THE FAIR CO-ED"
(M-G-M)

RICHARD BARTHELMESS
IN "THE PATENT LEATHER KID"
(FIRST NATIONAL)

RONALD COLMAN, VILMA BANKY
IN "THE NIGHT OF LOVE"
(UNITED ARTISTS)

BILLIE DOVE
(FIRST NATIONAL)

311

JOHN GILBERT, GRETA GARBO IN "LOVE" (M-G-M)
Above: JOHN GILBERT, GRETA GARBO, MARC MacDERMOTT IN "FLESH AND THE DEVIL" (M-G-M)

GRETA GARBO, JOHN GILBERT IN "FLESH AND THE DEVIL" (M-G-M)

GRETA GARBO, JOHN GILBERT IN "FLESH AND THE DEVIL" (M-

HAL COOLEY, RAYMOND GRIFFITH, ANN SHERIDAN IN "WEDDING BILLS" (PARAMOUNT)

ARTHUR HOUSMAN, CLARA BOW, REED HOWES IN "ROUGH HOUSE ROSIE" (PARAMOUNT)

JOBYNA RALSTON, EDDIE CANTOR, DONALD KEITH, DOUGHERTY IN "SPECIAL DELIVERY" (PARAMOUNT

RICHARD WALLING (FOX)

MARION NIXON (UNIVERSAL)

DAVID ROLLINS (FOX)

KATE PRICE (UNIVERSAL)

RAYMOND GRIFFITH (PARAMOUNT)

VIRGINIA VALLI (FOX)

WALTER McGRAIL (COLUMBIA)

GWEN LEE (M-G-M)

IVAN PETROVIT (M-G-M

POLLY MORAN, MARIE DRESSLER IN "THE CALLAHANS AND THE MURPHYS" (M-G-M)

GEORGE K. ARTHUR, CHARLOTTE GREENWOOD IN "BABY MINE" (M-G-M)

JEANNE EAGELS, JOHN GILBERT IN "MAN, WOMAN AND SIN" (M-G-M)

GARY COOPER, EVELYN BRENT IN "BEAU SABREUR" (PARAMOUNT)

GEORGE WALSH IN "HIS RISE TO FAME" (EXPRESS)

'S "BUDDY" ROGERS   RICHARD ARLEN, GARY COOPER
Above: JOBYNA RALSTON, RICHARD ARLEN

CHARLES "BUDDY" ROGERS, CLARA BOW
SCENES FROM "WINGS" (PARAMOUNT)

CHARLES "BUDDY" ROGERS, CLARA BOW, RICHARD ARLEN

NAR HANSON, POLA NEGRI, CLIVE BROOK
IN "BARBED WIRE" (PARAMOUNT)

GUSTAV FROELICH, BRIGITTE HELM
IN "METROPOLIS" (PARAMOUNT)

ESTHER RALSTON, GARY COOPER, CLARA BOW
IN "CHILDREN OF DIVORCE" (PARAMOUNT)

THONY
WITT
MOUNT)

BARBARA
WORTH
(UNIVERSAL)

EINAR
HANSON
(PARAMOUNT)

DOROTHY
REVIER
(FIRST NATIONAL)

JOHN
DARROW
(FOX)

DOROTHY
PHILLIPS
(M-G-M)

J. FARRELL
MacDONALD
(FOX)

POLLY
MORAN
(M-G-M)

MATTY
KEMP
(UNIVERSAL)

M HAINES, JUNIOR COGHLAN
IN "SLIDE, KELLY, SLIDE"
(M-G-M)

SUE CAROL, DOUGLAS MacLEAN
IN "SOFT CUSHIONS"
(PARAMOUNT)

RICHARD ARLEN, NATALIE KINGSTON
IN "FIGURES DON'T LIE"
(PARAMOUNT)

BEBE DANIELS
IN "SHE'S A SHEIK"
(PARAMOUNT)

313

ELEANOR BOARDMAN, WILLIAM HAINES LOWELL SHERMAN, DOROTHY MACKAILL, WILLIAM FRANCIS X. BUSHMAN, JR., JOAN CRAWFORD, JOAN CRAWFORD, JOHN
IN "TELL IT TO THE MARINES" COLLIER, JR., LAWRENCE GRAY IN "CONVOY" ROCKCLIFFE FELLOWS IN "THE UNDERSTANDING IN "TWELVE MILES O
(M-G-M) (FIRST NATIONAL) HEART" (M-G-M) (M-G-M)

1927 "The King of Kings" rates as one of the greatest films of all times. In the years since its release, it is estimated that over half a billion people have seen the picture, largely without charge to audiences in recent years. During Lent there are 600 prints available. The picture's subtitles have been translated into 23 languages. In remote regions, Paulist Fathers have shown it to audiences who have seen no other films. Missionaries have taken prints in canoes up the Ganges and the Congo. Cecil B. DeMille considers it his greatest effort. Will Rogers said at the time, "There will never be a greater picture because there is no greater subject."

CHARLES "BUDDY" ROGERS DOLORES COSTELLO
(PARAMOUNT) (WARNER BROS.)

GEORGE O'BRIEN MARY ASTOR
(FOX) (PARAMOUN

NORMAN KERRY, JOAN CRAWFORD, LON CHANEY FRANCIS X. BUSHMAN, CORINNE GRIFFITH WILLIAM BOYD, MARY ASTOR, LOUIS WOLHEIM
Above: NORMAN KERRY, JOAN CRAWFORD WARD CRANE IN "THE LADY IN ERMINE" Above: WILLIAM BOYD, LOUIS WOLHEIM
SCENES FROM "THE UNKNOWN" (M-G-M) (FIRST NATIONAL) IN "TWO ARABIAN KNIGHTS" (UNITED ARTIST

HARRISON FORD FAY WRAY IN ROD LA ROCQUE IN GILDA GRAY IN WILLIAM BOYD MYRTLE STEDMAN BEN LYON
IN "NO CONTROL" "THE LEGION OF THE "THE FIGHTING EAGLE" "THE DEVIL DANCER" IN "DRESS PARADE" IN "ALIAS THE DEACON" "FOR THE LOVE O
314 (PDC) CONDEMNED" (PARA.) (PATHÉ) (PATHÉ) (PATHÉ) (UNIVERSAL) (FIRST NATION

"CHANG"
(PARAMOUNT)

HAROLD GOODWIN, CLIVE MOORE, DUANE
THOMPSON, SALLY BLANE IN "HER SUMMER
HERO" (F.B.O.)

BUSTER KEATON
IN "COLLEGE"
(UNITED ARTISTS)

FORREST JAMES, HELEN MUNDY
IN "STARK LOVE"
(PARAMOUNT)

VARCONI. Center:
QUELINE LOGAN

SCENES FROM CECIL B. DE MILLE'S "THE KING OF KINGS" WITH H. B. WARNER AS JESUS, VICTOR VARCONI AS
PILATE, JOSEPH SCHILDKRAUT AS JUDAS, WILLIAM BOYD AS SIMON, JOSEPH STRIKER AS JOHN, JACQUELINE LOGAN
AS MARY MAGDALENE, MAJEL COLEMAN AS PROCULLA (above center)

H. B. WARNER. Center:
WILLIAM BOYD. Top: JOSEPH
STRIKER. H. B. WARNER

WINDSOR, JACKIE COOGAN
"THE BUGLE CALL"
(M-G-M)

CHARLES RAY, HARRY C. MYERS
IN "GETTING GERTIE'S GARTER"
(PDC)

IVAN PETROVICH, ALICE TERRY
IN "THE GARDEN OF ALLAH"
(M-G-M)

COLLEEN MOORE, DONALD REED
IN "NAUGHTY BUT NICE"
(FIRST NATIONAL)

LAWRENCE GRAY, NORMA SHEARER
IN "AFTER MIDNIGHT"
(M-G-M)

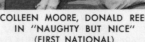

ANNA MAY WONG (PARAMOUNT)   KENNETH THOMSON (PATHÉ)   IVAN LEBEDEFF (FOX)   MARY NOLAN (M-G-M)   WILLIAM BAKEWELL (M-G-M)   CLAUDE GILLINGWATER (WARNER BROS.)   EVELYN BRENT (PARAMOUNT)   BOBBY VERNON (CHRISTIE)   BELA LUGOSI (UNIVER...

SOJIN, MYRNA LOY IN "THE CRIMSON CITY" (WARNER BROS.)   LE ROY MASON, DONALD CRISP, PAULINE STARKE IN "THE VIKING" (M-G-M)   CHARLES FARRELL, GRETA NISSEN, MAE BUSCH, JOHN BOLES IN "FAZIL" (FOX)   GLENN TRYON, MARION N... IN "HOW TO HANDLE WO... (UNIVERSAL)

WILLIAM HAINES IN "THE SMART SET" (M-G-M)   COLLEEN MOORE IN "LILAC TIME" (FIRST NATIONAL)   MICKEY MOUSE IN "PLANE CRAZY" (WALT DISNEY)   RALPH GRAVES IN "THE CHEER LEADER" (GOTHAM)   NANCY CARROLL "ABIE'S IRISH RO... (PARAMOUNT)

ANDERS RANDOLF, DON TERRY IN "ME GANGSTER" (FOX)   PHYLLIS HAVER, VICTOR VARCONI, ROBERT EDESON IN "CHICAGO" (WARNER BROS.)   CORINNE GRIFFITH, H. B. WARNER IN "THE DIVINE LADY" (FIRST NATIONAL)

SALLY EILERS (FOX)   CONRAD VEIDT (UNIVERSAL)   FRANKLIN PANGBORN (M-G-M)   FLORENCE LAKE (UNIVERSAL)   PAUL LUKAS (M-G-M)   MISCHA AUER (UNIVERSAL)   ANITA PAGE (M-G-M)   RICHARD "SKEETS" GALLAGHER (FIRST NATIONAL)   BER... ROAC... (M-G...

SHARON LYNN (FOX)   BILLY SULLIVAN (UNIVERSAL)   MARTHA SLEEPER (F.B.O.)   DANNY O'SHEA (F.B.O.)   BOB STEELE (F.B.O.)   CAMILLA HORN (UNITED ARTISTS)   DON TERRY (FOX)   BORIS KARLOFF (UNIVERSAL)

S MEIGHAN, LOUIS WOLHEIM IN "THE RACKET" (PARAMOUNT)

EMIL JANNINGS, EVELYN BRENT IN "THE LAST COMMAND" (PARAMOUNT)

IRENE RICH, WARNER BAXTER IN "CRAIG'S WIFE" (PATHÉ)

COLLEEN MOORE, MICKEY ROONEY IN "ORCHIDS AND ERMINE" (FIRST NATIONAL)

ST TORREN... MBOAT BIL... TED ARTIST...

...IN "...BLONDES" (...MOUNT)

DON ALVARADO IN "DRUMS OF LOVE" (UNITED ARTISTS)

NORMA TALMADGE IN "THE DOVE" (UNITED ARTISTS)

RICHARD BARTHELMESS IN "THE LITTLE SHEPHERD OF KINGDOM COME"

RAQUEL TORRES IN "WHITE SHADOWS IN THE SOUTH SEAS" (M-G-M)

1928 Producers were apathetic as to the public reaction to the sound screen, but it wasn't long before they realized that the "talkies," as they were labeled, were just what was needed to shake the motion picture industry out of the doldrums. Motion picture theatres throughout the country were being wired for sound and exhibitors were profiting by the novelty. Musical backgrounds were synchronized to silent films, and in some instances dialogue was added. They were advertised as "part-talkie." "Abie's Irish Rose" was an example of this. Originally made as a silent film, talking and singing sequences were added. Released in two versions, advertisements read "Silent *or* with sound."

SEPH SCHILDKRAUT, LEATRICE JOY, NILS STHER IN "THE BLUE DANUBE" (PATHÉ)

(Right) BILLIE DOVE, GILBERT ROLAND IN "THE LOVE MART" (FIRST NATIONAL)

NER ...ES (...M)   ROBERT ARMSTRONG (PATHÉ)   GLENN TRYON (UNIVERSAL)   BARBARA KENT (M-G-M)   EDDIE QUILLAN (PATHÉ)   FRED KOHLER (PARAMOUNT)   RUTH TAYLOR (PARAMOUNT)   REX LEASE (F.B.O.)   REX BELL (FOX)

EMILY FITZROY, ALICE WHITE, MACK SWAIN, RUTH TAYLOR
IN "GENTLEMEN PREFER BLONDES" (PARAMOUNT)

HAROLD LLOYD
IN "SPEEDY" (PARAMOUNT)

CHARLES ROGERS, NANCY CARROLL, BERNARD G
IN "ABIE'S IRISH ROSE" (PARAMOUNT)

JAMES MURRAY (also above), ELEANOR BOARDMAN
IN "THE CROWD" (M-G-M)

MARY PHILBIN, LIONEL BARRYMORE, DON ALVARADO
IN D. W. GRIFFITH'S "DRUMS OF LOVE" (UNITED ARTISTS)

LON CHANEY, NILS ASTHER, LORETTA YOUN
IN SCENES FROM "LAUGH, CLOWN, LAUGH" (

ROY D'ARCY, VIRGINIA PEARSON, WILLIAM HUMPHREY,
NORMA SHEARER, GWEN LEE, LEE MORAN
IN "THE ACTRESS" (M-G-M)

EMIL JANNINGS
IN "THE PATRIOT"
(PARAMOUNT)

JAMES HALL, RUTH TAYLOR
IN "JUST MARRIED"
(PARAMOUNT)

CLAUDETTE COLBERT
(FIRST NATIONAL)

JOHN BOLES
(FOX)

OLGA BACLANOVA
(PARAMOUNT)

WILLIAM HAINES
(M-G-M)

NANCY CARROLL
(PARAMOUNT)

NEIL HAMILTON
(PARAMOUNT)

JOAN CRAWFORD
IN "OUR DANCING DAUGHTERS"
(M-G-M)

SHERMAN, GRETA GARBO, JOHN MACK BROWN
Above: LARS HANSON, GRETA GARBO
NES FROM "THE DIVINE WOMAN" (M-G-M)

RLES CHAPLIN (right) PLAYS HIMSELF WITH
WILLIAM HAINES AND MARION DAVIES IN
"SHOW PEOPLE" (M-G-M)

REED HOWES
(PARAMOUNT)

MICKEY McGUIRE
(MICKEY ROONEY)
(FIRST NATIONAL)

JOAN CRAWFORD
IN "OUR DANCING DAUGHTERS"
(M-G-M)

GEORGE MEEKER, MARGARET MANN, FRANCIS X.
BUSHMAN, JR., CHARLES MORTON IN "FOUR SONS"
(FOX)

GEORGE MEEKER, JAMES HALL,
CHARLES MORTON, FRANCIS X.
BUSHMAN, JR. IN "FOUR SONS"

RONALD COLMAN, VILMA
BANKY IN "TWO LOVERS"
(UNITED ARTISTS)

JEAN HERSHOLT, POLA NEGRI, KENNETH
THOMSON IN "THE SECRET HOUR"
(PARAMOUNT)

MYRNA LOY
(WARNER BROS.)

JAMES HALL
(PARAMOUNT)

JOAN CRAWFORD
(M-G-M)

JOHN MACK BROWN
(M-G-M)

JANET GAYNOR
(FOX)

RICHARD ARLEN
(PARAMOUNT)

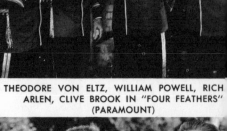

W. C. FIELDS, LOUISE FAZENDA, CHESTER CONKLIN
IN "TILLIE'S PUNCTURED ROMANCE"
(PARAMOUNT)

THEODORE VON ELTZ, WILLIAM POWELL, RICH
ARLEN, CLIVE BROOK IN "FOUR FEATHERS"
(PARAMOUNT)

WILLIAM BAKEWELL, SALLY O'NEIL, JEAN HERSHOLT,
BELLE BENNETT IN "THE BATTLE OF THE SEXES"
(UNITED ARTISTS)

GLORIA SWANSON, RAOUL WALSH
IN "SADIE THOMPSON"
(UNITED ARTISTS)

LOUIS WOLHEIM, JOHN BARRYMORE
IN "TEMPEST"
(UNITED ARTISTS)

BOB STEELE, BETTY WELSH
IN "COME AND GET IT"
(RKO)

WILLIAM HAINES, JOSEPHINE
DUNN IN "EXCESS BAGGAGE"
(M-G-M)

CONRAD NAGEL, GRETA
GARBO IN "THE MYSTERIOUS
LADY" (M-G-M)

LARS HANSON, LILLIAN GISH
IN "THE WIND"
(M-G-M)

RT ROLAND, NORMA
GE IN "THE DOVE"
NITED ARTISTS)

ALICE WHITE, ARTHUR LAKE
IN "HAROLD TEEN"
(FIRST NATIONAL)

JANET GAYNOR, CHARLES FARRELL
IN "STREET ANGEL"
(FOX)

ROLAND DREW, DOLORES
DEL RIO IN "RAMONA"
(UNITED ARTISTS)

COLLEEN MOORE, GARY
COOPER IN "LILAC TIME"
(FIRST NATIONAL)

BETTY COMPSON, GEORGE BANCROFT
IN "THE DOCKS OF NEW YORK"
(PARAMOUNT)

1928 A young man named Walt Disney produced a silent animated cartoon, "Plane Crazy," which featured a newcomer who was destined to become one of the most famous of all film stars—Mickey Mouse. Others new to the screen included Claudette Colbert and Ruth Chatterton, from the stage, and child actor Mickey Rooney, then being billed as Mickey McGuire. In "Power," a silent film starring William Boyd, the cast lists Joan Bennett, a blonde, and Carole Lombard, another blonde. Of the producers, Irving Thalberg, who had started his career as Carl Laemlle's office boy, was well on his way to a brilliant career at M-G-M. Greta Garbo, Emil Jannings, Clara Bow, Harold Lloyd and John Gilbert were now the biggest drawing cards.

RAQUEL TORRES, MONTE BLUE
IN "WHITE SHADOWS OF THE SOUTH SEAS"
(M-G-M)

S HALL, ESTHER
IN "THE CASE OF
TH" (PARAMOUNT)

KARL DANE, GEORGE K.
ARTHUR IN "BROTHERLY LOVE"
(M-G-M)

CARROLL NYE, LON CHANEY, ANITA PAGE
IN "WHILE THE CITY SLEEPS"
(M-G-M)

CLARA BOW, JAMES HALL
IN "THE FLEET'S IN"
(PARAMOUNT)

SUE CAROL, ROD LA ROCQUE
IN "CAPTAIN SWAGGER"
(PATHÉ)

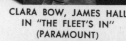

RUTH CHATTERTON
(PARAMOUNT)

EMIL JANNINGS
(PARAMOUNT)

JOAN CRAWFORD
(M-G-M)

LEW AYRES
(M-G-M)

JOAN BENNETT
(PATHÉ)

NILS ASTHER
(M-G-M)

NORMAN KERRY, THELMA TODD, SALLY EILERS
IN "TRIAL MARRIAGE" (COLUMBIA)

GEORGE K. ARTHUR, KARL DANE
IN "CHINA BOUND" (M-G-M)

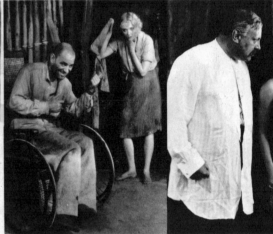

JOAN CRAWFORD, DOUGLAS FAIRBANKS, JR.
IN "OUR MODERN MAIDENS" (M-G-M)

JOHN BARRYMORE, CAMILLA HORN
IN "ETERNAL LOVE" (UNITED ARTISTS)

LON CHANEY, MARY NOLAN
IN "WEST OF ZANZIBAR" (M-G-M)

EMIL JANNINGS, RUTH CHA
IN "SINS OF THE FATH
(PARAMOUNT)

WAMPUS BABY STARS OF 1929

RAMON NOVARRO, DOROTHY JANIS
IN "THE PAGAN" (M-G-M)

COLLEEN MOORE, NEIL HAMILTON
IN "WHY BE GOOD?" (FIRST NATION.

ALLAN
LANE
(FOX)

MARGARET
MANN
(FOX)

HUGH
TREVOR
(F.B.O.)

ANNA Q.
NILSSON
(FIRST NATIONAL)

FRANCIS X.
BUSHMAN, JR.
(M-G-M)

JEANETTE
LOFF
(PATHÉ)

VICTOR
VARCONI
(PARAMOUNT)

LLOYD
HUGHES
(FIRST NATIONAL)

JA
LU
(PARA

A GARBO WITH LEWIS STONE and WITH NILS ASTHER, IN "WILD ORCHIDS" (M-G-M)

GRETA GARBO, NILS ASTHER. Above: GARBO WITH JOHNNY MACK BROWN AND NILS ASTHER IN SCENES FROM "THE SINGLE STANDARD" (M-G-M)
Top row: PORTRAITS OF GRETA GARBO

JOHN GILBERT, GRETA GARBO (also above with DOUGLAS FAIRBANKS, JR.) IN "WOMAN OF AFFAIRS" (M-G-M)

GRETA GARBO IN "THE KISS" (M-G-M)

1929

The film industry was hysterical over plans for the new audible screen. They realized that talkies could no longer be treated as a novelty but were here to stay. Silent screen stars with no stage experience were frantically taking voice lessons. Companies were scrambling to sign stage stars. Pictures were advertised with the magic words, "A talking picture." By the end of the year the majority of the theatres were "wired for sound," and the majority of the films, whether all-talkie, part-talking or silent, were synchronized with sound effects. The whole country was talking talkies.

GRETA GARBO, LEW AYRES IN "THE KISS" (M-G-M)

EAN RSHOLT VERSAL)

JAMES GLEASON (UNIVERSAL)

JOEL McCREA (M-G-M)

AUDREY FERRIS (WARNER BROS.)

GUINN "BIG BOY" WILLIAMS (WARNER BROS.)

MARY DUNCAN (FOX)

LUPINO LANE (EDUCATIONAL)

MAY ROBSON (PATHÉ)

GILBERT ROLAND

THE LAST OF THE SILENT FILMS

By the end of 1930, with rare exceptions, silent pi[ctures] were film history. The outstanding hold-out was C[harlie] Chaplin. In 1931 he released "City Lights," and in [1936] he released "Modern Times." Both these films were [made] with synchronized sound effects and a musical score[. His] leading ladies were Virginia Cherrill, a lovely blonde [from] Illinois with no previous acting experience, and Pa[ulette] Goddard, whose only stage experience was gleaned [from] Florenz Ziegfeld when in 1926 she appeared in his [show] "No Foolin'." In 1931, Robert Flaherty's "Tabu" wa[s the] only other outstanding silent film to be released.

CHARLES CHAPLIN IN "MODERN TIMES"
Top: CHARLES CHAPLIN, VIRGINIA CHERRILL IN "CITY LIGHTS"
Center: VIRGINIA CHERRILL, CHARLES CHAPLIN AND HIS CLOTHES

324

PAULETTE GODDARD, CHARLES CHAPLIN IN "MODERN TI[MES]
Top: VIRGINIA CHERRILL, CHARLES CHAPLIN, HARRY C. MYER[S IN]
"CITY LIGHTS." Center: PAULETTE GODDARD
(UNITED ARTISTS)

333

334